The Handbook of Race and Adult Education

The Handbook of Race and Adult Education

A RESOURCE FOR DIALOGUE ON RACISM

Vanessa Sheared
Juanita Johnson-Bailey
Scipio A. J. Colin III
Elizabeth Peterson
Stephen D. Brookfield
and Associates

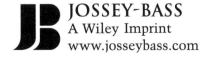

JOSSEY-BASS
A Wiley Imprint
www.josseybass.com

Published by Jossey-Bass
A Wiley Imprint
989 Market Street, San Francisco, CA 94103-1741—www.josseybass.com

Jossey-Bass books and products are available through most bookstores. To contact Jossey-Bass directly call our Customer Care Department within the U.S. at 800-956-7739, outside the U.S. at 317-572-3986, or fax 317-572-4002.

Jossey-Bass also publishes its books in a variety of electronic formats. Some content that appears in print may not be available in electronic books.

Library of Congress Cataloging-in-Publication Data

Sheared, Vanessa, 1956-
  The handbook of race and adult education : a resource for dialogue on racism / Vanessa Sheared . . . [et al.].
     p. cm.—(Jossey-Bass higher education series)
  Includes index.
  ISBN 978-0-470-38176-2 (cloth)
  1. Racism in education—Handbooks, manuals, etc. 2. Discrimination in education—Handbooks, manuals, etc. 3. Adult education—Handbooks, manuals, etc. I. Title.
  LC212.5.S54 2010
  374'.1829—dc22

                                                                          2010006969

Printed in the United States of America
FIRST EDITION
HB Printing   10 9 8 7 6 5 4 3 2 1

The Jossey-Bass Higher Education Series

CONTENTS

THE EDITORS

Stephen D. Brookfield, PhD, is currently Distinguished University Professor of the University of St. Thomas in Minneapolis-St. Paul, where in 2008 he won the university's Diversity in Teaching and Research Award. He has written and edited twelve books on adult learning, teaching, leadership, and critical thinking, four of which have won the Cyril O. Houle World Award for Literature in Adult Education. He is a straight Anglo-American and leads a punk rock band, *The 99ers.*

Scipio A. J. Colin III, EdD, is associate professor in the Department of Adult and Continuing Education at National-Louis University, Chicago, Illinois. She is the coeditor (with Elizabeth Hayes) of *Confronting Racism and Sexism.* She has held positions as an administrator and faculty member in community college and university settings. Her research interests include Africentric pedagogy and womanist consciousness, Africentric educational history and philosophy, African Ameripean adult education history and philosophy and culturally grounded curriculum and community-based programming.

Juanita Johnson-Bailey, EdD, is professor of adult education and women's studies at the University of Georgia, Athens (UGA). She is a member of the International Adult and Continuing Education Hall of Fame, and her book *Sistahs in College: Making a Way out of No Way* (2001) received the Phillip Frandson Award for Literature in Continuing Higher Education and the Sadie Alexander Award for Outstanding Scholarship in Black Women's Studies. She currently serves as UGA's interim director of the Institute for Women's Studies.

Elizabeth Peterson, EdD, served as associate professor in the Department of Adult, Continuing and Literacy Education at National-Louis University. She published extensively in the field. She is the author of *African American Women: A Study of Will and Success,* and the editor of *Freedom Road: Adult Education of African Americans.* She codirected the Gidwitz Center for Urban Policy and Community Development. Elizabeth Peterson passed away before the completion of this book, in January 2009. We will miss her as a friend and colleague.

Vanessa Sheared, EdD, is dean of the College of Education at California State University, Sacramento. She is the author of *Race Gender and Welfare Reform: The Elusive Quest for Self Determination,* the coeditor (with Peggy Sissel) of *Making Space: Merging Theory and Practice,* and the author of chapters and articles on giving voice, polyrhythmic realities, gender and welfare reform, and womanist pedagogy and ways of knowing and being. She has taught in and served in administrative positions at several universities. She is the African American single parent of college graduate Jamil.

THE CONTRIBUTING AUTHORS

Mary Alfred is associate dean for faculty affairs and associate professor of adult education in the College of Education and Human Development at Texas A&M University. As an immigrant from the Caribbean island of Saint Lucia, her research interests include the sociocultural contexts of immigration and globalization, low-income/low literate adults in education and in the workplace, and learning and development among people of the African Diaspora.

Carole Barlas is a member of the European-American Collaborative Challenging Whiteness. She is an adult educator and independent consultant in the field of organizational development and transformative learning. She has been an adjunct professor at the California Institute of Integral Studies and St. Mary's College. Carole is now retired and is an exhibited painter and a yoga practitioner. She is a White Jewish woman and has two adult children and two grandsons.

Lisa M. Baumgartner is associate professor in the Counseling, Adult and Higher Education Department at Northern Illinois University, DeKalb, where she has worked since 2003. She is a coauthor of *Learning in Adulthood: A Comprehensive Guide* (third edition), which won the Cyril O. Houle Award for Outstanding Literature in Adult Education in 2007, and *Learning and Development: Multicultural Stories* (2000). She is a White, childfree woman in her midforties from the upper Midwestern United States.

Rose Borunda is chair and associate professor of counselor education at California State University, Sacramento, where she has served for seven years. She identifies with her indigenous roots as a descendant of the Purépecha tribe. Her recent publications include "Lived Stories: Participatory Leadership in School Counseling," and "Collaboration and Community Transformation Center Stage: When Teachers, Youth and Parents Actively Value Difference." She travels this journey with her husband, Mike, two adult children, and many adopted family members and friends.

Ronald M. Cervero is professor and associate dean for outreach, engagement, and strategic initiatives in the College of Education at the University of Georgia. He has researched and written about power and politics in adult education, including *Working the Planning Table: Negotiating Democratically for Adult, Continuing, and Workplace Education* (with Arthur Wilson, 2008) and, in the *Harvard Educational Review,* "Different Worlds and Divergent Paths: Academic Careers Defined by Race and Gender"(with Juanita Johnson-Bailey, 2008).

Rosemary B. Closson is on the adult education faculty at the University of South Florida in Tampa. Her research focus is on what is learned from experience in academic and service learning settings in adult education. She has published several articles on learning experientially about race and racism, particularly when Whites are in the minority and African Americans are in the majority. Currently, she is exploring and critically examining critical race theory and its relationship to adult education.

LaJerne Terry Cornish is assistant professor of education at Goucher College in Baltimore, Maryland. A Baltimore native and Goucher alum, LaJerne returned to Goucher as an instructor in the fall of 1998, after spending fifteen years in the Baltimore City Public School System, serving as teacher, project coordinator, and assistant principal. In addition to her career in education, LaJerne is a commissioned lay pastor in the Presbytery of Baltimore. LaJerne and her husband, Wayne Cornish Sr., have one son, Wayne Cornish Jr.

Barbara Ford is professor of elementary education at San Francisco State University and also teaches classes in Africana Studies, with extensive work in Black child development. She was formerly an adult education and elementary school teacher in Los Angeles, and she is a proud mother and grandmother.

Doris A. Flowers is professor in the College of Education at San Francisco State University, where she teaches courses in adult education, language and equity, and social justice. She is the coordinator of the Center for Adult Education Master Degree and the Equity and Social Justice Education programs. Her research focus is on language and literacy in adult learning, race, class, language, gender, educational policy, and African-centered perspectives in teaching and learning.

Raquel A. González is professor in the Department of Special Education, Rehabilitation, School Psychology and Deaf Studies at California State University, Sacramento. Her research focus is on students with emotional and behavioral disorders, English learners in special education, and mental health issues affecting Hispanic children and families. She has published several articles centered on her research. Raquel credits her parents for teaching her the meaning behind *bien educada.*

Catherine A. Hansman has been professor of adult learning and development at Cleveland State University since 1998, and received a Cyril O. Houle Emerging Scholars in Adult and Continuing Education scholarship that allowed her to explore her research interests: power in mentoring relationships; race, class, and gender; and low-income adults in higher education. Among her publications are two books that reflect these interests: *Understanding and Negotiating the Political Landscape of Adult Education* (with Peggy Sissel), and *Critical Perspectives on Mentoring.*

Taj Johns teaches transformative leadership from a cultural and social justice perspective. She is adjunct faculty at St. Mary's College in Moraga, California, and Bainbridge Graduate Institute in Seattle, Washington. Taj has a strong interest in understanding the effects of internalized oppression on human development. She is the founder of a Black scholars' writing group and has published her research in the *Handbook of Action Research* (second edition, 2007).

Elizabeth Kasl has fostered collaborative learning through scholarly work, curriculum development, and pedagogical practice. When she helped form the doctoral program in transformative learning at the California Institute of Integral Studies, students of color challenged her and supported her initial exploration of issues of racism and White privilege. As an independent scholar, she continues to learn about Whiteness and to benefit from the power of group learning as a member of the European-American Collaborative Challenging Whiteness.

Luis Kong is a Peruvian Chinese American educator and director of the Alameda County Library's adult literacy program in the San Francisco Bay Area. He is the author of "Immigrant Civic Participation in

Citizenship Schools"; "Race, Gender and Economic Self-Sufficiency in a Worker-Owned Housecleaning Cooperative"; "The Role of Citizenship Schools in the Construction of Racial Identity Among Older Adult Immigrants"; and "Moving Without Moving: An Exploration of Somatic Learning as Transformative Process in Adult Education."

Ming-yeh Lee is an Asian Chinese American associate professor of adult education and equity and social justice programs at San Francisco State University, where she has been a member of the faculty since 1998. Born and raised in Taiwan, she immigrated to the United States around twenty years ago. She has received outstanding teaching and research awards and published in the areas of adult immigrant students, adult learning, transnational education, and equity and social justice in education.

Alec MacLeod is a member of the European-American Collaborative Challenging Whiteness. He has been on the faculty at the California Institute of Integral Studies since 1993. A middle-aged, middle-class, straight White male, he recently launched a Web project, *The Canine in Conversation,* that reflects on the ways in which colloquial references to dogs, especially name-calling references, can be signifiers of dehumanization (www.metaphordogs.org).

Elaine Manglitz is assistant vice president for student affairs at Clayton State University near Atlanta, Georgia. She has researched and written about challenging White privilege and in particular how White adult educators can challenge racism and White privilege.

Maria Mejorado is professor in the Bilingual/Multicultural Education Department at California State University, Sacramento, and has taught courses there since 2001. She is a member of the core faculty in the Educational Leadership Doctoral Program and is the director of the High School Equivalency Program (HEP), which prepares migrant farmworkers for the GED examination.

Mitsunori Misawa is assistant professor in the qualitative research program at the University of Georgia and an educational and training specialist at Central State Hospital. His research interests include adult bullying; antioppressive education; the intersectionality of race, sexual orientation, and gender; feminist pedagogy; positionality; qualitative research; narrative inquiry; critical race theory and queer theory; and multicultural issues in higher education and health care settings.

Catherine H. Monaghan, is assistant professor and program coordinator for the Adult Learning and Development Master's Program, Cleveland State University, Ohio, since 2004. One of her current publications is "Working Against the Grain: White Privilege in Human Resource Development" (in S.A.J. Colin III and C. Lund, eds., *White Privilege and Race: Perceptions and Actions,* 2010). She is White, single, female, middle-class, Irish, Catholic, heterosexual, midfifties, and able-bodied.

Lesley Ngatai was born in New Zealand; her descent lines are Scottish, Danish, and Ngapuhi from her mother and Ngai te Rangi from her father. Raised by a single working mother who had left school at the age of fourteen, she is the mother of a twenty-four-year-old son. She is currently a senior manager in a major research university library in Sydney. Her research interests embrace organizational learning, indigenous pedagogies, Generation Y learners, and issues of cultural legitimacy.

Doug Paxton is a learner and educator who is passionate about how we learn from our experience and connect to people and places around us. His PhD in transformative learning led to his dissertation research on how White people can work together to address racism in themselves and in organizations. He is a member of the European-American Collaborative for Challenging Whiteness. Born in Kentucky, he now lives in San Francisco with his domestic partner, Joe Vassallo.

Nichole M. Ray is currently lecturer in the Institute for Women's Studies at the University of Georgia. In addition to teaching in women's studies, she has taught courses in qualitative research, adult learning, program planning, and adult development. Her research interests focus on African American women in higher education, women and career development, and qualitative research methods.

Penny Rosenwasser is a member of the European-American Collaborative for Challenging Whiteness. A part-time instructor at the City College of San Francisco, she is a social justice practitioner and a White, queer Ashkenazi Jew. Penny is completing a book on internalized anti-Semitism and its relationship to justice in Israel and Palestine and also to the construction of race in the United States. Her previous books include *Voices from a 'Promised Land'* and *Visionary Voices: Women on Power.*

Linda Sartor teaches research in a master of education degree program at Dominican University, leads wilderness trips for Rites of Passage, and is a field team member with the Nonviolent Peaceforce, which is attempting to bring forth a Gandhian vision by placing trained, unarmed foreigners in places of violent conflict to provide a protective presence that reduces fear and violence. Linda is part of the European-American Collaboration Challenging Whiteness and lives in an intentional community in Sonoma County, California.

Yolanda Sealey-Ruiz is assistant professor of English education at Teachers College, Columbia University. Her work on African American reentry women, culturally relevant literacy instruction in secondary schools and colleges, and the preparation of teachers for urban high schools has appeared in the *Journal of Negro Education,* Kappa Delta Pi's *Educational Forum,* and *Adult Education Quarterly,* among other publications. She is currently involved in research projects investigating culturally responsive literacy practices in community college and secondary school English classrooms.

Derise E. Tolliver is associate professor and Chicago director of the School for New Learning, DePaul University B.A. Degree Program at Tangaza College in Kenya, and a program director for DePaul University's travel study course to Ghana. Her teaching and scholarship interests include African-centered psychology, spirituality, and culture in adult learning; teaching practice; personal and social transformation; study abroad; and internalization of the curriculum. She is a clinical psychologist in the state of Illinois.

ACKNOWLEDGMENTS

We began this journey as five colleagues, all interested in pursuing a better understanding about how race and racism intersect with and influence our lives, our dialogue, and how we interact with and react to others of different racial identities. For the five of us, it seemed simple enough to just tell our stories—with four of us talking about how our lives had been influenced by race and racism in the United States, and one of us talking about experiences in both England and the United States, and with four of us being Black women born when African Americans were still being called *Colored* and growing up over a period of time in which that descriptor shifted to *Negro* and then to *Black* to *African American* and to *people of the African Diaspora,* and one of us being a White male of European descent, born in England and now living in the United States in the Midwest. Our coming together was a very unlikely grouping outside of our intense desire to explore the meanings and impact of race and racism as it exists in the United States.

There are now four of us, and we will take time here to acknowledge our colleague and friend Elizabeth A. Peterson, who passed away from this life in January 2009. Elizabeth played an instrumental role in bringing the five of us together, and we want to say farewell to our friend and colleague, as well as saying thank you for bringing all of us to this table and to this journey. You will be missed, but your words and your ideas will find their way into the hearts and minds of those who read and go on this journey with us, as they read through the pages of this book.

In addition to thanking Elizabeth for starting this journey with us, we'd also like to say thanks to the many authors who gave of their time, ideas, and perspectives. Without you this book would have been just five voices, and instead it offers many more voices of those who believe, like us, that dialogue is one way of improving how individuals approach and deal with the subject of race and racism. We thank each of you for your contributions to this book.

We also thank our families and friends who have vicariously gone on this journey with us. It is your life stories and your histories that brought us this far. So we thank our parents, siblings, children, other family members, and friends. We each want to take a moment to say just a few words of thanks.

Scipio

I want to thank my beloved mother, Mrs. Mickey C. Colin (1921–1996), for her unwavering support and love and for teaching me by example the true meaning of righteous commitment. She taught me that we are representatives of our family and that daughters are their mother's legacy to the world. May those who read this endeavor say, "Well done, Ms. Mickey, well done." Promise made, and, I hope, promise kept. And I thank my brother, Curtis DuBois Colin, for always being there and keeping me grounded.

Juanita

I am indebted to the women of my family and the people of my 13th Street neighborhood who imparted a sophisticated analysis of race to me, the child who paid attention to their conversations about what was happening in and to our fragile and isolated segregated world. Thank goodness these women also shared their wisdom on how to rise above what they called the "ignorance of prejudice and discrimination." And I am especially grateful to Marvin and Brandice, who are there for me when the analysis and the wisdom can't keep me from the cumulative pain of the daily racial microaggressions and openly hostile racist acts that I experience as a Black feminist woman in twenty-first-century America.

Stephen

I want to thank my coauthors for inviting me along on this journey, and in particular I'd like to thank Scipio Colin and Elizabeth Peterson for some wonderful collaborations down the years.

Vanessa

I want to thank my mother, Ida Sheared, my stepmother Daisey, and my father, James Lee—your story has made my story and life experiences possible. I thank you for showing me how to love and to think outside the box. I also thank my son, Jamil Sheared, for teaching me what it means to be a mom, a parent, and a scholar. At the age of ten he said to me when I thought about quitting the doctoral program to work, "You like school, and I like to eat, you should do both." I thank my sisters and all my dear friends, colleagues who have supported me on this journey.

And finally, we want to conclude by thanking David Brightman for saying yes to this book and for working with us patiently for the last three years. We thank the editorial team of Robin Lloyd and Anessa Davenport at Jossey-Bass for taking us to the finish line. This has been a collaborative effort, and we thank all who played a small or a major role in making this edition possible (Brandon Abell, Georgia Gonzales, Katy Romo, La Tina Gago, Sheng-Yun Yang, and Cynthia Vessel).

The Editorial Collective
Vanessa Sheared
Juanita Johnson-Bailey
Scipio A. J. Colin III
Stephen D. Brookfield

FOREWORD

This book is not limited to adult education or even to education—it shows how racism's location within our social structures causes us to become internally racist as well as entrapped in structural racism without being explicitly conscious of the situation. So this book is for all individuals working with others in formal and nonformal settings.

This exciting book is brought to us by a powerhouse of leaders in the field of contemporary adult education: Sheared, Johnson-Bailey, and Colin III (the articulate proponent of Africentrism) are three of the most quoted African American adult education professors in the United States, and Brookfield is an internationally known critical theorist. These four editors introduce us to over twenty other experientially grounded authors who understand racism from many points along ethnic and color lines.

As the senior editors invite us to join them around the kitchen table, we are plunged into the debate within the first few pages and the discussion turns deadly serious: Can an African American framing her assumptions within the Africentric paradigm escape racism? Yes, I can. No, you can't. Three days later, I don't believe the argument was ever settled. This reminds us that racism is complicated and multifaceted. Even the senior editors were deadlocked on what some consider an already solved issue in the present-day United States.

Many people today believe we have moved beyond racism, pointing to our major achievement in electing an African American president.

And though we have indeed come a long way since the civil rights struggles of the 1960s, the sociopolitical and the personal structures of racism have become so entrenched over the years that they continue to resist destruction.

Therefore, agreeing that racism is still with us, the authors set out to offer an opportunity to engage in a discourse on race and racism and provide strategies for dealing with the issues in practice.

This book is carefully put together and is divided into four major parts. In Part One, "The Myth Versus the Reality," we get a dose of reality from representatives of Native America, African America, Chicana America, feminism, and Maori New Zealand, who present their experiences of racism in the raw. Clearly they understand our struggles with both the myths and the realities of racism, and they provide evidence of both. The process of writing the book is also revealed: each group of authors within a section talks together with a senior editor before submitting their manuscripts, so the sharing of content is promoted in developing each section.

After providing a broad and diverse base of racist reality, the authors analyze Whiteness in Part Two, which may be one of the more important sections of the book. When racism is discussed, many White people focus on those of color. Whiteness is still widely taken for granted and thus remains invisible. Ranging from Chapter Six's "White Whispers," which addresses how rarely White people acknowledge their complicity in racism, to a critical analysis of White supremacy and power as they operate in groups, this section makes Whiteness explicit. Especially unnerving is Chapter Nine, "White on White," which might make many White persons think twice about their racial behavior. Concepts such as critical humility, disdain, and proselytizing are all new behaviors for Whites to assign to themselves. But it is all fair game in examining racism.

Part Three is the theoretical section, and through the discussion of critical race theory (CRT), more and more subtleties of racism are exposed. Elizabeth Peterson served as senior editor for this section, and I am sorry to report that she died during the writing process. These authors agreed with Peterson that exploration of CRT and its spin-offs led them to greater optimism about the eventual eradication of racism—a view not usually supported by CRT and many others. This is one of the most important questions raised in this book.

Four strategies for combating racism are presented in the final chapter. Colin III presents Africentrism in practice, which is a summary of her lifelong work on cultural and philosophical approaches to Africana studies. Sheared discusses womanist in practice **as a strategy** that encompasses her theoretical work on giving voice and polyrhythmic realities arising from an Africana womanist perspective. Johnson-Bailey utilizes a critical psychosocial approach to elaborate on Black feminism in practice as a way of combating racism. Finally, Brookfield turns his critical skills to not only analyzing his own unconscious racist behavior but also summarizing the salient points in Part Three that deal with Whiteness. This part of the book is particularly challenging, as it forces major issues of racism into the foreground. Here we are asked how White identity is established. Do we reproduce a dominant White epistemology? Are we familiar with more than one tradition in other ethnic paradigms? Are we aware of our own practice of supremacy over others? Is the White supremacy in global capitalism reproduced in our classrooms and curricula?

In Part Four, Reframing the Field Through the Lens of Race, the authors describe a specialized approach to educational practice in combating racism. They present alternate ways of responding to racism that include language-based analysis, make White identity development explicit, expose a White supremacy power model, and operationalize the Africentric concept of twinness.

This book has many strengths: it is well written, well organized, and it synthesizes the best scholarship on the topic of racism in education. It does not view racism narrowly, but gives the reader multiple views from which to look at the phenomenon. For a long time we have needed a book that asks questions rather than giving answers, and this volume fills that need. I believe every professor of adult education should read it, regardless of her teaching assignment. It would make an excellent basis for discussing racism within professional associations. This may be too tall an order for the American Association for Adult and Continuing Education (AAACE), but perhaps the Commission of Professors of Adult Education (CPAE) would be up to the task. If we can't critically examine our own associations, why should we ask more of our students?

Phyllis M. Cunningham
Distinguished Teaching Professor Emeritus
Northern Illinois University

The Beginning
Kitchen Table Dialogue

VANESSA SHEARED
JUANITA JOHNSON-BAILEY
SCIPIO A. J. COLIN III
STEPHEN D. BROOKFIELD

We began this project with the intent of engaging a group of scholars from various backgrounds, disciplines, races, languages, and social classes around the issue of race and racism. More important, we wanted them to engage in a dialogue about how race and racism have shaped their lives and lived experiences, not only in their disciplines but also in the ways they interact with others generally. We initially chose individuals within the field of adult and continuing education, but quickly learned and decided that to narrow our book's focus only to this discipline would obfuscate the impact the issues of race and racism have had on all of us. We also chose a dialogical model, seeking to construct a wide-ranging discussion of race and racism (sociocultural, sociohistorical, and intellectual) from social, educational, political, and psychological perspectives in order to articulate a conceptual challenge to the ethnocentric focus that is generally applied to this topic.

When we began this project, we thought that if change is going to occur in our field's theoretical frameworks and practices, then all adult and higher educators must be challenged to "practice what they preach" and to engage in a critically reflective process in examining their own racial identity and how it shapes their worldview. To that end, this book is aimed at offering adult and higher education scholars and also all those in other fields who are engaged in research and teaching about race with an opportunity to engage in a discourse about race and racism in an effort to determine (1) how racism has dictated how they think about people of varying backgrounds and socioeconomic circumstances; (2) how racism has affected their lived experiences at work, at home, and in educational settings; and (3) how racism has served to privilege some and not others. In addition, we wanted to provide possible strategies for ourselves and other educators and researchers to use in order to *give voice* (Sheared, 1994, 1999) to the lived experiences of those who have been marginalized or negated in this country's discourse, history, policies, classrooms, communities, and services.

Just as we and others in the academy are grappling with the stark realities and impacts of racism in the classroom, discussions are being held in homes, churches, and other organizations about whether race and racism are still factors in how individuals operate and communicate in these various settings. Moreover, a number of events in the media in 2008—such as radio talk show host Don Imus calling African American members of the Rutgers women's basketball team "nappy-headed hos," presidential candidate Newt Gingrich referring to the Spanish language as the "language of the ghetto," and George W. Bush remarking on presidential candidate Barack Obama's ability to "articulate well"—sparked much debate on race. Such comments along with the continuing debates being heard on public radio and television, at community events, and throughout the halls of the academy lead us to believe not only that racism is alive and well but that it is being used in reverse by both the oppressor and the oppressed. Racism exists when one racial group has power and authority over another racial group because of beliefs about race. So the term *racism*—which was once used to describe how Whites treated all other racial groups who lacked power and authority in political, historical, or economic arenas because of their racial identity—is now being used by Whites and even those who once were marginalized to describe how minority groups relate to majority group members, namely the White men and White women considered to have power and authority over how others are treated.

We believe that this book is a timely addition to the intense debate that is occurring in this country and beyond. The public, we believe, is looking for ways in which to have a discussion about this subject. It is long overdue, and we look forward to providing a medium through which those in higher education as well as in the general adult education field can engage in a discussion that leads to a critical understanding and moves individuals into meaningful change.

These issues are not new, for as early as 1897, W.E.B. DuBois noted that people's histories are interconnected by how they see themselves as groups through the lens of race. And even though people might attempt to ignore race as being a factor, it inevitably has served to define how people operate and communicate with each other as individuals and within groups. DuBois (1897) stated that "the history of the world is the history, not of individuals, but of groups, not of nations, but of races, and he who ignores or seeks to override the race idea in human history ignores and overrides the central thought of all history."

Over the course of the last fifteen years, discussions have occurred on college and university campuses and at national and international conferences in adult education, as well as in all other areas of higher education, concerning the importance of including varied perspectives, ideologies, and racial groups in research studies, courses, publications, and media. Many of us in the field of adult and continuing education who have characterized our *lifework* as being focused on addressing the educational needs of the underserved who have been economically, socially, or politically disenfranchised because of their race believe that if these dispossessed are going to gain access, equity, and parity in society, then conversations like the ones proposed in this book are an important step toward that change. Even though the field of adult education has made a commitment to addressing these issues, we still believe that limited attention is being given to the role that race and racism play in how and why underserved individuals come to be in their present economic, political, and social conditions. Some have argued that race and racism are not influential factors here, but we believe that race and racism, as DuBois noted in 1897, are critical factors and must be examined if people are to change how they interact and communicate with one another. Moreover, we think that engaging in discourse about race and racism may lead to changing structures and systems of oppression and marginalization as experienced by those whose realities and possibilities may be determined by the color of their skin.

So even as we acknowledge that much attention has been given to inclusion, diversity, and multiculturalism within the field of adult education, we also believe that the members of our discipline have yet to engage in a dialogue specifically about race or racism and the ways in which these factors operate to foster or produce marginalization or oppression of specific groups and individuals within multiple educational, political, and corporate settings. Even though multiculturalism, gender, and sexual orientation have begun to receive increasing attention in the field of adult education, along with the impact of these factors on the teaching-learning context, adult education literature and practitioners have given relatively little attention to race and racism as an area of discourse. Given the relative invisibility of these two factors, their impact has yet to be problematized within the field of adult education (or within higher education as a whole). For the most part these factors are often ignored or relegated to the dialogical sidelines. In short, our field has tended to engage in what we would describe as an act of intellectual ethnocentrism.

One way to understand ethnocentrism is as a racialized perspective. To take a *racialized* view of something is to see it through the distinctive lens of one racial group's lived experiences (Sheared, 1999) and to assess its educational value relative to the expansion of the field's knowledge base and the impact on practice (Brookfield, 2002). As Outlaw (1996) in general and Brookfield (2002) specifically have noted, the intellectual world of the field of adult education is racialized in favor of the Eurocentric perspectives that are predominant in many other endeavors as well, and therefore our field has been unwilling to create a dialogical context or seriously consider how and in what ways other culturally grounded, intellectual racializations could positively influence theory, practice, and research (Colin III, 1988). However, discussions about race and racism should not nor do they occur in a vacuum. Stories and histories have been written to correct or insert a new paradigm (or framework) for thinking about how various racial groups have contributed to the fabric of our field and this society. For instance, the history of our field and its leaders presented in the work of Johnson-Bailey demonstrates how the field boldly incorporated issues pertinent to African Americans through acknowledging the work of such early scholars as Alain Locke and W.E.B. DuBois (Johnson-Bailey, 2006), and then goes on to examine the ebb and flow in the ways race has been discussed across the years in the various editions of the *Handbook of Adult and Continuing Education* (Johnson-Bailey & Cervero, 2000), and in the field's prominent journals and student dissertations (Johnson-Bailey, 2001a).

We see these attempts as being a part of our beginning conversations and understandings. We know that these steps are important and can provide adult educators and others with a way to reflect on and change how they think, talk, and act in various settings. We believe that we and others have a long way to go, and we see this book as a vehicle for changing thoughts and actions. Conversations about multiculturalism, gender, and sexual orientation should be viewed therefore as good first steps.

Clearly, adult educators must be challenged to practice what they preach and to engage in a critically reflective process in examining their own racial identity and how it shapes their worldview. In any great novel or book, as in life, there is a beginning, middle, and end. For us and the contributing authors in this book, our beginnings involved unveiling ourselves and sharing our stories about how we have come to this phase in our professional, personal, and social journeys.

OUR BEGINNINGS

When we began this book there were five of us, but one member of our editorial group, Elizabeth Peterson, passed away in January 2009, while we were still working on this project. We pay homage to our colleague, and believe that her voice and her spirit were with us throughout this project.

In keeping with the principle of practicing what one preaches, we now share with you portions of our discussions and work around our metaphoric kitchen table, to give you a glimpse into the difficulties everyone faces when the subject of race and its antecedent racism are discussed. The first step we call the uncovering of who we are. You will see the steps and beginnings taken by all the editors and contributing authors throughout this book. This uncovering, we believe, is a good first effort toward moving from the self to the necessary act of placing ourselves in the shoes of others. What better place to begin than with the editors, engaging in an exploration with each other about this topic.

WHO ARE WE?

Vanessa

I am a single parent African American woman, born in the 1950s to a young single Black woman—in a very segregated South. I never dreamt that in 2010, I would be able to say that I had graduated from high school or had obtained a bachelor's degree, a master's degree, and a doctoral degree, let alone that I would go on to become a professor and an administrator in a university setting. Twenty-three years ago I accidentally entered the field of adult education. When I applied for the position at Northern Illinois University, I did so only with the intent of acquiring a salary in order to take care of my son and myself. Although I believed that racism existed and had experienced it as a child growing up in the South—where I recall having to drink out of the "colored only" fountain, going to the theater through the door that said "coloreds only," and going to an all-Black Catholic school for my first three years of schooling—little did I realize that twenty-three years later I would be engaging in a project with four other colleagues on the topic of racism. Back then, if I had been asked to place a label on my experience of attending a Catholic school, I would have had to say that I thought of myself as being privileged. So even as a child I knew that there was something different about the schooling I had been given access to—at least while living in the South. In the mid-1960s, my three sisters and I moved to Chicago to live with my mother. Even though I had witnessed the "no colored allowed" signs earlier, it was while living in Chicago that I got a firsthand glimpse into poverty and the real struggle for financial and economic survival. My mother left home early in the morning to work as a waitress in a local restaurant, and after a year or so of doing this, she determined that there was a need for her to leave that job and get help from the Aid to Families with Dependent Children (AFDC) program. This was not an easy decision, but with four girls, she decided that she needed to stay home with us, especially the younger ones. She did not let this stop her; she later decided to go back to school to get her GED, and while assisting in the classroom with my youngest sisters' Head Start class, she obtained a job there as an assistant teacher, and worked there for twenty-five years, eventually becoming the head teacher. This new job was over an hour away by bus, so my sisters went to a baby sitter, but because I was old enough to have a key, I could go straight home after school. All four of us finished high school, and two of us went on to obtain college degrees. Looking back on those days—and despite the stories I've heard since in the media or read in newspapers or research journals about the possible economic or educational success of children growing up in a single family household, no father in the home, and a family income based on minimum wages—I now realize that even though the racialized construct of our society had a bearing on my life, it did not prevent me from being able to move forward. The reason for this was found in the strength and persistence of a single Black woman—my mother.

On the school front I became the kid who studied hard, did her homework, and never caused any trouble. I was so studious in my classes by the fifth grade that when a teacher failed to show (and there were many such days), another classmate and I were the ones excused from class so that we could substitute for the absent teachers (usually in first- or second-grade classrooms) for that day or week. As a child I felt special when this happened, but reflecting back on those days I now realize that this was an example of how racism afflicts low-income or racially disadvantaged communities. The children in my school were not valued enough to warrant sending an adult substitute teacher out to work with them. For me, now, this represents the epitome of marginalization. As I noted in my dissertation (Sheared, 1992), when people are marginalized, adequate resources are not given to ensuring their success. While I didn't know what any of this meant as a child, I now recognize that my life story is replete with examples of the perpetuation of racist acts, even though at the time I did not have a name for them.

Over the course of the years I witnessed the events of the 1960s and 1970s, when rioting occurred in Black neighborhoods, and police routinely visited neighborhood homes, walking through without a warrant, looking for that Black criminal that none of the home's inhabitants knew or had ever even heard of.

I witnessed the positive waves of the 1970s into the 1980s, as those of us who had grown up going through "colored only" doors now, as a result of the civil rights movement and the laws it produced, found that for the first time we could dream of possibilities. For myself this meant the possibilities of going on to college, even though my family were not able to factor that into the family budget; attending one of the most prestigious Christian liberal arts colleges, where I obtained a BA degree; attending a southern school, one that once upon a time did not even admit Blacks, but now there I was receiving an MA degree; and finally earning that EdD degree from another state school in the North.

Ultimately, I discovered that I could have a career in higher education as a professor and now as a dean in a teaching institution. So without a doubt this subject matters to me, for not only have I witnessed racist acts against others but I have also felt the slings and arrows of racism in my personal life. My beginning was growing up in the racially divided South, and multiple acts of racism have invaded my life story, but this beginning did not mean that I, a child of a single parent African American woman, would never be where I am now or that I would not one day make space for other voices to tell their stories—stories describing beginnings that shaped us yet did not determine our possibilities. So even though racism is alive and well, it need not define our endings—especially if those of us who have gone through it tell the stories and seek the actions that can redefine our possibilities and realities.

Juanita

My childhood experiences of growing up in 1950s segregated Columbus, Georgia, crystallized my understanding of race and racism by the time I was five years old. Although my happy, carefree existence was informed by race and racism, it was not ruined or spoiled by it. Segregation just defined and confined my world in this American apartheid called Jim Crow. My personal existence was more often than not determined by three factors. First, I lived a privileged life in the world of the Catholic mission school that I attended, with White nuns, my extended family, whom I dearly loved and who, I felt, loved me. Second, I had my group of girlfriends that included my best playmate, Dianne, a White girl. Although Dianne and I lived worlds apart, we often played together because she spent many nights and weekends with her family's maid, our neighbor. And finally, my world was shaped by my precious freedom: my parents allowed me to run around with abandon as a wild girl child. The only occasional threats to my world were a few neighborhood kids who thought I didn't fit in and wasn't Black enough because I went to a Catholic school instead of public school. When their hatred was at its highest they'd chase me from my school bus stop to my home or they'd throw rocks. But they didn't much frighten me or impact my way of life. However, my near-perfect existence was disrupted when Dianne's mother ripped us apart because school-age children could not have friendships that crossed racial lines. So when we began first grade our play dates ended; we could only watch each other from the vantage of our respective porches. As a child, I was helpless and only able to miss my friend Dianne and to wonder about her occasionally in the years to come.

For the next eight years I was sheltered in a secure all-Negro, Catholic grade school environment (we had moved from *colored* to *Negro* by 1968), where I was privileged. I recall such highlights as riding on the school's float in the Columbus Christmas parade as Suzie Snowflake and playing Portia in a fifth-grade production of *The Merchant of Venice*. Reflecting from the distance of time and a critical race theoretical frame, I now know that even in the segregated grade school environment I was advantaged because of my light skin color, a vestige of *White racism*.

After grade school I attended the newly desegregated Catholic high school, and for the four years of high school I was the only Black girl in my class. My new classmates were different—driving new cars like convertible T-Birds and having maids who looked like me. I always wondered if, given my working-class status, some of their maids even knew my people. But I could never judge this from the maids' expressions because they avoided looking at or acknowledging me when I visited my friends' homes. Nevertheless, high school was a place where I thrived academically and socially—I served as the editor of the school newspaper and one year was even elected the Mardi Gras representative for our biggest annual social event.

By my college years my world perspective was set, and I moved through the world as a free thinker, a feminist, and a Black person with a consciousness about race regardless of what life threw my way. It was during my undergraduate years at a small, predominantly White Southern Baptist university that I met the real world, a world unsupervised by liberal, do-gooder nuns, and came to understand that the Catholic schools had been controlled and artificial environments where we were all made to play fair. Schooling in this new place meant constantly fighting to prove that I had earned my academic scholarship, challenging grades so that I could stay on the dean's list, and barely graduating cum laude.

So fifteen years after finishing my BA degree, when I attempted to enter graduate school and encountered racism yet again, I was prepared for the struggle. I was refused admission to the University of Georgia's Journalism School because the graduate coordinator felt that my insistence on being a part-time student conveyed a lack of dedication. I had heard about the university's Adult Education Program, and because training was a large part of the state government job I had then, I did what so many of my colleagues have done—stumbled into an adult education program, where I was also initially refused admission. The rejections didn't deter me. One appeal hearing later and I entered the graduate program in adult education. Being turned down by the J School has been the best redirect of my life.

Looking back and viewing these collective experiences, I know the following: I understood at an early age what it meant to have cross-cultural friendships; I had an extended family that did not look like me; and I had experienced the pain of being rejected by members of my own race. As a first grader who had been ripped away from her best friend, I came to know that there were racist systems in place that the Black adults who ruled my world were powerless to challenge or change. It is obvious to me that my stance as a Black feminist adult educator who researches race and gender is grounded in those early years. I have been emboldened to step out of the shadows of my segregated world and to exist as a fearless scholar by the women in my family and neighborhood who talked back in resistance to a system that disrespected them and by the courageousness of my grade school missionary nuns. It is no accident that my research agenda—expressed in a dissertation and subsequent book, *Sistahs in College* (Johnson-Bailey, 2001b)—flows from a lifetime of trying to figure out how race has affected the schooling experiences of Black women in mostly White settings. Throughout my life I have encountered racism and shed many tears over the setbacks, detours, and attacks resulting from this powerful force. The daily microaggressions have taken their toll on my spirit, but I go on with my work because it is so important to me. I guess I'm still desperately seeking answers as to why I couldn't play with Dianne, or maybe I just want the world to be a place where my girl child can truly run free and not live with the threat of having her world and life choices controlled by structural inequalities established to protect and ensure the continuance of White supremacy.

Scipio

There are those times in my life when I sit myself down and ask, "Why are you still battling White racism?" I first met my opponent when I entered first grade at Carter School. All we had done in kindergarten was to take naps; color, and sit in a circle and be read to. Well, I could sleep at home; I already knew how not only to color but to color within the lines; and I knew how to read, so I didn't need to be read to. I expressed my disappointment to my parents, probably on a daily basis, and was always reassured that better times were ahead, reminding me of all the things I had to look forward to in first grade. After suffering through the silence in kindergarten, I approached first grade with joy and excitement about entering the real world of learning. Little did I know that *White racism* would be greeting me at the doors of first grade with open arms.

I was overjoyed on my first day when the teacher said that one of the things we were going to do was to learn how to read, and then she passed out the book. I know I am dating myself, but the book was one of the infamous Dick and Jane readers. Little did I know what was between the covers: "See Dick run. See Jane run. See Dick and Jane run." Huh? What world am I in? I thought to myself, "OK, they are running; so what?" And then as my brother would say, with my silly self, I raised my hand and asked a question. I asked the teacher if I could bring one of my books, *Black Beauty,* from home. Welcome, White racism, to my world—or more accurately to yours. First, the teacher in responding mispronounced my first name again, calling me "Scripto"; I thought we had cleared this up when she took attendance. Reflecting back, that exchange was my first introduction to White racism. After I said "present," I had told her that my name was pronounced Scipio, and she had asked me, "How did somebody like you get a name like that?" I told her and mistakenly thought that was it.

But her response brought me deeper into the world of White racism. She got up out of her chair, walked to my desk, and as she hovered over me said in a tone that I would hear throughout my life, "This is my classroom and I am the teacher; you will do what I say. Who do you think you are?" She then accused me not only of lacking this book in my home but of not being able to read. Thus began my family's almost daily trips to school, sometimes one of my parents, at other times my grandmother or one of my uncles. In resistance I decided that I would not answer "present" if she did not call me by my name, which she had decided not to do, and when called upon to read aloud, I read with a closed book. How many times do you have to read "see Dick and Jane run" before you know it by heart?

Thus began the "war of the worlds": the world of those who exercised the power and privilege of pigmentation in attempts to rename me (in more ways than one) and to place limits based on racist assumptions of who I was and what I was capable of doing, and my home world, where I was taught racial pride and that my intellectual capabilities were not limited.

This battle continued in various ways throughout my educational journey, and given the lessons learned from it, I vowed that my career would not be in education. Be careful about what you say you will never do. I think the lived and learned lessons of my journey prepared me to challenge this enemy of humanity on its home court. My commitment to not allowing White racist ideology to be the paradigm through which others are viewed and, most important, through which others view themselves frames my practice.

Stephen

Why am I in this book? Well, apart from the joy of working with four colleagues I respect immensely, my participation sprang from my conviction that discussions of race should not be solely the province of authors of color. If this happens, then the White majority can easily marginalize the issue as the province only of non-White adult educators, as something that *they* (the generalized non-White *others,* whose only distinguishing characteristic is defined as their lack of Whiteness) should take responsibility for exploring. This effectively keeps racial analysis conveniently (for the White majority) on the periphery.

But if White adult educators acknowledge and critique their own complicity in a field racialized in favor of Euro-Americans, and if they engage seriously with racialized analyses drawn from a range of racial perspectives—many of which will focus on racism as the salient experience of people of color in a racist country—questions of race and racism cannot so easily be pushed aside by White colleagues.

Like all Whites in Britain, I grew up in a world in which Whiteness and all things White were taken as the "natural" order of things. I have had six decades of ideological conditioning into White supremacy, and as a result, I do not expect it ever to leave me. However, external events, and sometimes acts of my own will, are helping me to name and challenge it. Two pivotal events in adolescence and early adulthood helped to disrupt and challenge the way White supremacy moved in me. The first was at the age of seventeen when I was being beaten up by a gang of White youths (they were *rockers,* I was a *mod*) in Banbury High Street one Friday night. A Black American GI from Upper Heyford Air Force base crossed the street and broke up the fight, telling us "everybody's got to be cool now." That man saved me from potentially severe injury. In my memory I was on the verge of falling to the ground as the GI intervened. Having been born in Bootle (Liverpool), I knew that once you were on the ground things got a lot worse, because then people could kick you in the kidneys and head. That event formed what critical race theory calls a *counterstory,* which disrupted the White supremacist script forming in my head (which said that Black people are violent and start fights and White people are peacemakers who sometimes have to use force to rein in Black instigators of violence).

The second event was rooming with Terry, an Afro-Caribbean, in college. We shared a love of cricket (the West Indies were regularly thrashing England at the time), and I naively assumed that all Black people, and particularly all West Indians, shared a common identity. White supremacy trivializes the vigor of Black intellectual life by assuming that all Black people think alike and that therefore one needs to speak to only one Black person to get the "Black" perspective on a topic. That this is not true was brought home to me when I came home after attending a meeting addressed by a Trinidadian revolutionary activist, Michael X. Terry was appalled. "Why do you want to go and hear him?" he asked, "he's nothing but a rabble rouser." In the ensuing conversation it became clear I had been woefully ignorant of the debates, different positions, ideological divides, and multiple analytical constructs present in Caribbean, let alone Black, intellectual life. Once again, White supremacy was interrupted.

But despite disruptive moments and events such as these, White supremacy moves in me as it does in all Whites. First, my skin color means that for my whole career I have been used to seeing, as the gatekeepers in adult education, people who look like me. Now, I suppose, I am one, continuing the unproblematized White supremacy norm. I never have to question my right to publish something, and White epistemology is something bred into my neural synapses (more on this later). Racism—the ugly operationalization of the ideology of White supremacy—moves in me in ways that constantly catch me by surprise. I see a Black pilot enter the cockpit of the plane on which I'm traveling and catch myself thinking, "Will this flight be safe?" In classes I catch myself holding back from challenging students of color and realize that my so-called concern masks an embedded racist consciousness that says that *they* can't take a strong challenge from a White person. Clearly, racism moves in me. I find myself quickly granting paper extensions to Black students and can only assume it springs from a White supremacist judgment that Black students are not as intelligent as White students so of course they will need more time to complete their work. I keep silent in a presentation given by a scholar of color because (so my internal calculus goes) my voice is so powerful it will diminish the voice of the presenter. It is deeply sobering to realize how strong and enduring is the successful ideological conditioning of White supremacy.

So as I come to the end of my career, I wish I were at the beginning so I could have another forty or fifty years to disrupt the White supremacist narrative embedded in my consciousness. Nevertheless—seeing the glass as half full—I have had the chance to participate in a project that has helped me understand better how to recognize that narrative instead of letting it run unchallenged in my head, in my classes, in my workplace, and in my community. And as we discuss at the end of this book, this project has helped all of us understand better how to take practical steps to challenge that narrative when we encounter it.

MOVING FROM HISTORY TO ACTION

These are our stories. We believe that as you begin your dialogues and conversations about race and racism within your classrooms, your offices, your homes, and your spaces—personal, professional, or social—you must be willing to unveil a part of your history, your life with others. We recognize that this is not easy, and as you will see throughout the pages of this book, some find it easier to reflect on the self than others.

The next step is to move from talking about one's self to engaging in a dialogue with others about how lived experiences influence or direct current interactions and actions. This next step in the process, for those of us in the academy, will occur around the table in our classrooms, and for those of us in other settings it may be around some other frequent or informal gathering point, what this book is calling the *kitchen table.* Whether the conversation begins in your classroom or at your kitchen table, we ask that you be open to exploring and engaging in a critique and reflection about yourself and also be willing to listen to others—releasing any preconceived beliefs or expectations about what may be unveiled. This second step begins with a conversation about race and racism.

OUR KITCHEN TABLE DIALOGUE

The four of us spent a total of two and a half days with each other sitting around a table in a Chicago hotel, grappling with the meaning of race and racism, and discussing whether we in fact—as three Black women (from the U.S. Midwest, South, and West) and one White male (from

Liverpool)—could provide a medium through which others might dialogue with one another around these issues. We are bringing you the reader into the midst of our dialogue, with the four of us trying to describe our assumptions as well as define racism. We are sharing portions of our dialogue with you in an attempt to demonstrate the difficulties, the challenges, and the rewards of engaging in dialogue about subject areas we value but find difficult to explore in mixed groups.

The first thing we uncovered was that although we held similar definitions of race and racism, our assumptions about whether we could be the object or the subject of racism differed. So in spite of our commitment to writing and engaging in dialogues about race and racism, our varying assumptions caused us to pause and engage in a very heated and healthy conversation. For instance, in this brief exchange, as we discussed and tried to describe what our assumptions were, Scipio commented:

> I'm not sure that we share the same definition of racism. I see racism as being different from prejudice. I'd be willing for us to go around, but I would say I don't have racist assumptions.

She went on to share how her experiences had affected her understanding of race and racism. Then she continued:

> And my perspectives are probably different from others'. My experiences and my understanding initially of racism are not grounded in the Eurocentric context but in the African American and African Diaspora context. That's how I understand racism. Not from the perspective of a perpetuator, because I believe there's a power differential that is based upon White racist ideology regarding the idea of the power and privilege of pigmentation.
>
> And there's sociocultural racism and there's intellectual racism. So if I say I don't have racist assumptions because when I look at Stephen I don't have certain assumptions about his intellectual capabilities because of his racial group membership, do you know what I'm saying? So I would say I don't have racist assumptions.

Because we had no consensus about whether our assumptions about race and racism needed to be similar in order to pursue a conversation about race and racism, might we be using the wrong questions to frame our discussions? In an attempt to move the conversation to another level, Vanessa said:

> So, maybe the question is wrong. I mean, we framed it in terms of what racist assumptions frame our actions. "What assumptions do you hold about race and racism in terms of actions and/or behaviors you've experienced?" might be a different way of framing it.

What we discovered was that when, despite our best intentions, our conversations stall because we discover we have differing opinions or understandings, one of the first things we find ourselves doing is questioning whether we have the right question, issues, or tools to move forward. Although we believe that it is good to stop and reflect, we encourage you in these circumstances to move on, to push the dialogue further. Do not stop pushing each other to find a way to continue sharing and listening to one another.

PUSHING FORWARD

So ask the question or questions, and then allow for differences in thought to be brought into the conversation and then move forward. For us this meant allowing for very different points of view. As we continued the conversation about our assumptions about race and racism, it led the three of us who are African Americans to talk about whether we could be considered racist or could inflict racism on others, and just with whom and under what circumstances this might occur. Juanita responded to the question of whether African Americans could engage in racist acts with this observation:

> I think that you have to have racist assumptions because you grew up in a society that's racist. I understand the academic position that people of color cannot be racist because the power structure does

not support us to act on that racism. I understand that it's a macro-level kind of thing. Unless you're perfect, and God—if you grew up in American society then there's no way you cannot have racist assumptions, 'cause nobody's perfect.

This led to a lively back and forth between Juanita and Scipio. For example, Scipio responded to Juanita's comment by challenging her assumptions:

But what I would say to you is that there is another interpretation of that experience. The point is that you can't grow up in this society without understanding racism, but it's back to the same point. The assumption on the table is that we all have a shared definition of that, when really we don't. Because what I'm saying is that I don't have racist assumptions. I do not treat other people in that manner, whether it's scientific racism, first visual pigmentation, or anything else. So I am not going to respond to that theoretical interpretation but from my perspective. That may not be true from your perspective but neither you nor anyone else can tell me that's not true from my perspective, which is based upon the meaning of my lived experiences.

After much debate, we did come to a rather interesting turning point in the conversation. Just perhaps, given one's worldview and set of experiences, one might be considered to have both a theoretical view of racism and an experiential view. As Vanessa stated:

So when I think about race, I have a set of assumptions about what that means. You know? And whether or not [they're] true or not…[they're] my assumptions [and they] have some bearing on how I view what happens to me in a situation. So I have an understanding about that as well as about what is racism. So maybe the initial question did not get at the heart of what we intended it to address. And how we frame or reframe the question has a bearing on what we intend to discuss concerning race and racism.

Addressing both this idea and her own earlier exchange with Juanita, Scipio went on to say:

> We need to stick with the point of the kitchen table. And this...how shall I put this? Here, here we have a situation, two members of the African Diaspora, and one calls the other a liar...—let me finish—because that person says I am not racist. And the response is, well, I don't believe that you can't be racist. Now on some level we have a shared experience at different levels, just by simply being members of the African Diaspora in America, and although we have [these] shared experiences, I've come away with a whole different definitional frame of what a racist is, and she's come away with a whole different definitional frame of what a racist is.

Juanita summed up her position by reiterating that

> In this universe it's not possible for any human who has grown up within these hierarchies to not have racist assumptions. We may not act on them. We may say, "I know that I have racist assumptions, but I've worked enough on myself to try not to act on them."

And the conversation continued on, with three of us debating back and forth—one pointing out that the question was not getting at the heart of the topic, the other two embroiled in a debate about what it meant to be racist and whether either of them were racist, and the fourth member of our group listening intently. We pressed on, hoping that we'd reach consensus with each other. After several hours of discussion, we finally reached a juncture for departing to end our first evening. We recognized that there are two types of conversations and places of entry into conversations on race and racism. One begins in the academy, in the classroom, and the other begins in our homes around the kitchen table. Where one begins and or ends is relevant to obtaining an understanding about race and racism and its ensuing impact on our lives and our work. Vanessa described it this way:

> I think part of this for us, being in the academy, is that we hold positions of power over others. And now we're in positions where

we're making decisions that could be skewed or viewed as being racist, even when we employ the same tactics used...by Whites who were in power or authority before us. So, since we are now in positions that previously [had] been denied to us, we must be doing the same [to others] as had been done to us. And if that's what racism is about—having power and authority over someone else and...[deciding] whether or not someone outside of a [race similar to] yours gains access or not, or what is valuable about...[that person]—then, yeah, I guess that could be racism. But, I think, traditionally, when we talk about racism in America, it's been described as racism between Blacks and Whites or Whites and others. Or between Whites and everybody else. So it hasn't been necessarily viewed in the context of Blacks and other groups being racist or committing racist acts towards Whites. So what happens when we take on the positions of power in a classroom? Or when we take on positions of power as an administrator? What does that mean? And how do we exert that power? And do we use our racial identity as a sense of power and authority over others? Now I suspect we could, but somehow, I think, the tendency of those of us in administrative positions is that we don't—and maybe that's the issue.

So our conversation moved from whether we were racist or had racist assumptions to a discussion about power and power relations and how issues of power may affect whether a person of color could be considered a racist. We struggled to determine whether those of us who are African Americans could in fact be racist or whether that was something that could or would occur only if one were White or Euro-American. Did we come away with any answers after spending two days with each other or reading through the stories of the individuals we've included in this book? We daresay we decided there were no exact answers. But the dialogue gave us an opportunity to express how we felt about the topic. We decided that much more time was needed for such conversations, and that we had to work diligently to stay on task. We came away saying that this was a beginning and not an end to our need and everyone else's need to engage in these kinds of conversations—especially if we all want to change our perceptions about each other with regard to race and racism.

THE GOAL: ENGAGEMENT IN DIALOGICAL DISCUSSIONS ON RACE AND RACISM

To that end, the purpose of this book is to offer both adult and higher education scholars and those engaged in research and teaching about race an opportunity to engage in a discourse that addresses (1) how race and racism have been examined through multiple theoretical frameworks; (2) how race and racism have affected their own and others' lived experiences at work, at home, and in educational settings; (3) how race has served to privilege some and not others; and (4) how race and racism need to be further explored. The ultimate intent of this discourse is to provide as many individuals as possible, whether they are in the margins or the center, with ways to think about creating changes in their classrooms, communities, and homes.

OVERVIEW OF THIS BOOK

Following this Introduction, this book is divided into five parts, each aimed at fulfilling a specific part of our work's purpose and essential to obtaining a greater understanding of race and racism. These sections are titled "The Myth Versus the Reality of Race and Racism"; "Problematizing 'Whiteness,' Supremacy, and Privilege: Their Impact on Race"; "Theoretical Responses to Race and Racism"; "Reframing the Field Through the Lens of Race"; and "Individual and Collective Responses to Race and Racism." The chapters in each part offer a point of entry into the discourse on race and racism, ultimately taking readers to a place of recognizing themselves and their roles, and revealing what actions they need to take in order to change the impact and weight of race and racism in their institutions, their communities, and their lives. We do not believe that anyone can do this alone or apart from others. At the same time, we do believe that individuals will need to engage first in conversations with same-race and same-gender groups. You will note our efforts to move these conversations along in these ways, as well as to recognize that in the end there is a need to move from individual to collective reflections and actions.

Our contributing authors assisted us in these efforts. One or more of us acted as editors for the chapters in each part of this book, and took responsibility for leading the chapter authors through a series of guided questions, the same questions with which we ourselves had grappled:

1. What racist assumptions have framed your actions and behaviors? And what have you learned and/or are learning about yourself?

2. Do you believe that racism is endemic and permanent in our society?

3. As you read through the chapters in this section, what new insights have you gained about how race, racism, and sexism impact the teaching, learning, and administration within adult or higher education?

4. How might the chapters in the section where your chapter appears help lead to deeper or new understandings about the ways in which race and racism impact how we work/operate within our various settings?

5. How might this book help us change this situation, or have we gone so far along on this path (with race and racism) that there is no turning back with regard to how we see ourselves in relationship to and/or work with others outside of our racialized identities?

We also asked the contributing authors to reflect on these questions as they shared their stories and reflections with us. One or two members of the editorial team guided each of the smaller group discussions (see the Reflections at end of each part). We also asked each author in this book to read drafts of the other chapters in the portions of the book in which his or her chapter appeared, so that each author could give the others feedback and also engage in informed and rich conversations with each of the other authors on the meaning and relevance of racism and its effect on their lives, their lived experiences. In addition to this, we also attempted to employ technology to expedite our conversations in cyberspace. At the heart of this project was a belief that it is only through dialogue and discussion that each person will begin to enhance his or her understanding of the ways in which race and racism influence different individuals' lives and direct how each person engages with others within the global community. For each of us this was an eye-opening experience. Yet it also solidified some of our preconceived notions about the difficulties each of us has engaging in conversations about racism, especially in mixed audiences.

We hope that this book will be used by those who teach and prepare master's and doctoral degree candidates in the fields of adult education, equity and social justice, multicultural education, curriculum and instruction, sociology of education, and other areas of education. As you reflect on the stories and voices of the authors in this book and the editorial reflections at the end of each part, we ask that you take a step outside of your everyday comfort zone to inquire whether you see a glimpse of yourself, recognize your own realities, or hear your own voice in the stories that unfold throughout this book.

We now invite you to read, listen, and deliberate about the ways in which you may exhibit racist tendencies or acts in your personal, social, or professional lives.

REFERENCES

Brookfield, S. (2002). Teaching through discussion as the exercise of disciplinary power. In D. Lieberman & C. Wehlburg (Eds.), *To improve the academy: Resources for faculty, instructional, and organizational development.* Boston: Anker.

Colin, S.A.J., III. (1988). *Voices from beyond the veil: Marcus Garvey, the Universal Negro Improvement Association and the education of African Ameripean adults.* Unpublished dissertation, Northern Illinois University, DeKalb, IL.

DuBois, W.E.B. (1897). The conservation of races. *American Negro Academy Occasional Papers* (Vol. 2). Washington, DC: American Negro Academy.

Johnson-Bailey, J. (2001a). The road less walked: A retrospective of race and ethnicity in adult education. *International Journal of Lifelong Education, 20*(1–2), 89–99.

Johnson-Bailey, J. (2001b). *Sistahs in college: Making a way out of no way.* Malabar, FL: Krieger Press.

Johnson-Bailey, J. (2006). African Americans in adult education: The Harlem Renaissance revisited. *Adult Education Quarterly, 56*(2), 102–118.

Johnson-Bailey, J., & Cervero, R. M. (2000). The invisible politics of race in adult education. In A. L. Wilson & E. R. Hayes (Eds.), *Handbook of adult and continuing education: New edition* (pp. 147–160). San Francisco: Jossey-Bass.

Outlaw, L. (1996). *On race and philosophy.* New York: Routledge.

Sheared, V. (1992). *From workfare to Edfare: African American women and the elusive quest for self-determination: A critical analysis of the JOBS plan.* Unpublished dissertation, Northern Illinois University, DeKalb, IL.

Sheared, V. (1994). Giving voice: An inclusive model of instruction— A womanist perspective." In E. Hayes & S.A.J. Colin III (Eds.), *Confronting racism and sexism in adult education* (New Directions for Adult and Continuing Education, No. 61). San Francisco: Jossey-Bass.

Sheared, V. (1999). Giving voice: Inclusion of African American students' polyrhythmic realities in adult basic education. In T. Guy (Ed.), *Providing culturally relevant adult education: A challenge for the twenty-first century* (New Directions for Adult and Continuing Education, No. 82, pp. 33–48). San Francisco: Jossey-Bass.

PART ONE

The Myth Versus the Reality of Race and Racism

This section examines the ways in which race and racism have affected and marginalized the life stories, histories, and research of "people of color," in this case women of various ages and languages and from varied geographies. These women discuss how race and racism are maintained and perpetuated within their particular educational, work, or personal spaces or contexts. They address the ways in which the myths and the realities of race and racism have served at times to obfuscate and at other times to inform their practice and their lived experiences.

A *myth* is what we have come to believe about a phenomenon. And the *reality* is what we feel we know about a phenomenon. And so what are the myths and realities around race? It's simple: the myths and realities around race are dependent on one's perspective. The authors of the chapters in this section share a belief that race is a powerful social construct that shapes our society and often determines the actions of people intentionally and unintentionally. Even when we try to deny the existence of race and its partisan adherent, racism, the construct exists nevertheless—constant yet changing, powerful yet pathetic, unyielding yet compliant. Despite their knowledge of race and racism, the authors of this section readily admit that their experiences and expertise about race, their comprehension of it, is as shifting as the phenomenon. They collectively acknowledge that even though they have an understanding of race and racism, they continue to struggle with these constant companions.

What is voiced in the collection of chapters in this section is that the authors are on a journey to understand the myths and the realities of race, and they feel that this journey is an ongoing sojourn in which they negotiate between a state of double consciousness (knowing of a normed existence while being seen as the other) and a single-minded, quintessential realization of home. The disorienting dilemma of *otherness*—of being seen as the one with "race"—is tiring. However, the lessons and teachings provided by the authors' indigenous cultures have given them a refuge and the strength to maintain their humanity. Overwhelmingly, the section authors expressed again and again that they sustain a spiritual connection with a place that provides them comfort, voice, acceptance, and strength.

Although it was not deliberate, all the authors in this section are women of color, albeit from different backgrounds, races, tribes, regions, and hemispheres. Furthermore, they are all feminists and consequently stand on a shared political base and common existence—the communal intersection of race and gender—a location in the margins or of being marginalized.

In the first chapter, "Rebirth of the Indigenous Spirit: Turning the World Right Side Up," Rose Borunda, a Native American, has a powerful spiritual message borne out of the pain of being an indigenous scholar whose voice emerges from an American apartheid with a message that is filled with love and kindness. Yet this author first created a bridge that melded bits and pieces of her lost and then discovered native world with the culture of the colonizer in an effort to find balance. But finally, this bridge of acculturation led Borunda back to her home culture and provided her with a methodology for showing and teaching others. Although she does not speak specifically of theory, her teaching approach is strategic and developed from trial and error, from observations, and from making connections using the specific to explore and make conjectures. Borunda is grounded in the theory of her people.

Yolanda Sealey-Ruiz, the African American author of Chapter Two, "Reading, Writing, and Racism: Developing Racial Literacy in the Adult Education English Classroom," has taken a different path to developing her educational practice. Sealey-Ruiz has decided to use theory merely as a base to inform her practice. She is unflinching in dealing directly with the untidy, ugly clutter that race and racism has deposited on our academic doorstep, and she has developed strategies to use in the classroom to help students of color and White students deal with the issues and dilemmas that arise when race is discussed.

Although the two Chicana writers who speak to us in the third chapter of this section, "Experiencing the Race, Gender, and Socioeconomic Divide in Academia: A Chicana Perspective," are also sending us messages learned from their lives in the academy, their voices are their lived experiences, telling cultural narratives aimed at empowering their sisters and brothers who may still live in fear of the telling. Raquel Gonzáles and Maria Mejorado speak of the prejudice and pain that hides behind the seemingly liberal walls of academia, where polite behavior and detached sanitized words and texts miseducate the disenfranchised to places of self-loathing, hopelessness, passivity, and gratitude. As activist scholars, Gonzáles and Mejorado want to openly express love for their community, and pledge to each other and their community to engage in an agenda of uplift.

Just as the authors of Chapter Three have used higher education as a base for establishing a shared plan for survival and struggle, Nichole Ray, the author of the fourth chapter, "Transforming Teaching and Learning: Teaching Race," uses her teaching practice to sharpen her Black feminist consciousness and to engage her White students, who are often encountering her as their first Black professor. She wades through resistance, attacks, and cries of alleged colorblindness to "speak race" to her students while they are in moments of cognitive dissonance, in an effort to make change and to take advantage of those teachable moments that will be transformative.

And magically, as if summoned to this place, Lesley Ngatai, a Maori woman and the author of the final chapter in this section, " 'Who Is This Cowboy?' Challenging the Cultural Gatekeepers," calls from New Zealand to give a précis of Part One, "The Myth Versus the Reality of Race and Racism," by embracing theory, academic practice, lived experiences, and the pains of struggling in higher education to find healing in the spiritual exercise of teaching from a place of peace, acceptance, and cultural truth.

1

Rebirth of the Indigenous Spirit
Turning the World Right Side Up

ROSE BORUNDA

I am now considered well educated because of the formal degrees I hold. Yet I somehow have also held onto the value of being *bien educada,* the essence of having respect for one's elders and living in harmony within one's community. On my journey toward becoming *bien educada,* I also discovered that Columbus did not "discover America." No one told me, but I came to know this as being a lie. I also came to understand when to and when not to speak of this truth, because speaking such truths publicly challenges the illusion created by a people who need to believe in what Loewen (1995) refers to as "heroes," however symbolically violent (Anderson and Herr, 2003) this position may be to those of us who claim roots in this land.

We are all born into a world, a situation, a story over which we do not have control but ultimately must understand. In order to gain control over how we live in this world, I believe that a rebirthing of one's self, a reconnection to one's spirit, is necessary. It is a journey that requires us to let go of stories and images that have caused us to devalue ourselves, and it is a journey in which we each reframe our story, rediscover and rewrite the story as it is told through the voices and stories of our ancestors, thereby turning the world right side up so that ultimately we each take control of our own story. Taking control of the story is not enough though. We must share the story through our life's work. This is the journey, the story, the reclaiming of truths, and the sharing of those truths that I repeat with the students I teach in my classes.

THE JOURNEY: MY STORY

A family friend recently reminded me that as a child I used to gleefully announce to anyone who would listen, "I was born on Columbus Day!" This statement from a young child of indigenous ancestry—but what else could I say? In elementary school I was required to memorize facts about Christopher Columbus, the Italian-born mariner hailed "discoverer." Later in life I learned how this man had turned this side of the world upside down. Subsequently, even though my ancestors lived in the "New World" for thousands of years, I have no knowledge of their language and only limited knowledge of their history. I can, however, readily name the three ships under Columbus's command when he first voyaged across the Atlantic; the *Niña,* the *Pinta,* and the *Santa Maria.* This is one of many "truths" I was taught about "his"tory. This chapter addresses my voyage to uncover "my" story and the subsequent impact that my discoveries have had on my teaching as a university professor.

"In fourteen hundred ninety-two / Columbus sailed the ocean blue." As children we were taught this song that immortalized this "discoverer." I remember outlining the images of the three ships with my color crayons. Blue construction paper provided the backdrop of a vast blue ocean. This child's artistic rendition was proudly displayed on the classroom wall. It was a fitting tribute to a man portrayed to be gallant and valiant and whom we honored with song, study, and artistry. I was taught to believe that we were indebted to this mariner, whose feats warranted a day off from school, holiday sales and promotions, and parades in tribute.

The activities in which I engaged during my childhood *expected* me and *conditioned* me to show *gratitude* and to celebrate the fact that I was being introduced to an advanced "civilization" attributable to this momentous "discovery." From the perspective of my childhood eyes, it seemed appropriate that we honor someone who brought this advanced culture to fill the void of nothingness assumed to have existed prior to Columbus's arrival. Yet, even while we sang praises to Columbus and I exclaimed, "I was born on Columbus Day," I intuited that I was not *intended* to be where I was, in the United States, and that somehow *who* I was, a descendant of indigenous people, was a source of contempt, disdain, and even inconvenience to many confronted by my existence.

Even as a child I sensed an existential chasm between the society in which I existed and the home in which I lived. Attempting to bridge the two worlds, I drew from my home culture's tradition of storytelling and created my own story. This tale was repeated to teachers and classmates in order to justify my existence in a land in which I subconsciously recognized that I was the "other."

> I came from a walnut that grew in a tree that is south of here. One day I fell off the tree and landed in a creek below. Protected by the outer shell I traveled on the water for many miles. I came to rest in Walnut Creek, California, and that is where I came out of the shell and so I was born here.

Americanization had claimed my identity by omitting to explore my heritage and instead, in its place, attempting to inculcate me with a homogeneous, nonethnic identity. To integrate myself into the colonizer's story, I instinctively adapted to the fixed reality (Freire, 1970/1998) and creatively merged "my" story with "his"story, and in my story the attempt of a child to rationalize her existence where she is otherwise absent is evident. I was too young to understand that without the use of chains and locks, my mind had been enslaved by "edification" skillfully designed to ensure that the reality of the world in which I lived reflected the reality of the conqueror, the subject, and not the vanquished, the subjugated.

This enforced alien worldview is not new to the people from this land. My ancestors experienced this force through the violence of guns, swords, biological warfare, relocation, genocide, broken treaties, and rape. My generation came to know this force through the violence of the pen that erased the existence of anything *pre-Columbian* and that characterized anything related to my culture as *savage* and *uncivilized*. Conquered people are rendered harmless as long as the conqueror's weapons remain visible to remind the conquered of the pain they can cause. Sustaining the bondage of the descendants entails convincing these oppressed people that "true knowledge" came from beyond the ocean to the East, thus rendering their minds harmless.

A child's mind is malleable and can be easily deceived. Absence of knowledge about my heritage, my origins, my ancestry, rendered me harmless and therefore incapable of posing threat. Weaponry of pen replaced physical violence to dominate a conquered people. My coping mechanism rendered me incapable of recognizing that I had been culturally invaded and historically raped. Born, I was, on Columbus Day.

READING AN UPSIDE DOWN WORLD

Freire (1970/1998) posits that most children do not have the capacity to read their world from beyond their state of submersion. So, being born on the day that Columbus discovered America meant that who I was, who I am, was shaped by how those in America treated and celebrated this date. For me, hanging onto the coincidence of my date of birth with the "discovery" of America made my reality more palatable. The teachers who shaped my day-to-day reality provided history books that bore nothing positive about anyone whose origins might be traced to my own heritage. The absence and invisibility of my ancestors implicitly conveyed the value they were to be given.

As I moved into adolescence, my eyes began to perceive a world that revealed *my place* in it. In my community, those who looked like me worked long hours in agriculture, steel mills, or canneries. On weekends and vacations, we worked in the fields of those who owned them, but on weekdays we attended school alongside the owners' sons and daughters, where self-imposed segregation commonly occurred. My childhood illusion of being exceptional due to my coincidental date of birth no longer satisfied my adolescent mind, which perceived this reality differently. The seed of anger sprouted. The adolescent and the child were now at odds with one another.

My child self found validation through a meaningless, coincidental connection with a significant historical date. My adolescent self detected an unspoken silence that encapsulated my reality. And this silence grew louder each day. Unwritten rules spoke to an implicit understanding, that the way of being and using language that mattered in one context, my home, was not accepted or valued in the dominant context represented by school. And while I academically excelled in this dominant context, there was a growing spiritual void. Silent anger—my adolescent self swallowed it like a pill.

SEARCHING FOR THE RIGHT MEDICINE

Freire (1970/1998) notes that differences in culture, language, and worldview exist where conquest and colonization have led the way for forces of cultural invasion. The pen follows the swath left by guns, swords, biological warfare, and rape, then holds the power to write history from the vantage of the colonizer. The colonized, indigenous child is left to endure the differentiated outcomes of a world devoid of her essence. Yet her *place* in the existing class structure is clearly prescribed. This same child is also indoctrinated to believe that she can *make it* in this world because there is a *meritocracy* and that only those who work hard will *succeed*. What the indigenous child is not told is that there is a cost to her soul for engaging in ways that disassociate her from her authentic self. That cost often leads to alienation and isolation from a person's family and community.

Even though on occasion there is an exception in how this person is perceived, all too often he or she becomes known in the community as a *coconut*. The person is accused of *selling out*. Such derogatory terms reflect the community's perception of individuals who *forget who they are*. So how does a child begin to understand a world in which she is encapsulated with knowledge other than her own? The shackled self lacks the key.

From my position as the subjugated, I had ample opportunities to see the world from the bottom rung of the social class ladder. Working the fields of my classmates' parents, being placed in classes with "troubled" youths (most of whom were children of color or low-income Whites), being excluded from programs such as Gifted and Talented Education (GATE) due to my limited English vocabulary, and getting dirty looks for speaking my home language in public, spoke loud and clear, implicitly and explicitly, that *who and what I was* was not acceptable. To gain acceptance I had to learn to live by *their* rules, so I adapted. According to Davidson, Phelan, and Yu (1998), during such times one separates one's two worlds by employing navigational skills to cross back and forth between them. For me, this meant that I had to learn to succeed in one world while struggling to retain the other; subsequently, an empty void filled my soul.

As I entered my adulthood the unresolved anger from my adolescence resounded. An internal confrontation centered on what had been inculcated into my mind as a child. The adolescent spoke through the adult to the child and asked critical questions, "How do you reconcile the absence of 'self' in historical accounts touted as 'truth'?" "Why do you celebrate the accidental fact that the date of your birth coincides with the memorializing of the first person to bring the transatlantic slave trade and genocide to your ancestors?" "Why do you listen to 'teachers' who teach lies and vilify your ancestors?" The child in me fell silent. I did not have an answer. My ears stopped listening to the world around me. My spirit began searching.

REDISCOVERING MY WORLD OF ORIGIN

My first teaching experience in higher education was as a faculty member at California's only tribal college, D-Q University, in the summer of 2001. The students, adults who were either from First Nations or whose ancestors had been indigenous to what is now referred to as *Latin America*, became my teachers. Though I was the one with the formal education, they were the ones who taught me about who I am culturally. They taught me that through our collective identity we can create a world that is not dominated by individualism, competition, and self-interest.

My true education began with my primary teacher, Angelbertha Cobb, a member of the Mexica tribe, and her understudy, Benjamin Torres. Together, they provided me with an authentic education that helped me realign my frame of reference and that spoke to what Cobb (personal communication, January 2002) refers to as "my" story. Mama Cobb, as she is affectionately and reverently called in our community, taught me the cultural values that are embedded in the sacredness of the medicine wheel, or, in *Nahuatl*, the language of the Mexica, the *Xantotl*.

The medicine wheel teaches cultural truths about our relationships with one another. As shown in Figure 1.1, a cardinal point resides at each of the four directions on the sacred circle. Each point is opposite to another without being *oppositional* to the other. They exist on the same plane, which means that each holds equal worth, and yet they are interdependent. In the direction of the East, the place of the rising sun, is the place of men. The element of fire resides in the East. Opposite to the place of men, in the West, is the place of women. The element of water is held sacred at this point. To the South is the place of children, where the element of earth is recognized, and to the North is the place of our elders, where we honor the sky, the air we breathe, the fourth vital element. Together, the four directions create balance to the whole in this realm of existence.

The elements of the medicine wheel come alive through an immersion in a community of collectiveness, selflessness, and cooperation. For me, this began when I began undoing forty-plus years of what

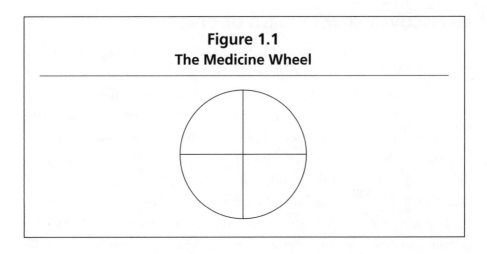

Figure 1.1
The Medicine Wheel

Woodson (1933), a noted African American historian, refers to as one's *miseducation.* This miseducation occurs whenever one is told that others' ways of knowing and being are to be valued over one's own culture and history. For me, this meant that I had to rid myself of these other ways of knowing. In this new world, my students modeled how to believe and act—such as sharing without being asked. They considered the needs of others without being reminded. They sought resolution and consensus without ego. There was respect for elders and for teachers. There was a relational respect that did not require being written. Children and women were valued in a way the outside world has yet to achieve, and even though the soul wound from years of genocide and relocation was present in the form of alcoholism and other ills, there was a sense of pride that comes with being a survivor and in reclaiming one's (my) authentic self.

TURNING THE WORLD RIGHT SIDE UP

The answers I would discover came in my reclaiming my truth, my world as seen through the stories of my parents and my ancestors. Through this quest, I discovered that truths about my father's ancestry had also been taught. His tribe, the Purépecha, originated from Aztlátan, a region now known as the southwestern United States. Other indigenous people have called this land Turtle Island. His tribe resided in an area called the Land of the Cranes, also known as Salt Lake City. In the central region of Aztlátan reside the Hopi, where they have lived since the beginning of the Fifth World, and whose connection to Mother Earth is analogous to a child's umbilical connection to its mother. Through the oral tradition I learned about the twelve tribes that originated from this region. Seven of these twelve, including the Purépecha, traveled south of Aztlátan after the great flood waters receded during the beginning of the Fifth World, to the region known as Aztlanahuac, which consists of Mexico and Central America.

Learning about such truths began to feed my spirit—one that had long been silenced. No longer was there joy in proclaiming, "I was born on Columbus Day," because for the first time I understood the significance of not only the physical and cultural violence that took place as a result of the acts of conquest and colonization but also the pain of cultural invasion which had left me devoid of my *authenticity*. Once I began to peel away the layers of this story, the next act was to remove the pill of anger that had turned into a cancer in my spirit. I began to consciously and spiritually reconcile the true meaning of my date of birth coinciding with a day that marked the physical, cultural, and spiritual genocide of my people. And so on my forty-fourth birthday, I was spiritually reborn. I participated in a ceremony that allowed me to symbolically emerge from the womb of my mother, Mother Earth, a Lakota sweat lodge. This rebirthing took place after having undergone hours of chanting, singing, and praying.

HEALING WHILE TEACHING: REBIRTHING

The rebirthing was the first step toward gaining an appreciation of who I am in relation to my family, my community, and the world. The next step was taking this awareness into my work and the relationships I would ultimately encounter in my journey. A gentleman employed as a resident adviser at D-Q University told me, "You are my other me," meaning that the "other" is merely our spiritual self in another physical body. For this reason, we must treat the other as we would want ourselves to be treated. So as an example of this, this man once a year gave away all of his material belongings so that he would not become attached to the things of this world and be owned by his possessions. He valued the harmony of relationships with others and was resolute in considering the needs of others as a primary objective in his life. His values made him empathic and caring, dispositions that I believe are needed by people who endeavor to become educators and counselors.

For me, this is a very important example, for I now am responsible for helping graduate students uncover and share themselves with others in the field of counselor education. For me, as a faculty member in an institution of higher education, teaching is not just solely about the content; it is also about the journey we take our students on while they are in our classes. It is a journey that for many will be about their own rebirthing and reclaiming of stories yet to be told. Throughout my years as a faculty member, I have discovered that many graduate students do not have the cultural self-knowledge to foster the disposition required to become caring counselors. My challenge, then, is to create a classroom experience in which the student can go on the journey of rebirthing, learning, and sharing.

Given the ethical expectations of my profession, I find challenge in undoing values fostered by years of conditioning and modeling in a society whose values reflect materialism, self-centeredness, disassociation, and extrinsic gratification.

I believe that undoing the miseducation of students requires a recognition that we—teachers and students—all have equal value in the classroom. In order to achieve this, teachers must set a tone for learning, collaborating, and sharing with one another. There are several tools that I use and that I believe are essential to achieving and going through the rebirthing phase. Drawing upon the medicine wheel—the circle—I believe that having students arrange their chairs in a semicircle or full circle reframes the power dynamics in the classroom. Students often say that they feel vulnerable and exposed as a result of not being able to "hide" behind a desk. The physical structure of a circle forces them to *see* one another; subsequently all of us in the room begin to overcome what Schaefer (2005) refers to as years of interracial social distance. I ask students how this might help them gain an understanding of how their clients might feel when they expose them to similar circumstances in their counseling sessions. In addition to changing the seating arrangements, I walk around the class and introduce myself to each and every student.

Acts of inclusiveness are preceded by valuing the other. Adults raised on values of exclusion, competitiveness, independence, self-centeredness, and future orientation can only be what they know. The next generation learns what is modeled. After I model civility, students begin to see and ultimately deconstruct what they observed and how they felt as a result of being acknowledged by their teacher on the first day. In a classroom where inclusion is valued from the heart and not just the head, we are then able to talk about what happened, and this becomes not only a teachable moment but the beginning of their rebirth.

From acknowledgment we move to listening and ensuring that everyone is heard. Often students share that they have lost their voices by the time they reach graduate school. After years of "educational" conditioning that has taught them to regurgitate what their teacher tells them, they find it difficult to believe that someone is actually interested in what they think. Their capacity to think critically has been stolen, so they rarely question what they are told, whose perspective it is taught from, and why it is even relevant to their lives. Then I tell them to question *me*. I give them permission to restore their voices.

They talk about how they have never experienced a class such as this and how they hope to replicate the *feeling* of it in their practice. They begin to reach out, smile, and talk with one another. They anticipate their classmates who may arrive late and prepare a seat for them in the circle. They begin to share notes and conduct study groups. They suggest holding potlucks at the end of the semester, and everyone brings something to share. It is then that I know that the world is right side up again. I, as my authentic self, have something of worth to offer my students because in my classroom I have created the conditions through which my students have made the ultimate discovery—they have discovered themselves and each other, their indigenous spirit, reborn, and alive.

REFERENCES

Anderson, G., & Herr, K. (2003). Violent youth or violent schools? A critical incident analysis of symbolic violence. *International Journal of Leadership in Education*, 6(4), 415–433.

Davidson, A. L., Phelan, P., & Yu, H. C. (1998). *Adolescents' worlds: Negotiating family, peers, and school*. New York: Teachers College Press.

Freire, P. (1998). *Pedagogy of the oppressed*. New York: Continuum. (Original English translation published 1970)

Loewen, J. (1995). *Lies my teacher told me*. New York: Touchstone.

Schaefer, R. (2005). *Race and ethnicity in the United States*. Upper Saddle River, NJ: Pearson Prentice Hall.

Woodson, C. G. (1933). *The mis-education of the Negro*. Washington, DC: Associated Publishers.

2

Reading, Writing, and Racism

Developing Racial Literacy in the Adult Education English Classroom

YOLANDA SEALEY-RUIZ

One of those "defining moments" in my teaching career happened several years ago when I gave a talk to a group of high school teachers on English language arts (ELA) standardized tests. My goal was to provide an overview of the use of ELA standardized tests in public education and discuss the antitesting movement that was gaining momentum across the country. I spoke to forty novice teachers who worked in urban schools and were also graduate students at the predominantly White university that sponsored the event. At the end of the three hours, an Asian woman came to the front of the room, where I was talking to a group of teachers. Our eyes locked just as she said, "I just want you to know that I was expecting to have a White, male professor today. You actually did OK with the material. Better than I expected."

She left before I could respond to her comment. I thought to myself, "Was that supposed to be a compliment?" and, "What gave her the right to speak to me that way?" A range of emotions flooded over me: I was embarrassed that she had made this bold statement in the presence of others; but most of all, I was confused and incensed by what she said to me. I wanted to ask her, "Why do you think only White males are capable of discussing standardized testing?" I wanted to know why she *couldn't* expect that I, a former student and teacher in the public school system, would speak adequately on the topic of standardized tests. I also wondered what myths about African Americans she summoned that day to make her final judgment about me. Her assumptions about my ability, surely based on my race and gender, had silenced me in that moment. It was an incident that I have never forgotten, and one that has been instrumental in shaping my pedagogy as an adult educator.

As an African American adult educator, I have experienced challenges and difficulties in the classroom that have centered on my being Black, and I have developed a method of teaching that has *racial literacy* as a major component. Racial literacy can be developed when explicit conversations about race and the ill effects of racism are central topics of course readings and writing assignments and when discussions are held in a safe classroom environment.

THE IMPACT OF RACE AND RACISM ON MY TEACHING

When I reflect on that defining-moment incident and other experiences I have had as an educator of adults, DuBois's concept of *double consciousness* comes to mind. African American adult educators and their African American students experience an obstinate external pressure, a "sense of always looking at one's self through the eyes of others, of measuring one's soul by the tape of a world that looks on in amused contempt and pity" (DuBois, 1903/1995, p. 45). That critical incident happened nearly a decade ago, and yet it remains one of the principal reasons why I currently initiate and encourage explicit conversation about race and racism in my adult education English classroom. In my class, students who hold negative opinions about people of color, including African Americans—opinions like those that Asian teacher most likely had of me—are given the opportunity to interrogate their beliefs and assumptions. In my classroom, my Asian students, just like my African American students, are expected to explore racial stereotypes (as reflected in the *model minority* label, for example) that exist about them.

It has been my experience that notions of race and racism affect my students' perceptions of my qualifications to be their professor. The critical incident with that teacher made me acutely aware of the ways in which my knowledge and pedagogy are scrutinized by all of my students, including my White and African American students. Once students realize that my course requires them to discuss the role of race in their lives and the lives of others, White students suspect that I will browbeat them with the tragic history of Blacks in America and evoke the White guilt that comes when they confront their White privilege. Similarly, my African American students investigate the syllabus with a careful eye, wondering about the deliberate focus on race and racism in a class that is supposed to improve their writing skills and increase their chances of getting a better job. For many of them, the notion of spending a semester talking about race and racism, especially in the presence of Whites, is daunting. Further, internalized racism has them experiencing some cognitive dissonance—many appear to believe—as did that Asian teacher, that college teachers are usually White and male. These criticisms of me manifest in different ways: in the looks students give me as soon as I walk into the classroom, in their questions about my choice of texts, in their scrutiny of the syllabus and what I say in class, and in their complaints that the class is "just so much work."

Racism triggers their inquiries about where I went to school, how long I've been a professor, and where I grew up. As we share more about our lives during the semester, my students expect me to tell idyllic stories of middle-class life and a private school education. Instead, I talk about growing up in a poor-to-barely-working-class family and my mediocre K–12 public school education (Sealey-Ruiz, 2005). Over the years I have faced the painful observation that many of my students find it hard to believe that someone who went to neighborhood schools in the South Bronx, New York, could go so far as to earn a doctorate and land a job teaching at a predominantly White institution. They anticipate tales of amazing feats and pulling oneself up by one's bootstraps stories. When I do not offer any of this, they ultimately settle on the idea that I was one who "made it through." Overall, my experience as an African American woman in America has framed my academic teaching career in these ways: I know that I will not be given the benefit of the doubt. I know that I will not be granted a "pass" and have students take for granted that my doctorate means I know something about English and have some ideas on how to teach it. Moreover, as a junior professor with publications and "extensive research experience for someone at this stage in her career," I know I must work twice as hard to gain the respect that is so easily given to White assistant professors and even doctoral students who are just beginning their journey into the academy. White professors and doctoral students are seen as knowledgeable and credible because they are White—this is a benefit of their White privilege. Racism causes my students to make assumptions about me and compare me to other (White) professors they've had in similar courses they've taken during their academic experience.

Developing Racial Literacy Through Explicit Discussions

As an English educator, I have chosen race and racism to be central topics in my courses because they are common points of reference in our American identity. Certainly, there are other shared characteristics for what it means to be American, but race and racism are topics that have unique power to join us together and tear us apart. It is important to me that my students and I interrogate that which prevents us from being truly united as Americans.

Jane Bolgatz (2005) defines *racial literacy* as "a set of competencies that allows us to engage with others to challenge undemocratic practices" (p. 2). Students are able to challenge the construction of race and racist practices because they are equipped with ways to talk critically about them. The development of racial literacy in my adult education English classroom means that students are taught to critically analyze canonical, popular, media- and student-generated texts for stereotypical representations or deliberate exclusions of people of color. My students and I investigate the influence of race and the ill effects of racism in texts written by novelists, playwrights, essayists, and poets who tackle these topics in their work. They read texts by writers such as James Baldwin, Toni Cade Bambara, Herb Boyd, BeBe Moore Campbell, Jayne Cortez, Ernest Gaines, Lorraine Hansberry, Langston Hughes, Toni Morrison, Suzan-Lori Parks, Sonia Sanchez, Roberto Santiago, Brent Staples, and others. These texts are a springboard to help students problematize race and the fundamental ideals behind structural racism. We talk about dreams deferred, hopes lost, and opportunities missed because of institutionalized racism.

My experience with this method of teaching has confirmed for me that the adult education English classroom must be a site for critical discourse, a space where adults examine their social, historical, and political realities. In this type of English classroom they engage these topics through reading a diverse range of literature that highlights critical moments in history. Students investigate language and culture within communities that are similar to and unique from the ones in which they were raised and now live. Students have shown that they understand how to apply their racial literacy when they initiate discussions and raise *their* own questions.

Another possible outcome of racial literacy, for African American adult students in particular, is self-empowerment and transformation. Outlaw (1983) has asserted that "as the contours of African Americans' response to racism are learned," this will lead to "increased self-transparency—a broadening and intensification of our personal and collective self-understanding" (as quoted in Brookfield, 2003).

This critical approach to English education has gained popularity (Morrell, 2005) as a move toward better preparing secondary teachers to engage their students in critical conversations around race and power. Critical English education expects educators to position themselves as activists (Morrell, 2005). Students who engage with a critical English education embark on a journey to deconstruct race and liberate themselves from the binds of a racist society. I have witnessed that when adults are able to participate in this type of learning environment, they consider their learning experience to be meaningful and rewarding.

Practicing Racial Literacy

At the start of my course, students are grappling with how to adjust to the focus of the class as well as to my egalitarian approach to teaching. The intense conversations about race and racism are not always easy for students to participate in. I spend a considerable amount of time creating a safe classroom environment where these conversations can thrive. A safe classroom environment is achieved by creating a community where it's common for my students and me to share information about ourselves. I am able to achieve this through activities that ask students to talk about themselves (as shown in the accompanying examples). Through these activities, personal stories are shared and cultural connections and differences are explored. The first activity, "Name Story," asks students to talk about their names.

NAME STORY

We all have a unique connection to our names—some of us have love or hate relationships with our names, while others of us feel that our names signify a special family tie. This activity asks you to explore this connection by reflecting on your own name.

With this in mind, write a brief story about your name. Remember, it's your story. Feel free to focus on your full name, middle name, last name, or even your nickname.

Source: previously published by Diversity Resource Collaborative.

The "Jump Street Odyssey" activity asks students to discuss where they grew up and a particular time when they were made to feel like the "other." This activity often elicits painful moments of experiencing prejudice and discrimination and also often leads to "aha" moments for students who have discriminated against others.

JUMP STREET ODYSSEY

Briefly respond to the following questions. Then share your answers with the members of your small group. Take no more than 5 minutes per person to share your responses.

- Where were you born?
- What language(s) or dialects(s) was(were) spoken in your home?
- Where did you grow up? Describe your neighborhood.
- Where did you attend school? Describe your classmates. Did you perceive your teachers to be similar to or different from you and your family? In what ways were they similar or different?
- Recall the first time you interacted with someone different from yourself. Describe this interaction.
- Recall the first time that you felt different from everyone else. Describe the situation.

Source: previously published by Diversity Resource Collaborative.

Another activity I often use with my students involves "unpacking the cultural knapsack." The image of the knapsack suggests that our culture is something we carry with us wherever we go. This activity requires students to jot down the practices, beliefs, and interests that influence their lives and make them unique.

WHAT'S INSIDE YOUR CULTURAL KNAPSACK?

Culture is the shared perceptions of a group's values, expectations, and norms. It reflects the way people give priorities to goals, how they behave in different situations, and how they cope with their world and with one another. People experience their social environment through their culture.

Culture is transmitted from generation to generation.

Unpack your cultural knapsack.

Source: © Yolanda Sealey-Ruiz.

In addition to these and other activities, students journal and share their responses to quotations and other phrases that promote social justice, self-affirmation, and community. The students in my class must adjust to my practice of letting them control the conversations and helping them to feel at ease in making connections between literature and their lives without my assistance.

Adult education research (Imel, 1998; Kassworm, 1997) reveals that adults come to the classroom with a variety of experiences with which they wish to connect by using them as points of departure for discourse in the classroom. They bring with them beliefs and practices they've relied on to form perspectives, raise children, and negotiate personal and professional relationships. Even so, I have had students who have been away from the classroom for a long time, and they rely on their memories of schooling to help them fashion their classroom behaviors. They recall sitting in rows, teachers "giving" knowledge and their "receiving" it. This *banking* concept of education (Freire, 1970/1992) categorizes most of their learning experiences, especially if they attended public schools.

Although the adults in my class have come to school with some hope and expectation of discussing their experiences, overall, many of them experience difficulty when the conversations get very personal or center on a controversial topic like race. Building community is a key element for practicing racial literacy—without it, this type of discourse would not be possible.

Critical discourse in my English adult education classes has promoted a critical awareness of structural racism and prompted an examination of how systems in society are beneficial for some and detrimental for others. Such criticality in classroom discourse is important because it situates learning in the daily lives of the students (Shor, 1987) and provides them with a sense of ownership and responsibility for what they are learning.

ARE WE THERE YET? THE ELUSIVE PERMANENCE OF RACISM

Developing racial literacy in students is not an overnight process. Even though all students show gains in their racial literacy by the end of the semester, they admit that this type of *undoing* may take them a lifetime. I have learned to appreciate the struggles my students experience in confronting their racist beliefs, including beliefs they have about me as their professor. Although many African Americans have made gains, and more of us are entering the professoriate, with numbers now reaching an all-time high, we still earn only 7.1 percent of all doctoral degrees awarded in the United States ("Doctoral degree awards to African Americans . . . ," 2006). Racism, undoubtedly, has played a role in these dreadful statistics. Moreover, with so few Black professors in predominantly White institutions, White adult education students are simply not accustomed to having a professor who doesn't look ethnically or racially like them, while African American adult education students are not accustomed to having a professor who does look like them.

Racism is endemic and permanent in our society. It is deeply embedded in our psyche and spills over into the things we say to each other and how we treat one another. Even though America elected its first African American president, Barack Obama, I still don't have much hope that racism will end. In his national bestseller, *Faces at the Bottom of the Well,* Derrick Bell (1992) wrote:

> Indeed, the racism that made slavery feasible is far from dead in the last decade of twentieth century America, and the civil rights gains, so hard won are being steadily eroded. Despite undeniable progress for many, no African Americans are insulated from racial discrimination. Our careers, even our lives are threatened because of our color [p. 3.].

I believe Bell is right, and I live this out at the start of every new semester. I do not think racism will disappear, not only because it is entrenched in our society but also because too much is riding on it. It is a principle factor in our capitalist system; those who are at the bottom (often the poorest and persons of color) serve those who are at the top (mostly wealthy and White). To do away with racism is to take away the basic ingredient in America's melting pot. To do away with racism would require the rewriting of texts that describe the African American's role in establishing American democracy. America may be too young a nation to take this on. After all, with African Americans just 151 years out of slavery and only 46 years from having secured their civil rights, America may simply be too immature to honestly discuss and work toward the elimination of structural racism.

Our educational institutions mirror our society. The issues we struggle with in society are some of the same battles we confront in our classrooms. Candid conversations about race and racism in adult English classrooms have the potential to increase understanding about how race and racism affect the daily lives of our students and our own lives. Using a racial literacy approach to learning equips students with the skills to problematize the prevalence of racism in our society. Adult educators must give students the opportunity to work out their issues around race and, particularly if they are White, to critique their role in perpetuating racism. More adult educators must respond to the call of this book to engage both students and faculty colleagues in dialogue about race. Moreover, adult educators must be "reflective thinkers who challenge social adaptation, and struggle with complex issues such as race and racism" (Ooka Pang, 2006). The teachers, the students, and the field of adult education will reap the benefits this type of dialogue brings.

REFERENCES

Bell, D. (1992). *Faces at the bottom of the well: The permanence of racism*. New York: Basic Books.

Bolgatz, J. (2005). *Talking race in the classroom*. New York: Teachers College Press.

Brookfield, S. (2003). Racializing criticality in adult education. *Adult Education Quarterly*, *53*(3), 154–169.

Doctoral degree awards to African Americans reach another all-time high. (2006). *Journal of Blacks in Higher Education*. Retrieved February 25, 2008, from http://www.jbhe.com/news_views/50_black_doctoraldegrees.html.

DuBois, W.E.B. (1995). *The souls of Black folk*. New York: New American Library. (Original work published 1903)

Freire, P. (1992). *Pedagogy of the oppressed*. New York: Continuum. (Original English translation published 1970)

Imel, S. (1998). *Transformative learning in adulthood* (Digest Series No. 200). Columbus, OH: ERIC Clearinghouse on Adult, Career, and Vocational Education.

Kassworm, C. (1997, March). *Adult meaning making in the undergraduate classroom*. Paper presented at the annual meeting of the American Educational Research Association, Chicago.

Morrell, E. (2005). Critical English education. *English Education*, *37*(4), 312–321.

Ooka Pang, V. (2006). The outsider within multicultural education: Understanding the field from a marginalized viewpoint. In D. S. Pollard & O. M. Welch (Eds.), *From center to margins: The importance of self-definition in research* (pp. 87–102). Albany: State University of New York Press.

Outlaw, L. T., Jr. (1983). Philosophy, hermeneutics, social-political theory: Critical thought in the interests of African Americans. In L. Harris (Ed.), *Philosophy born of struggle: Anthology of Afro-American philosophy from 1917* (pp. 60–67). Dubuque, IA: Kendall/Hunt.

Sealey-Ruiz, Y. (2005). Getting to here from there: One woman's journey from the South Bronx to the academy. *WILLA, 14*, 40–42.

Shor, I. (1987). Educating the educators: A Freirean approach to the crisis in teacher education. In I. Shor (Ed.), *Freire for the classroom: A source book for liberatory teaching* (pp. 7–32). New York: Third World Press.

3

Experiencing the Race, Gender, and Socioeconomic Divide in Academia

A Chicana Perspective

RAQUEL A. GONZÁLES
MARIA MEJORADO

We are two Chicana faculty members who have taught in different teacher preparation programs at the same institution since 2001. We come together here to tell the story of our lived experiences as faculty in order to gain what Witherell and Noddings (1991) refer to as "meaning and belonging" in this large public institution of higher education. Our telling attaches us to our own histories and to the histories of others by providing a tapestry rich with threads of time, place, character, and even advice on what we might do with our lives.

Cuádraz (2005) makes the point that "since the inception of the field, Chicanas have used lived experiences as a basis from which to discuss the issues facing Chicanas and higher education" (p. 216). Their stories are used as a way of "capturing the complexity, specificity and interconnectedness" (Carter, 1993) of the challenges Chicana faculty face teaching adults in teacher education. The power of narratives allows them to have a voice within a social and cultural context. They tell stories because in the last analysis, human lives need and merit being narrated (Ricoeur, 1984). Thus in this chapter's two spools of threaded stories, we bring forth the tapestry of our own lives as Chicana faculty. Yet we ask ourselves why it took us six years to come together to collaborate on such a project. We found that Cuádraz helped us answer this question. She states that to understand the issues facing Chicana faculty in higher education is to "acknowledge the presence of three elements; the unique combination of traditional scholarship, lived experiences and a legacy of activism ... although not necessarily at the same time" (Cuádraz, 2005, p. 217). Upon reflection, we concluded that a major reason for coming together was our shared research interests in advocating and supporting the voices of Latino parents in our respective communities. As Chicana faculty we found in each other a *safety net* for openly speaking about issues that we were reluctant to raise with others; that safety net has provided us a means of support in an environment that has a history of marginalizing women of color. We approach this project with a certain level of trepidation, unsure if by telling "our truth" we might offend those who closely identify with either of our departments or with particular individuals described (but not named). One senior Latina faculty member expressed, on a more serious note, the concern that our speaking out might have a negative impact on gaining tenure and promotion. Yet, with faith, we embark on these uncharted waters, on the raft of academic freedom, hoping these stories will help to transport others in the future to safety, and do so without incident.

Chicana faculty are grossly underrepresented in U.S. institutions of higher learning. In 2005, the National Center for Education Statistics (NCES) documented the number of full-time Hispanic female faculty engaged in instruction and research at 10,332, compared to 214,215 White female professors. Breaking this number down further, the

NCES found that 1,113 Hispanic females were full professors, 1,768 were associate professors, 2,725 were assistant professors, 738 were lecturers, and another 1,308 held "other" teaching positions. One of the many explanations provided for these disproportionate numbers is Hispanics' "cumulative disadvantages early in life" as students and graduate students, and also their low tenure rates and overrepresentation in the lower academic ranks (Clark & Corcoran, 1996). This resonates for both of us, as professors who completed our doctoral degrees by overcoming such "cumulative disadvantages early in life" as poverty and being migrant farmworkers. Yet even with the major obstacles overcome through the educational process, we continue to be perceived as the "other," for the academic environment assumes the "male experience as normal" (Goffman, 1963, p. 128). In describing minority women faculty on predominantly White campuses, Vargas (2002) argues that they are not seen as White teachers are and are likely to be perceived as "other teachers," a view based on stereotypes. This leads us to have classrooms experiences very different from those of our male counterparts and of White faculty.

IDENTITY: ¿QUIEN SOY YO? (WHO AM I?)

It is important to understand the context of our self-identifying as Chicanas (Vera & de los Santos, 2005). The sociopolitical movements that took place in the 1960s and 1970s—the civil rights movement, the women's movement, the United Farm Workers movement, and the Chicano movement—greatly shaped our social consciousness and provided us opportunities not previously available, such as affirmative action and financial aid. It was the combination of these experience and opportunities that, together, set out the paths to our ultimately becoming university professors.

The Chicano movement came into popularity during the 1960s as Mexican American activists sought to define a social, cultural, and political identity for themselves (Espinoza-Herold, 2003; Vera & de los Santos, 2005). The term *Chicano* was coined by a generation of activists who had pride in their Mexican heritage and demanded that White America acknowledge historical and persistent patterns of racial inequality in legal and political, education, and social opportunities for Mexican Americans (Urrieta & Méndez Benavidez, 2007). *Chicanas* refers to women of Mexican descent raised or both born and raised in the United States. These identities specifically reject the idea that anyone must deny his or her Mexican heritage in order to be a "real American" (Cuádraz, 2005; National Association for Chicano Studies, 1990). However, the Chicana identity also recognizes that sexism is prevalent in this society, especially among our own ethnic group, and must be addressed if we and other Chicanas are to take up our rightful place in society.

Raquel

I was marginalized at birth, as my mother named me Raquel yet the spelling on my birth certificate is "Rachael." My mother recalls that the nurse advised her that it was best if I had an American-sounding name, since being a Mexican was going to be hard enough for me. At that time the climate toward Mexicans in Colorado, my birthplace, was one of rampant discrimination. Although my legal name is Rachael, I prefer Raquel. At an early age, working in the cotton fields, I recall the experience as fun, exploring with my older brother, being close to my parents as they came to check on us while we sat under the belly of the truck. I cannot remember a time that I was not working. During my middle school and high school years, I cleaned the homes of White students who attended the same school that I did. I was invisible in their homes as well as in school. Thus from the start I was placed in a marginalized position, without having an understanding about what that would mean for me later in my schooling experience.

Maria

My birth name is Mary Guadalupe, after the Mexican patron saint to whom my mother prayed daily for a daughter after giving birth to six sons. Mary is the Americanized version of Maria, a choice made by my mother due, in part, to internalized racism and the particularly racist environment of South Texas in the mid-1950s. Upon graduating from college, armed with an understanding of the political challenges of Chicanos in the United States, I felt that the name Mary no longer seemed to fit who I was, and I changed it to Maria. I often reflect on both the harsh environmental conditions of being a farmworker in the 1960s and the skills I learned that have served me well in my career. In speaking engagements I share with individuals that as the youngest child, I learned about teamwork and carrying my own weight. My first role, at the age of four and five, was to carry the water jug and paper trays from row to row to my family members in the vineyard. Later I acquired my own grape bin and knife. My proudest memory was being teamed up with my oldest brother to "turn trays" (for drying grapes into raisins). I felt I had finally earned my place after this "promotion" at ten years of age.

FACTORS INFLUENCING ACADEMIC ACHIEVEMENT

For first-generation college students like us, from low-income families, higher education was considered to be the great equalizer. However, with a lack of role models and mentoring, our college and career options were limited. K–12 White teachers and counselors were well meaning but never seriously engaged in discussion about our future as professionals. In fact for many of our peers, some counselors discouraged college altogether. Raquel and her peers were told by their high school counselor that they "shouldn't waste their time" applying to college. They applied anyway, without any assistance, and were admitted. For Maria, the hands-on support to attend college came from the community staff of such agencies as the Fresno County Economic Opportunities Commission (FEOC). But long before she came in contact with FEOC, it was her peers who set the academic standards, from elementary school through high school. It was a friendly competition, which resulted in four peers attending four different four-year colleges away from their small agricultural town. Gandara (1995) speaks about the power of peer influence, especially among super-high-achieving Latinos. Of the original four, one became a medical doctor, another a banker, and Maria became a college professor.

Being English language learners also presented challenges, as the cultural capital of the English language was unavailable until we attended college. In college the academic vocabulary was almost inaccessible when every other word used by professors sounded like a foreign language; yet we prevailed. In spite of poverty, ever present were clear and consistent rules and structure, love, and the message of the importance of education. In other words, in our families, poverty did not define us but was viewed as a temporary situation. Our parents believed that one could overcome poverty with an education leading to a good job; a job not requiring the use of our backs and out of *el santo sol* ("the blessed hot sun").

Our stories closely resemble those described in Gandara's *Over the Ivy Walls* (1995), which reports the reflections of fifty Chicanos and Chicanas, born into poverty, who achieved high levels of education leading to prestigious careers as, for example, doctors, lawyers, and college faculty. Gandara identified several factors reported to have made a difference in their early academic achievement, such as the importance of parents supporting their children's educational goals, encouraging literacy in many different ways, helping with schoolwork, repeating family stories of past successes, and believing in a culture of possibilities (p. 112). Having a strong work ethic, connecting with high-achieving peer groups, and taking advantage of opportunities made available to minority groups were equally important (p. 114). The stories in *Over Ivy Walls* are our stories as well.

Raquel

My parents valued education and encouraged my brothers and myself to get a good formal education so that we "would not have to use our backs for a living." They also emphasized the concept of being *una persona bien educada*. A person *bien educada* is a well-educated person who has been taught skills in human relationships and who understands the importance of interacting and relating to others with respect and dignity (Lynch & Hanson, 1992, p. 165). Within our community my parents were considered properly educated because they had attended and graduated from a Spanish-speaking theological school in southern Texas. My father had credentials as a minister, pastoring Protestant churches for over twenty years. My mother was an outspoken voice for having women take an active, decision-making role in church business. The only time my father ever went to my school was to insist that the counselor admit me into the college prep classes. I was the first in my family to attend college—starting off at a community college and later transferring to a four-year university and then going on to complete my doctorate.

Maria

It was my mother who set and maintained the high academic expectations. She made many sacrifices so that her children had the basics needed to earn a high school diploma. As an example, the opportunity to purchase volumes of an encyclopedia with coupons from the grocery store was very important to her.

Neither my family nor my peers' families ever completed the entire set, so we often borrowed the books from one another. My earliest recollection of my mother's direct support of my academics involved my weekly spelling test in the second grade. Although she was tired from having worked all day in the fields, after feeding a large family and taking care of all the household responsibilities, she sat with me for a few minutes as I spelled out words aloud. The little English she knew she had learned from the basal readers my older brothers brought home from school. Fortunately for me, she knew the English alphabet to the degree that she could tell me if I spelled each word correctly. But by the time she sat down with me, usually the night before the test, I had memorized all the words. Thus her gesture served more as moral support and sent the strong message that these tests were important. When we worked in the hot sun picking grapes or cotton, my mother would often tell stories of her wealthy ancestors who owned land and businesses. These talks were strategically timed for when the sun was at its highest peak and we were experiencing the most miserable physical conditions. Her proudest moments were attending her children's high school graduations! She also attended my next three graduation ceremonies, in 1978, 1985, and 2000.

THE EVOLUTION OF OUR SOCIAL CONSCIOUSNESS

Both of us have dedicated ourselves to being vocal advocates for social, economic, and political justice in communities that are generally ignored by the mainstream culture. We continue to give back to the community, to act as role models to the community, to mentor, to be the voice for those who cannot use their voice, to teach, to fight the race, class, and gender oppression in our society—in other words, to practice our consciousness.

Raquel

My social consciousness came into full swing during my transfer from community college to the university. I became actively involved in the Brown Berets, a national activist group that arose during the Chicano movement, whose roots were centered on the civil rights struggle. I was a community activist involved in supporting a Mexican American parents' discrimination lawsuit against a local school district. The *Serna* v. *Portales, New Mexico* lawsuit became the authority used in *Lau* v. *Nichols* in support of bilingual education. Entering a graduate program in California, I chose the field of special education. For many of my Chicano colleagues that choice was considered a sellout against the community. I was asked, "How can you participate in such a program, whose practices have been documented as racist toward our children?" But that was exactly the reason I chose special education, to break the racist practices of the past and create new practices for students from culturally and linguistically diverse backgrounds with special needs.

Maria

My social consciousness first raised its head when I was in middle school and learned that through César Chávez's efforts, porta-toilets were now required in the vineyards, where I once had to hide to relieve myself. Due to my parents' relationship with *los rancheros,* who depended on our family to pick their grapes each year, my parents could not publicly support Chávez. In college I was the first female and the first Chicana ever elected student body president, but not without incident, for a certain section of the student body were from rancher families. Thus each morning I would see the corners of my beautifully silk-screened posters burned at the edges. The campus talk was that if elected, I would rename the school Colejio de Santa Maria.

ENGAGING IN ADVOCACY AND ACTIVIST SCHOLARSHIP

A study by Urrieta and Méndez Benavidez (2007) "highlights that all scholarship is political and that the activist scholarship of the Chicana/o professors is no different in rigor or in political inclination than any other type of scholarship. The difference is that White-stream scholarship is perceived as neutral, objective, and of quality because of its normalized status" (p. 234). Urrieta and Benavidez further make the statement that "activist scholarship is not unsound or non-rigorous research, but rather scholarship about issues undervalued or misunderstood in the White-stream academy and by White-stream researchers" (p. 230). The separation of scholarship and community involvement is not something that can be done easily if one is truly following one's social consciousness. The 1984 National Conference of the Association for Chicano Studies, Voces de la Mujer, signaled the arrival of Chicana scholars. An academic organization that formed at approximately the same time, the Mujeres Activas en Letras y Cambio Social (MALCS), "rejected the separation of academic scholarship and community involvement" and strived to bridge the gap between intellectual work and active commitment to their communities (National Association for Chicano Studies, 1990, p. xiii).

THE TRIALS, TRIBULATIONS, AND SYNCHRONICITY OF BEING A CHICANA PROFESSOR

We came up with the title "The Trials and Tribulations and Synchronicity of Being a Chicana Professor" as we discussed how to approach the telling of our story in relationship to the pain, anguish, and stress we experienced over a period of time. As part of our cathartic conversations, these terms helped us to divide our past trials and tribulations and explain how we came together via synchronicity to make sense of our experience and gain the strength to tell "our truth."

According to the *American Heritage College Dictionary,* a *trial* is an effort or attempt; a state of pain or anguish caused by a difficult situation or condition; or a test of patience or endurance. A *tribulation* is a great affliction, trial or distress, or suffering; or an experience or condition that causes such distress. According to the *Longman Dictionary of Contemporary English, synchronicity* is the relationship that exists when two or more events happen at the same time or place and seem to be connected in some way.

Raquel

Trials. My expectations of university life as a faculty member included the notion that all ideas would be valued, ethical standards would rule, individuals would be collaborative and respectful, resources would be shared or at least mentioned as a possibility, and accomplishments would be recognized. I was not prepared to find myself in such a competitive environment; to have my credentials questioned; to be rebuffed when I asked to see someone's grant proposal; to be passed over for the cream of the crop committees; to have students ask me how I could teach if I was from another country (New Mexico is a part of the United States, last I heard); or to have my scholarly work conveniently lost, thus losing an opportunity to be published. I often have asked myself, "Is this act one of racism or grossly unprofessional behavior?"

Tribulations. When I entered the university system the thought of filing a grievance on the basis of racism had never crossed my mind. Yet after a year of enduring a colleague's unprofessional behavior and elevated sense of entitlement, I approached my department chair and the dean of the college at the time to inform them of my intentions to file a grievance against the individual for emotional distress. I was naive enough to think that they would support my decision or at least speak to the individual. Instead, they strongly encouraged me not to pursue the grievance, pointing out that filing any grievance could hurt not only my position on campus but also the university. Based on their feedback, I did not pursue a grievance. It was during this time that I seriously considered leaving the university. Had it not been for the encouragement of colleagues outside my department, and the opportunity to teach a course in the Educational Leadership Department, I believe I would have followed my heart and left the university life altogether, as so many Chicana faculty do each year.

Maria

Trials. For my first four years as a junior faculty member, I lived under an accepted code that faculty would not discuss intra-ethnic politics, including sexism, beyond the department, a topic that remains taboo today for faculty of color. During my first year, faculty meetings were battlegrounds—people were bullying others, using profanity, having tirades, and ranting. I could not believe the tolerance for such unprofessional behavior. Most disconcerting was that even though some of my colleagues recognized the disruptive impact of this behavior, they excused it as "personality quirks" and quickly normalized it. The department chair advised me that openly disagreeing with colleagues at faculty meetings was not acceptable and that I had to watch what I said for it left the "wrong impression." As other junior faculty became more vocal, it was made clear that we were to be seen and not heard. Thus no one was *free* to speak freely, much less share these internal disagreements outside the department. While I was not going to be censored nor silenced, over time this stance became problematic for it led to a certain level of isolation. After trying to make sense of the nonsensical, I decided to take a personal leave of absence, with no intent of returning, after I learned that directions had been given not to provide any direct support to me as the department graduate program coordinator.

At that point my illusions of remaining a fully contributing faculty member in my department were shattered.

WHAT VALIDATES AND INSPIRES US TO STAY THE COURSE

In feminist scholarship, otherness is often spoken of as *difference*—a source of insight and thus of power (Anzaldua, 1987; Perez, 1999; Sandoval, 1991; Zavella, 1991). It is this insight and sense of power—internal, untouchable power—that helped us to recommit to our role as Chicana faculty and continue to create and honor our own reality rather than trying to conform to the traditional ways of academic life.

Raquel

There is an expression in Spanish, *no hay mal que por bien no venga.* Translated the phrase means, "there is nothing bad out of which good cannot come." I cannot say that the bad that occurred did not affect me emotionally, physically, and spiritually. However, in moments of reflection, I know that I can hold my head high knowing that I have never lost who I am or where I came from. Each day presents itself with new possibilities—a day of exploring what could be. I remain in public education because *I love teaching.* I find sharing knowledge with children, parents, and graduate students a most challenging yet rewarding experience. I have been able to diversify my teaching load by teaching courses in general education and educational leadership, which has allowed me to meet students and faculty from diverse educational backgrounds.

Being asked to teach in other departments has been an honor and a sense of validation. Teaching out of my department has given me a different perspective on what matters. Breaking away from the negativity of my department has presented me with pathways to collaborate with Maria and other faculty outside my department. It has also provided me with other support avenues and role models that I can seek out.

Maria

Following a one-year leave, I returned to my department part-time, which proved to be a positive experience. I resumed my tenure track and received much support. One day four different people stopped to acknowledge me. I then realized that my role as a Chicana faculty member was greater than being a member of a particular department. It was my service and relationships with others in the broader campus and in the community as a whole that mattered most. Furthermore, I was reminded that it is my lived stories, in and out of the classroom, that help students make sense of theory and practice. So I returned with a renewed sense of self-confidence and purpose, and as a result many new opportunities have come my way.

THE NEED FOR DIALOGUE

At the present time the individuals who are seeking teaching credentials are predominantly White middle-class women. Thus a dialogue on the impact of race and racism creates opportunities for current and future instructors to understand the impact of culture on teaching adults and to learn the value of cultural capital, so they can go on to create classrooms that build on the different experiences students bring to their learning (Moll, Amanti, Nedd, & Gonzalez, 1992). Yet we have to ask, if we cannot sustain an open dialogue about our own differences (and racism, sexism, and socioeconomic status) within our own departments, how can we expect to engage our students to reflect on their own?

The challenges facing K–12 educators include high numbers of students from low-income families, many students who are English language learners, and low rates of academic achievement among students, which leads to high dropout rates, especially among African American and Latino males. Thus the preparation of teachers to work effectively with these populations is critical. The remaining challenge is to transform the dialogue of social justice into action, so that all children reach their dream. As Chicana faculty, it is our charge to network with those committed to social justice, to use teaching as a tool for raising consciousness, and to mentor low-income students and students of color, which involves a responsible, respectful relationship.

SYNCHRONICITY

Ultimately, this chapter is a testament to the power of two women working in unison and in solidarity as Chicana faculty members of the academy. As we disclosed our individual trials and tribulations, we found parallel existences and occurrences. We know that other Chicana and Latina faculty have experienced similar circumstances at our institution and at other schools and have left permanently. We hope that our dialogue moves us and others to action for those that will come after.

REFERENCES

Anzaldua, G. (1987). *Borderlands/la frontera: The new mestiza.* San Francisco: Spinsters/Aunt Lute Book Company.

Carter, K. (1993). The place of story in the study of teaching and teacher education. *Educational Researcher, 31*(1), 5–12, 18.

Clark, S. M., & Corcoran, M. (1996). Perspectives on the professional socialization of women faculty: A case of accumulative disadvantages. In D. E. Finnegan, D. Webster, & Z. F. Gamson (Eds.), *Faculty and faculty issues in colleges and universities* (pp. 126–141). New York: Simon & Schuster.

Cuádraz, G. H. (2005). Chicanas and higher education: Three decades of literature and thought. *Journal of Hispanic Higher Education, 4*(3), 215–234.

Espinoza-Herold, M. (2003). *Issues in Latino education: Race, school culture and the politics of academic success.* Boston: Allyn & Bacon.

Gandara, P. (1995). *Over the ivy walls: The educational mobility of low-income Chicanos.* Albany: State University of New York Press.

Goffman, E. (1963). *Stigma.* Englewood Cliffs, NJ: Prentice-Hall.

Lynch, E. W., & Hanson, M. J. (1992). *Developing cross-cultural competence: A guide for working with young children and their families.* Boston: Brookes.

Moll, L., Amanti, C., Nedd, D., & Gonzalez, N. (1992). Funds of knowledge for teaching: Using a qualitative approach to connect homes and classrooms. *Theory into Practice, 31,* 132–141.

National Association for Chicano Studies. (1990). *Chicana voices: Intersections of class, race and gender.* Albuquerque: University of New Mexico Press.

National Center for Education Statistics. (2005). *Full-time instructional faculty in degree granting institution by race/ethnicity, sex, and academic rank.* Washington, DC: U.S. Department of Education.

Perez, E. (1999). The decolonial imaginary. *Writing Chicanas into history.* Bloomington: Indiana University Press.

Ricoeur, P. (1984). *Time and narrative* (Vol. 1). K. Blamey & D. Pellauer (Trans.). Chicago: University of Chicago Press.

Sandoval, C. (1991). U.S. third world feminism: The theory and method of oppositional consciousness in the postmodern world. *Genders, 10,* 2–24.

Urrieta, L., Jr., & Méndez Benavidez, L. R. (2007). Community commitment and activist scholarship: Chicana/o professors and the practice of consciousness. *Journal of Hispanic Higher Education,* 6(3), 222–236.

Vargas, L. (Ed.). (2002). *Women faculty of color in the White classroom.* New York: Peter Lang.

Vera, H., & de los Santos, E. (2005). Chicana identity construction: Pushing the boundaries. *Journal of Hispanic Higher Education,* 4(2), 102–113.

Witherell, C., & Noddings, N. (1991). *Stories lives tell: Narrative and dialogue in education.* New York: Teachers College Press.

Zavella, P. (1991). Reflections on diversity among Chicanas. *Frontiers, 12,* 73–85.

4

Transforming Teaching and Learning

Teaching Race

NICHOLE M. RAY

I began my academic teaching career as a graduate student in adult education teaching an introductory level women's studies class at a historically white university in the southeastern United States. With child-care responsibilities, a partner in graduate school, and a full-time class schedule, I maintained full course responsibility for approximately forty-five students in two women's studies classes. I entered into the women's studies classroom full of hope, wonder, and a firm belief that my classroom, according to hooks (1994), would

> Be a place where there is a sense of struggle, where there is visible acknowledgement of the union of theory and practice, where we work together as teachers and students to overcome

the estrangement and alienation that have become so much the norm in the contemporary university [p. 51].

Influenced by feminist pedagogy, a major goal was to create a teaching and learning community that fostered engaging dialogue and discussion of course topics (hooks, 2003), as well as an environment that encouraged the sharing of experiential knowledge along with theoretical concerns in the area of women's studies.

The course I taught, and continue to teach as a postgraduate, is one in which we examine the lives and concerns of women of color in the United States. In this class, race, ethnicity, gender, ability, orientation, and other markers frame our understanding of women's bodies, work and welfare, and sexuality and sexual identity, among other issues that are of concern to the demographic. Major learning goals for the students include developing and deepening critical thinking skills while learning how to examine course topics from a multicultural and feminist perspective. The majority of my students are white, heterosexual, conservative, Christian, middle- to upper-class young women and men. They come to class laden with laptops, designer handbags and sunglasses, cellular phones, and other distractions.

When they are asked why they decided to enroll in this course, their responses range from "it satisfies the college multicultural requirement" to "I heard that we will watch MTV in here." These students often enter my class inundated with negative and stereotypical images and understandings about people who are positioned differently in society, and become defensive when presented with information that counters their beliefs, values, and assumptions. In this chapter I explore and critically reflect on my experience as a feminist educator teaching race in the predominantly white, women's studies classroom. Within this frame of feminist pedagogical perspectives and relevant work on race in adult education, I then suggest new possibilities for transforming adult educator and learner perspectives on the ways that race can shape the classroom experience.

PERSPECTIVES ON FEMINIST PEDAGOGY

My teaching philosophy and resulting teaching practices are greatly informed by feminist pedagogy. Feminist scholars have varying interpretations and understandings of what can constitute a teaching and learning experience from a feminist perspective. Crabtree and Sapp (2003) define feminist pedagogy "as a set of classroom practices, teaching strategies, approaches to content, and relationships grounded in critical pedagogical and feminist theory" (p. 131). Maher and Tetreault (2001) view pedagogy in a different light, suggesting that "the term 'pedagogy' was not about teaching techniques, divorced from content, but rather about the whole process of knowledge construction, in the classroom as elsewhere" (p. 10). Lee and Johnson-Bailey (2004) support this definition and describe feminist pedagogy, in particular, "as a method of teaching and learning employing a political framework that involves consciousness raising, activism, and a caring and safe environment" (p. 57).

Although feminist pedagogy is defined in multiple ways, there are several overarching goals evident in the extensive body of literature. According to Webb, Walker, and Bollis (2004), feminist pedagogy is built on the principles of empowerment, building dynamic relationships between students and professors, creating a learning community, addressing individual student voices, challenging and critiquing beliefs and assumptions, and understanding the diverse array of subjective experiences that students bring into the classroom.

In particular, I find the works of bell hooks on liberatory and emancipatory pedagogies (hooks, 1994, 2003) and the black feminist and womanist pedagogies (Dillard, Abdur-Rashid, & Tyson, 2003; Omolade, 1993; Sheared, 1999) to be an inspiration and guide to teaching in the multicultural women's studies class. Similar to the argument of feminists of color regarding the *whiteness* and exclusionary practices of feminism and women's studies, black feminist and womanist educators are particularly troubled by and resonant about feminist pedagogical concepts and practices that neglect to address issues of difference, racism, and colonization, for example (Grande, 2003). These works are vital to my teaching practices in that they provide a space in which I can theorize my experience, engaging race as a black woman educator in a predominantly white classroom environment.

THE ELEPHANT IN THE ROOM: THE EXPERIENCE OF RACE IN THE CLASSROOM

As an educator in the multicultural gender studies classroom, I am confronted with a host of challenges that relate to my teaching of race as a raced individual, and I must navigate slippery, unstable terrain when race and racism are central topics of the course. A primary obstacle encountered by women of color adult educators involves the impact of positionality on the classroom experience. Women of color in the classroom continue to find their knowledge and authority to be suspect (Johnson-Bailey & Cervero, 1998; Lee & Johnson-Bailey, 2004). Johnson-Bailey and Cervero (1998) suggest that learners and teachers, or facilitators, bring with them their "positions in the hierarchies that order the world, including those based on race, gender, class, sexuality orientation, and disability" (p. 389).

Micro-level classroom dynamics are a direct reflection of larger, macro-level structural inequities. When a black woman is in a position of authority in the classroom, this can become problematic for both her and the students. There is a type of cognitive dissonance on her part in that she recognizes and is aware of her hard-earned credentials and her ability to provide a quality education to the students. This belief must be negotiated with students who enter the classroom with negative and stereotypical beliefs about black women. We are reminded by hooks (2003) that

> [o]ne of the manifestations of daily life in an imperialist white-supremacist capitalist patriarchy is that the vast majority of white folks have little intimacy with black people and are rarely in situations

where they must listen to a black person (particularly a black woman) speak for them for thirty minutes [p. 31].

My students are seldom in contact with black women who are in positions to directly influence their academic success. Many of these students have never experienced a black woman professor and often experience a disconnection between their preconceived notions about who black women are and the reality of being a part of a class in which a black woman is in a position of authority.

Understanding how my position as a black woman in the predominantly white women's studies classroom affects events in that classroom has been an important aspect of my practice as a feminist educator. On the first day of class of my first semester of teaching, I introduced myself and presented the class with my professional information—my research, awards, and other credentials. Quite certain that the students would have little to no doubt of my ability to teach them, I began the semester excited and comfortable with my knowledge base and five-plus years experience as a women's studies student. As the semester progressed, I expressed great frustration that students continuously challenged my knowledge base and my ability to teach about "other" cultural groups. To illustrate, the students often demanded statistics when we discussed matters that were, in a sense, unbelievable to them. I was and am often accused of holding a "biased opinion" when speaking about women of color, especially when the topic includes black women. In an effort to understand the nature of these disturbing experiences, I shared them with my adviser and with other graduate teaching assistants in women's studies.

Following my first year of teaching this course, I began to gain a deeper, more critical understanding of what it can mean to be a black woman in a position of authority. Eventually, I viewed these experiences as teachable moments, when I could encourage the students to think more critically about race.

Johnson-Bailey (2002) summarizes three overarching perspectives on race in the adult education literature, specifically as it relates to the classroom environment, understanding differences among adult learners, and how adult educators negotiate power and positionality in the classroom context. These ways of "talking race" are the color-blind, the multicultural, and the social justice perspectives. The color-blind perspective is noted as being the most widely adopted viewpoint in adult education. Johnson-Bailey (2002) asserts that the color-blind view "seems well suited to a stance that does not acknowledge race or that views all racial issues as inconsequential when not expressed as part of any classroom or curriculum equation" (p. 42). For example, class members almost always express such heartfelt sentiments as, "I don't see color," or, "I thought we were all just human." Despite the reality that race is central to the course topic, my students continue to question the validity of race and how it shapes women's experiences.

In conjunction with their color-blind perspective on race, I find that students are all too eager to speak to issues of gender and class while remaining silent about race. This problem occurs without fail near the beginning of each semester. In addressing this problem, I often turn the tables on the students and ask them why they find it so easy to talk about sexism, and even homophobia, but when it is time to talk about the "race thing," they are resistant and unwilling to participate. After a long silence, usually one student speaks up and readily admits to feeling uncomfortable and guilty. It then becomes my goal to encourage them to work constructively through the guilt so that they can begin to move beyond the silence and into critical discussion. In turn, they begin to think more deeply and critically about *how* they engage and understand race.

Although race is a central theme of the course on multicultural women that I teach, I find that students are overwhelmingly resistant and hostile when asked to consider race and racism as they operate on both the micro- and macro-levels of United States society. My students feel personally attacked when we, for example, go beyond examining beauty ideals on an individual level to examining how these ideals are shaped by larger social, political, and economic forces. Many students express sentiments such as, "We are not the ones responsible for the war in Iraq," and, "I don't believe heterosexism is oppressive," or even the classic, "My parents worked hard for what they have. So why shouldn't 'they'?" This has been especially the case when students are struggling with the reality that racism is endemic and persistent in our society. The prevalence of this type of response has been addressed by hooks (2003): "While it is a positive aspect of our culture that folks want to see racism end; paradoxically it is the heartfelt longing that underlies the persistence of the false assumption that racism has ended, that this is not a white-supremacist nation" (p. 29).

I agree with hooks's contention that on a certain level my students eventually come to realize that racism does exist and that it should be eradicated. However, the tension between their previous concept of racism, in which they viewed it in terms of specific acts, and their new knowledge is ever present. I feel their anger and frustration with my request that they expand their thinking on this topic through their journals, small-group discussions, and even conversations before class begins. They want desperately to believe that things truly are "fair" and "equal" among women and men, blacks and whites, the poor and the wealthy ("if only the poor people would work longer and harder, they'd be fine," lamented one student). Students in the multicultural course struggle with shifting their understanding about race, on both a structural and institutional level. In turn, they inadvertently excuse themselves from examining how they participate within and benefit from institutional and structural oppression.

We currently live and work in a critical time, one in which diversity, inclusion, and equity are of paramount importance in colleges and universities across the United States. In light of the current political climate, conversations about race and racism are reaching an all-time high as educators and students grapple with what can be an extremely sensitive and often elusive topic. Creating, surviving, and thriving in the feminist classroom at a historically white university is not without its challenges as well as its rewards. As evidenced in my experiences, the journey is by no means smooth and uncomplicated when we are seeking to work with and in a pedagogical perspective that asks learners to engage in critical thinking while bringing issues such as racism and heterosexism to the center of classroom discourse. In spite of the challenges, I continue to do the necessary work for potentially transforming students' understandings and perspectives on race.

TRANSFORMING TEACHING AND LEARNING: BEYOND SURVIVING RACE IN THE CLASSROOM

Much of the adult education literature that speaks to addressing adult learners' needs and issues neglects to articulate the needs of the adult educator, especially as they relate to the issue of race. This has been both a practical and theoretical issue in my teaching: What about me? What happens to me when I am accused by a student of being a racist? What do I do when I leave the classroom feeling defeated? In addressing these ongoing questions arising from my experience with race in the classroom, I find hooks's (1994) concept and practice of an engaged pedagogy to be appropriate.

A commitment to wholeness or to a union of mind, body, and spirit in academia is difficult, hooks maintains, because of the typical deemphasis on wellness and well-being in this setting. In contrast, an engaged pedagogy "emphasizes well-being. That means that teachers must be actively committed to a process of self-actualization that promotes their own well-being if they are to teach in a manner that empowers students" (1994, p. 15). Teaching race while navigating students' perceptions and limited understanding of race can be difficult to manage in conjunction with and maintaining a sense of well-being. One way that I practice this particular aspect of engaged pedagogy is through building relationships with other women of color educators who share similar experiences. Black women scholars writing on race in the classroom argue for the centrality of establishing sister-networks as they negotiate the various challenges associated with being a black woman in academia (Johnson-Bailey, 2006). I find that teaching race and feeling good about teaching race as a black woman become less of a burden and more thrilling when I am able to dialogue and build community with colleagues who share similar experiences.

Engaged pedagogy also involves making oneself vulnerable in order to facilitate one's own growth and empowerment as an educator. As students are encouraged to navigate the space between their experiential knowledge and what they are learning in the classroom, so must the feminist educator be willing to do the same. Theorizing feminist pedagogy from this perspective can allow feminist educators "to create pedagogical practices that engage students, providing them with ways of knowing that enhance their capacity to live fully and deeply" (hooks, 1994, p. 22).

To illustrate, the practice of engaged pedagogy became especially critical for me as I sought to create a *safe space* in the classroom not only for my students but for myself. I often struggle with the idea and reality of creating a less hierarchical learning environment, while understanding that my power is limited and that my position as a black woman requires a keen awareness of power relations in the classroom. I often find it challenging to understand, embrace, and implement the myriad ways in which creating a safe space is possible. The feminist classroom is one in which student and teacher positions are partial and in flux and affect multiple classroom dynamics (Lather, 1991). Several scholars have queried the idea and practice of creating safe spaces within the feminist classroom (Lather, 1991; Maher & Tetreault, 2001). Feminist scholars argue that this space is necessary so that students can feel comfortable with expression of ideas, beliefs, and opinions about course topics.

However, the practice of engaged pedagogy necessitates a more complex understanding of the ways in which power relations and dynamics influence my ability to create a safe space for the students. Moreover, my teaching practice and experience demands that I monitor my individual safety in a classroom environment that can be hostile and challenging. Emphasizing educator well-being does not negate my responsibility for the students. As a feminist educator, I firmly believe in taking a both/and perspective in terms of my desire to address the unique experience of multicultural issues in the classroom and the ensuing challenges in conjunction with a commitment to self-awareness and self-care.

TRANSFORMATION BEGINS AT HOME

As a black woman educator working for social justice within and beyond the university classroom, I, like many others similarly positioned, must find creative ways to manage the challenges I encounter with race. Although there are countless resources for educators who teach in this area, I am concerned about and find problematic the use of "strategies" as the be-all and end-all in "dealing with" or "handling" the issue of race. Whether they are wrestling with students' subjectivities and their own, or trying to explain how institutional racism permeates this society, I believe that adult educators who are of color and are women, in particular, must move beyond strategies, beyond day-to-day survival in what can be a hostile classroom environment.

I believe that transforming teaching and learning as it relates to race begins at home with a commitment to wholeness and individual and collective well-being. Not only must adult educators critically reflect on teaching philosophies and practices, but I would argue that they should also take a look inward and ask questions such as, "What do I need to do to be 'OK' in the classroom?" or, "What can I do to simultaneously create a sense of 'safety' for myself and for the students?" I think these questions are of paramount importance to our field as we continue to do the challenging work necessary to create optimal learning experiences for adult learners and to bring issues of social justice and inclusion to the foreground in our teaching.

REFERENCES

Crabtree, R. D., & Sapp, D. A. (2003). Theoretical, political, and pedagogical challenges in the feminist classroom. *College Teaching*, *51*(4), 131–140.

Dillard, C. B., Abdur-Rashid, D., & Tyson, C. A. (2003). My soul is a witness: Affirming pedagogies of the spirit. *Qualitative Studies in Education*, *13*(5), 447–462.

Grande, S. (2003). Whitestream feminism and the colonialist project: A review of contemporary feminist pedagogy and praxis. *Educational Theory*, *53*(3), 329–346.

hooks, b. (1994). *Teaching to transgress: Education as the practice of freedom.* New York: Routledge.

hooks, b. (2003). *Teaching community: A pedagogy of hope.* New York: Routledge.

Johnson-Bailey, J. (2002). Race matters: The unspoken variable in the teaching-learning transaction. In J. Ross-Gordon (Ed.), *Contemporary viewpoints on teaching adults effectively* (New Directions for Adult and Continuing Education, No. 93, pp. 39–49). San Francisco: Jossey-Bass.

Johnson-Bailey, J. (2006). Transformative learning: A community empowerment conduit for African American women. In S. B. Merriam, B. Courtenay, & R. M. Cervero (Eds.), *Global issues in adult education: Perspectives from Latin America, Southern Africa and the United States.* (pp. 307–318). San Francisco: Jossey-Bass.

Johnson-Bailey, J., & Cervero, R. M. (1998). Power dynamics in teaching and learning practices: An examination of two adult education classrooms. *International Journal of Lifelong Education*, *17*(6), 389–399.

Lather, P. A. (1991). *Getting smart: Feminist research and pedagogy with/in the postmodern.* New York: Routledge.

Lee, M., & Johnson-Bailey, J. (2004). Challenges to the classroom authority of women of color. In J. A. Sandlin & R. St. Clair (Eds.), *Promoting critical practice in adult education* (New Directions for Adult and Continuing Education, No. 102, pp. 55–64). San Francisco: Jossey-Bass.

Maher, F. A., & Tetreault, M.K.T. (2001). *The feminist classroom: Dynamics of gender, race, and privilege.* Lanham, MD: Rowman & Littlefield.

Omolade, B. (1993). A black feminist pedagogy. *Women's Studies Quarterly*, *3/4*, 31–38.

Sheared, V. (1999). Giving voice: Inclusion of African American students' polyrhythmic realities in adult basic education. In T. C. Guy (Ed.), *Providing culturally relevant adult education: A challenge for the twenty-first century* (New Directions for Adult and Continuing Education, No. 82, pp. 33–48). San Francisco: Jossey-Bass.

Webb, L. M., Walker, K. L., & Bollis, T. S. (2004). Feminist pedagogy in the teaching of research methods. *International Journal of Social Research Methodology*, *7*(5), 415–428.

5

"Who Is This Cowboy?"
Challenging the Cultural Gatekeepers

LESLEY NGATAI

I am a Maori woman connected in *blood memory* (Lawrence, 2004) to a cultural past and future. As an indigenous academic librarian I am an anachronism, representing 0.01 percent of an appallingly absent population. Add to this my passion as an educator who believes in the political nature of her profession, and you can see how I may easily be labeled "other." In my professional world, I am the "voice" of the oversensitive indigene. My *tupuna* (ancestors) use me to reach the exhausted spirits of my students. I help them crack a window onto a critical landscape; they do the rest.

I came to theory because I was hurting; I stuck with theory throughout my life because I was hungry and it fed me. It gives me a *turangawaewae*, a place to stand. Intergenerational racism helped me come to theory at a young age, and theory has kept me together, body and soul, when nothing else worked in my life. I am writing here about the hurt of constant rejection by my tribal family because of my connection to theory and the colonial constructs it represents, and how I came to see that the overstatic determination of identity by cultural elites was in all probability more about protecting individual power bases than it was about me. I have come to see that theories of cultural hybridity can counter such pinched approaches to legitimacy and provide increased depth and breadth for the culture itself; yet primordial and essentialist notions are important to indigenous people for two reasons: the continued recognition of native sovereignty and land ownership and the cultural belief that as First Nation people we have an essential life force passed down to us by our ancestors that connects us to the land, giving us legitimacy in all our relationships with the natural world and its bounty.

Through an ongoing commitment to theory I have come to see I have more political reach outside my tribal community. There are too many rules inside my tribal community. To survive my endangered life journey I have had to learn to break the rules. This is not tolerated: elders pull rank; self is subsumed by clan; tribal protocols cannot be broken; dissent must be formulaic; and boats are to be steadied, not rocked. If I went home I would be gagged, of this I have been assured. Nick Tilsen, a young activist from the Lakota nation, wrote, "when the people need to walk on top of you, you lay down" (LaDuke, 2005). I don't know how to lie down; my mother taught me that you get up and you fight, or you lose everything.

My relationship with criticality through theory has also made me suspect in my chosen profession, where reflective practice is not encouraged. I constantly critique the absence of "brown" voices in critical discourse, in my profession, and in my university. I am the recipient of racism every day, in my cultural life, where home is still denied me by the gatekeepers, and in my working life, where voices like mine are shamed into silence and colonial assumptions go unchecked. I have come to realize that the way I teach within a colonialized curriculum has been informed by both my endangered journey to theory and my internal claim to an indigenous heritage.

No one wants to talk about racism. In academic environments we talk about cultural diversity, ethnicity, multiculturalism, and inclusivity.

Situations, policies, and even people are either *culturally sensitive* or *culturally inappropriate*; here in Australia, having preparatory programs for indigenous students who want to be doctors and lawyers and social workers so they can heal their wounded communities is a good thing... isn't it? We pat ourselves on the back for our politically correct, *culturally responsive* support programs: indigenous homework centers, counseling programs, literacy programs, and specialized funding sources that are bursting out of our educational institutions. These are good things, but why do we need them in the first place? What are they born of? What is the real problem? No one wants to talk about racism.

Racism gave me my life. My mother's story is rife with rage and grief and the kind of harsh beauty women bring to pain. She suffered prejudice, rejection, and shame because she was Maori, a woman, and a single parent. The messages she passed to her only girl child came not from her public strength but from her most private thoughts: "You're no good, you never will be"; "Why bother? Just give up"; "Who do you think you are?" She denied her culture in the most public ways; she took us from the country *marae* to the city to protect us and keep us safe. As in Bonita Lawrence's family, "the price of this struggle for survival has been an absolute ruthlessness on her part about abandoning anything—including any identification with Native people—which might stand in the way of our survival as a family" (Lawrence, 2004, p. xii). My mum cut us off from friendships, because people can't be trusted and love hurts. Her young husband, dead at twenty-eight, taught her that; her father in a drunken rage taught her that.

MY LEGACY—THE JOURNEY

My legacy is a strength born of a desperate love and a trauma so deep it's almost mundane. At a young age I sought solace in school, in books and ideas. My mum let me be; she believed in the assimilationist dream, that a good education would make a difference. My coming to theory at such an age and with such desperation reflects bell hooks's experience: "Living in childhood without a sense of home, I found a place of sanctuary in 'theorizing,' in making sense out of what was happening. I found a place where I could imagine possible futures, a place where life could be lived differently.... Fundamentally I learned that theory could be a healing place" (hooks, 1994, p. 61). Learning was the only thing that was mine, the only thing my mum didn't stomp on to make me stronger. She never understood that for my brother and me this did not make us strong but broke our hearts and clawed at our spirits. My journey as a brown girl through a White man's world has been visceral. I was compelled to succeed; my journey away from my mother's racially induced heartbreak and violence bred its own pain but ultimately created a powerful context, giving me a purpose for my learning and development, giving me a reason to succeed.

My grandmother was Maori, soft-spoken and gentle. She died from cervical cancer because she didn't want to go to the big White hospital with the big White doctors; not until she had to, not until it was too late. She wrote me letters in a language I couldn't understand, her own heart-speak. It was an emotional time. So at eighteen I went to college in another city to learn our language, our culture, and to find my family. I thought I would be welcomed. When I walked into a Maori language class of native speakers, dressed in cowboy boots and a vintage thrift shop dress, with my blonde-streaked hair, I was greeted with snorts and a derisive, "*Ko wai tenei kaupoi?*" "Who is this cowboy?" Beneath this seemingly benign and humorous question lay a subtext of racist alienation and what bell hooks (1990) calls "notions of a static over-determined identity" (p. 28).

Years later, I realize that my walking into that room as a young girl had been a defining moment, a moment described by Karumanchery as "a Diasporic dilemma": "a culture clash between family, community and world resulting not only in a type of figurative erasure of culture and race, and a symbolic-literal denial of home, but more importantly a moment of psycho-social surrender from which emerges a dislocated and disconnected self" (Dei, Karumanchery, & Karumanchery-Luik, 2004, p. 140). As a result I wandered for years in a state of nihilistic confusion; each time the pain peaked I would turn to theory. So it was that at the age of forty, when I was finally brought to my knees and my life began anew, I had four university qualifications earned while folding myself into the only thing I knew would make the hurt go away. Like bell hooks, I unconsciously turned to theory because I was hurting; like hooks, I was "desperate, wanting to comprehend—to grasp what was happening around and within me" (hooks, 1994, p. 59).

THEORIZING—GROWING PAINS

This story is an effort to examine that hurt and how coming to theory has succored much of the pain. I hope to take a *racialized view* from the cultural margins, where identities are created, denied, and assumed. Using the lenses of critical theory and my own autobiography, I will examine multiple theoretical frameworks of indigeneity, race, and racism and consider the impact of such frameworks on adult learning and development in particular settings and how these same frameworks have informed my own practice and lived experiences. I hope my story will intersect with the conversations around the kitchen table by providing an indigenous lens fitted around my own lived experience and theory building as a Maori woman living outside her community, bound in blood memory to the past and present while also constructing new realities and localities for indigeneity.

Through theory building I have come to some understanding of the fearfulness with which my own people regarded me then as now, seeing me as an intellectual, dislocated, urban, half-caste woman, "colonised beyond recall" (Green, 2006, p. 17). Such racial ambiguity can be threatening, especially to elitist gatekeepers who see that it could undermine real or imagined power bases constructed around static boundaries of membership. Yet it was not always this way. Traditional Maori society was ever changing and inclusive; it had to be to survive, but after colonization there was a shift, and that which was not "truly" Maori was excluded (Meredith, 1998b, p. 10). I have come to see how the freezing of cultural boundaries is an instinctive reaction from a culture trying to survive, to arrest continued degradation of cultural, political, and social precepts. Back then I felt only hurt and rejection; today I feel sadness and understanding for "a culture so assaulted by the processes of a brutal and colonizing experience it had to grow a protective mindset to police its cultural boundaries, purify the impure and decolonize the colonized" (Barcham, 1998, p. 306). Barcham links this loss of dynamism and inclusivity to the refusal by some to acknowledge the legitimacy of new, multiply located Maori identities.

New Zealand Maori have a relatively short history in their adopted land. The particulars of this history are disputed among academics, tribes, and individuals. Oral histories clash with written, recorded with remembered. Some prevalent colonial myths have been dismantled only in the last decade. It is, however, generally agreed that the ancestors of today's New Zealand Maori population migrated from their ancestral homeland of Hawai'iki to the land they named Aotearoa around the period from 800 to 1000 A.D. Aotearoa was not *terra nullius*. What happened to the locals is part of the disputed history. Today most Maori (never a homogeneous group) can connect themselves with a tribal region or an urban community. Our most physical central place of identity is the tribal *marae,* where all important gatherings and meetings are held.

As with most indigenous people, land is fundamental to our identity; it is our primary ancestor, embodying the past and future (Ka'ai, Moorfield, Reilly, & Mosley, 2004, p. 50). We see ourselves as *tangata whenua* ("people of the land"), and as such we embody the spiritual authority of *mana whenua* (which gives us the right to undisturbed and continued ownership of our lands and the right to self-determination and cultural sovereignty) unique to First Nation people; this alone distinguishes us from other colonized groups sharing a geographical space. This long-standing bond with the land and the natural environment is a core feature of indigeneity; it arises from an ecological relationship and includes time, culture, an indigenous system of knowledge, environmental sustainability, and a native language (Durie, 2004, p. 2).

Despite some differences, there is a common reality between First Nation people and other colonized peoples, as we share common histories of invasion, resistance, dispossession, poverty, exploitation, racism, and exclusion (McDaniel & Flowers, 1999, p. 254). As a political half-caste, Meredith identifies an internal tension he describes as deriving from being both colonizer and colonized, yet he creatively sees his position as a potential "lubricant in a conjunction of cultures creating a richness and energy at the point of commonality." He thinks that a bipolar model can't account for "more complex polyethnic encounters," nor does it encompass a larger sociological reality that acknowledges an "increasing hybridity of human experience" (Meredith, 2000, p. 19).

As a member of the New Zealand Maori Diaspora, I have never lived within my tribal community for any length of time. This physical removal has rendered my cultural integrity suspect and open to criticism by those who have remained geographically located within their tribal homelands. Meredith (1998b, p. 15) supports the relational nature of identity: "Each of us is constituted by the other...we are Maori in relation to those who are non-Maori, urban in relation to those who are tribal. To dismiss the other is to dismiss the self." When exclusive boundaries are laid down between an *us* and a *them* in order to form notions of identity, then transgressions are bound to follow. Out of these transgressions the hybrid is formed and is viewed as a representation of "danger, loss, and degeneration" (Paperastergiadis, 1997, p. 258). If the boundary is inclusive and used to broaden and deepen that which it marks by welcoming change and diversity, then the hybrid may yield strength and vitality. So the hybrid's position is always relative to how much value is placed in purity, "along axes of inclusion/exclusion." "To be a hybrid can be a blessing or a curse, depending on the nature of the boundaries" (Paperastergiadis, 1997, p. 259).

THEORY RECONSTRUCTED

Much has been written about cultural hybridity and the spaces in between (Dei et al., 2004; Bhabha, 1994; Meredith, 1998a; Lavie & Swedenburg, 1996) in an effort to dispel essentialist notions of identity and culture bound in time by space and location. Bonita Lawrence is understandably cautious about nonessentialist definitions of Native identity; for to say it is something negotiated and continuously evolving can have dangerous repercussions for Native land claims and thus indigenous sovereignty (Lawrence, 2004, p. 3). Identities are constructed within, not outside representation. This is "about using the resources of history, language, and culture in the process of becoming rather than being: not 'who we are' or 'where we come from,' so much as what we might become" (Hall & Du Gay, 1996, p. 4). White supremacist structures, in which I have always lived, not only accept me but reward me for my exotic looks and my educational and professional "achievements." I am them.

There is a segment of Maori society that agrees and treats me with suspicion, as if I have entered into a Faustian contract in order to "succeed" in the colonialists' world, as if I have given up some essential part of my Maoriness. Yet my *whakapapa,* my descent lines, are undeniable; there is my mountain; this is my river; here is my canoe; these are my tribes. I know the descent lines for both my parents going back generations. For the gatekeepers, this in itself is not so threatening. But once I came into being as a teacher and once I saw how racism had informed my practice and where the energy behind the transformational nature of my teaching came from, I did the only thing I know to do to make a difference. I began to build theory and to teach others about it and through it. I took my passion to the academic streets in conference papers, lectures, and debates. I challenged my professional peers to conversations they did not want to have; I asked questions wherever I found visiting Maori academics and withstood their hostility and silence; I stood up in community centers and challenged visiting New Zealand politicians; I even volunteered to present on behalf of New Zealand in a Lifelong Learning Conference stream on international perspectives, in a room packed with New Zealand educators and librarians, because I knew other teachers would not talk about indigenous pedagogies from a place of transformational criticality, because no one in my profession ever does.

I have heard visiting Maori academics from tribal universities in New Zealand present the uniqueness of the indigenous framework in which they teach, with no more passion than if they were reciting a recipe, and perhaps they were; to me it was codified, sanitized, and packaged for White audiences who reacted on cue with wonderment, and in one fell swoop relegated it all to the exotic borderlands of "other." As a transformational teacher, I use the cultural and spiritual principles of my ancestors as the foundation of my pedagogical framework.

What is missing from today's university environment is heart, and without the heart the brain can't function. On a spiritual level our students are exhausted, our universities bereft. It is to the heart that indigenous pedagogies speak, bringing a unique voice to the educational world.

THEORY REALIZED—TRUTH TELLING

Maori pedagogies stream out of the ancient world of mythology and creation, anchoring themselves to the immediacy of death, birth, and the struggle of life. What better intrinsic motivation for the creation of a transformational pedagogy than that of community (*whanau*) built on an energetic flow of guidance and support (*manaakitanga*) and acceptance and compassion (*aroha*) in the interests of unity (*kotahitanga*)? Taking the time to create connection through conversations built on trust, interest, and respect helps our students feel listened to and part of, to feel loved and cared for; without this foundation they are unwilling to expose themselves to the emotional risks of learning (Ngatai, 2006). Because of my endangered life journey to theory, I create safe and loving spaces for learners; because of my alienating racial experiences, I create inclusive communities where difference can be negotiated and understood. I write, speak, and teach in a multitude of contexts from this foundation, constantly bringing into question the "missing voices" from the critical discourse. In the higher education context the discipline I teach is extremely political. I teach people how to find, use, and evaluate information to enable and empower their lives. I teach students about critical theory and that the real experience of people's lives is also a powerful form of knowledge.

Like my ancestors I am an orator; I tell stories and weave pictures from my own life and the lives of others to demonstrate agency and powerlessness, joy and despair, in the context of information literacy and lifelong learning. I make connections from where my students exist now (socially, intellectually, and culturally) to where they might exist in the future. The spiritual principles of my *tupuna* are living, energetic presences in my learning and teaching spaces. Somehow, as a result of all this, I move my students and as a result become moved also. They tell me I make a difference, but to what I don't know. I touch their spirits; I care about them and love them into learning. We are cautioned by bell hooks (2003) that "to speak of love in relation to teaching is to engage in a dialogue that is taboo" (p. 127). I don't care. I do much that's taboo. My journey to critical theory and my life from within it are my strengths.

My mother died in 2007 from inoperable cancer. Inoperable because a fifty-four-year career in smoking already had her on oxygen and with no lung capacity to survive the procedure. Nicotine is a drug, and it suppresses emotion. Today more than 50 percent of Maori women smoke cigarettes. In the last twelve years I have been more present in my life, available to those who love me, and I crossed the Tasman Sea many times in Mum's final year to be with her. We cooked and ate and laughed and argued. Whenever she wanted to speak to me honestly she would get angry first, because truth makes us vulnerable, and then she'd cry as she told me what she needed to say. We cried a lot. She told me things I had been waiting my lifetime to hear, about her pride in me and her regret for my loneliness as a child and pain as a lost adult. She told me how proud my father would be of me for reclaiming his language and culture. Funnily enough, it no longer mattered. I had built theory along the way to survive the pain and much had already been healed. The day before she died, I was told, she answered questions with simple Maori words and spoke of someone watching her. As she left this life I stroked her hair and sang her a Maori lullaby she'd sometimes sung to me. In the shadows her *tupuna* waited, ready to take her home.

Kua mutu.

REFERENCES

Barcham, M. (1998). The challenge of urban Maori: Reconciling conceptions of indigeneity and social change. *Asia Pacific Viewpoint, 39*(3), 303–343.

Bhabha, H. (1994). *The location of culture.* New York: Routledge.

Dei, G.J.S., Karumanchery, L. L., & Karumanchery-Luik, N. (2004). *Playing the race card: Exposing White power and privilege.* Washington, DC: Peter Lang.

Durie, M. (2004, November 25–26). *Race and ethnicity in public policy: Does it work?* Paper presented at the Social Policy, Research and Evaluation Conference, Wellington, New Zealand.

Green, T. (2006). *A case of mistaken (cultural) identity: Multiculturalism and the politics of culture.* Paper presented at Mini-APSA.

Hall, S., & Du Gay, P. 1996. *Questions of cultural identity.* Thousand Oaks, CA: Sage.

hooks, b. (1990). *Yearning: Race, gender, and cultural politics.* Boston: South End Press.

hooks, b. (1994). *Teaching to transgress: Education as the practice of freedom.* New York: Routledge.

hooks, b. (2003). *Teaching community: A pedagogy of hope.* New York: Routledge.

Ka'ai, T., Moorfield, J., Reilly, M., & Mosley, S. (Eds.). (2004). *Ki te whaiao: An introduction to Maori culture and society.* Auckland: Pearson Education.

LaDuke, W. (2005). Nick Tilsen: A new generation of activists protects the people, the land. *Tribal College Journal of American Indian Higher Education, 16*(3), 24–25.

Lavie, S., & Swedenburg, T. (1996). Between and among the boundaries of culture: Bridging text and lived experience in the third timespace. *Cultural Studies, 10*(1), 154–179.

Lawrence, B. (2004). *"Real" Indians and others: Mixed-blood urban Native peoples and indigenous nationhood*. Lincoln: University of Nebraska Press.

McDaniel, M., & Flowers, R. (1999). Adult education and indigenous Australians. In G. Foley (Ed.), *Understanding adult education and training* (2nd ed.). St. Leonards, NSW: Allen & Unwin.

Meredith, P. (1998a, July 7–9). *Hybridity in the third space: Rethinking bi-cultural politics in Aotearoa/New Zealand*. Paper presented at the Te Oru Rangahau Maori Research and Development Conference, Massey University, Wellington, New Zealand.

Meredith, P. (1998b). *Seeing the Maori subject*. Paper presented at the Maori Law Society 10th annual conference.

Meredith, P. (2000). A half caste on the half-caste in the cultural politics of New Zealand. In H. Jäcksch (Ed.), *Maori und Gesellschaft*. Berlin: Mana-Verlag.

Ngatai, L. (2006). *Indigenous pedagogies: Bringing back the heart*. Paper presented at the International Lifelong Learning Conference, Yeppoon, Australia.

Paperastergiadis, N. (1997). Tracing hybridity in theory. In P. Werbner & T. Modood (Eds.), *Debating cultural hybridity: Multicultural identities and the politics of anti-racism*. London: Zed Books.

Healing

A Journey Through Conversations on Race and Gender

The five chapters in Part One, "The Myth Versus the Reality of Race and Racism," make the argument that race and racism are permanent fixtures of our lifetime. The authors' words give a hopeful response and provide insights into how to fight the good fight in an effort to bring positive change into the world through our teaching practices. Their collective voices show us how to practice humanity in the face of those who would deny our humanity. The common denominator that unites these chapters is the understanding that love supports and drives the teaching process. Rose Borunda, Yolanda Sealey-Ruiz, Raquel Gonzáles, Maria Mejorado, Nichole Ray, and Lesley Ngatai all sow seeds of kindness (sometimes repackaged through constructive confrontation); they all love and accept themselves and others; they all share a fierce strength that allows them to teach from their place of acceptance and peace.

However, the five telephone conversations that we (the chapter authors and the editors) had during the preparation of Part One tell a different tale. These discussions contained burdensome and painful stories of how we had been injured in our classrooms by our students and in our practices by our colleagues. And in the moment of the telling, which was devoid and decoupled from future resolution, there were tears, silences, amens, and the all too common utterance of "me too." The women-of-color authors in this section realized that their struggles were common experiences among the group and that their solutions were also familiar to the others: those of us who are women of color seek out other women of color in the academy for support and sanity checks; we rely on lessons learned in our cultural community grounding; we reflect and debrief and arm ourselves anew with up-to-the-minute information and fresh innovative arguments; and we seek communion and comfort by turning to our individual spiritual belief systems—we pray.

When we authors and editors talked on the telephone about our practices, our conversations flowed with the ease and familiarity usually only afforded old friends. Although mostly new to each other, we found we had unknowingly been forging bonds in our university classrooms as we each had labored to talk about and to teach about race and the impact that race has had on each of our lives as well as on our students' lives. We had all arrived at this shared place of knowing, telling, and writing having taken different paths. And the straightforwardness of our dialogue came from the joy of unburdening. The tears, whether detectable in the once strong voice that was now quivering or disguised but still perceptible in the sharpness and tension of an occasional epithet, seemed to always lurk in the shadows. There were noticeable themes in our stories, from our shared lived experiences: discovery, betrayal, struggle, broken alliances, hard-earned lessons, and recovery. For several of the authors, the confrontational classroom resistance had taken its toll on the zest that they had once brought to their practices. Another story from the battlefront was the well-known scenario of the formal written student complaint that alleged a hostile classroom environment or uncomfortable atmosphere with "all of this talk about race," and the even more common harsh end-of-course evaluations. So, incrementally, as educators, we have had our enthusiasm replaced by cautious optimism or by the armor of experience that keeps us ready to assume a self-protective posture. Our conversations also featured the notorious narrative of the White colleague who seemed to "get it" and appeared to be an ally, but who later discovered that the perpetual journey to racial understanding was too complex and the fight too arduous and often costly. We each spoke of colleagues who had opted to disengage, a luxury afforded only to those who choose either to engage in denial or to shield themselves with their privilege. Even though, thankfully, we could also tell stories of associates, both White and Black, who were constant allies, more often than not, it seemed, we spoke of the colleagues who either didn't respect our knowledge base or who labeled our race work as second class. Another often-told combat story was of the White colleague who traded on our race work, expecting us to do the heavy lifting, or the colleague who expected more from us in a relationship than he or she was willing to give, because being the *White friend* should have benefits.

And yet the pain, although prevalent in our musings and front and center in our analysis, did not outweigh the joy. For we discovered that at some point, each of us had learned to heal quickly in order to get back to the battle—to move back to practicing with hope. How could it be that each of us had endured journeys of self-doubt, of feeling lost, of being alone, and of occasionally feeling inferior in our academic worlds to find this strength? How was the joy discovered?

With faces that have been occasionally stained with tears, contorted in anger, and awash with fear, we spoke in bewilderment about why our accomplishments in the academic world did not provide us with acceptance. Cursing the fact that they could not think or write their way out of the pain that comes from this rejection, the authors in this section moved on to more productive pursuits.

As editors we took notes of the ebb and flow of the telephone conversations. Yet we could not help but sigh as we listened to the experiences of our youthful colleagues, because we knew that the character of the incidents they related would not change as they became more accomplished in their careers. It was clear to us as elders that it was likely that the hostile incidents would become increasingly austere, because we recalled that as we progressed in the academy our accomplishments did not shield us from harm but instead threatened others' natural and accepted order. Therefore our occasional castigations have become more severe. In other words, women of color have not been expected to be at the top of their academic fields, because as women of color they are expected to be gratefully respectful, deferent, and busy with service work. It has not been our place to be deans or department heads. In fact, all of the authors in this section agreed that our very presence in the academy has been an affront to the *Paper Chase* image of what a professor looks like, a White male.

Yet, the women writing in this section have persisted, and it was stated either directly or indirectly in every phone call that they were about *surviving* and *thriving* despite the infertile soil in which they have chosen to implant themselves. And yes, it was decided in our conversations that it was the choice of all us to be here and to do this race work. Initially and naively, it was our belief that the academy was a better and higher plane of existence, where social justice and intellectual quests were the order of the day. Although it was quickly realized that higher education was not our real world—the community that we are recognized as being a part of as a particular race, gender, class, or other social category—it is now our chosen homeplace, our site of struggle. Our classrooms, our writings, our research are our way of making a difference—of attempting to make the way better for those like us who will follow.

As we fight for survival, it has been only natural to rely on the truths learned in our childhood or the certainties that were in some form embedded in our cultures and our set of lived experiences. Such lessons have been our salvation. Like the kernels of truth and strength concealed in the African axioms that became Aesop's Fables, we have discovered the truisms and proverbs that will save us: an open hand holds more than a closed fist; wrestle easy when your head is in the lion's mouth; nothing goes over the devil's back that doesn't come back to buckle under his belt; pretty is as pretty does; a hero rises to the occasion—a warrior is already there; the stories of the hunt will be tales of glory until the day when the creatures tell the story; and White fairy tales begin with, "Once upon a time"; Black fairy tales begin with, "You ain't gonna believe this s__t!"

With an understanding that is simultaneously culturally and linguistically rooted and experientially realized, together in our academic world we have found comfort in the knowledge that race is a myth and a reality. And it is our choice to struggle with and against the myth of race and racism—we aspire to have our teaching practices create positive changes in our classrooms, in our communities, and globally. We think and act locally and globally, bridging the racial, gender, and language gaps between the communities we come from and the academy in which we now find ourselves working as teachers and administrators. For us, race reflects who we are and racism reflects acts of negation, denial, and aggression against a people because of the color of their skins or the sound of their voices. Understanding the difference between the two means that we acknowledge that race and racism are not either/or; they are both/and. We are making an effort to have an impact on that reality of race and racism in which we all must live. To the editors of this section, the women who shared their lived experiences and stories throughout the first five chapters are activists. Their reach as activist educators is far, because each person they have taught and who embraces the message passes it on to others. And the collective is thereby made whole and "all the better" from the effort of these few.

PART TWO

Problematizing "Whiteness," Supremacy, and Privilege: Their Impact on Race

The chapters in this section offer a critical examination of *Whiteness*, supremacy, and privilege as they intersect with and affect the ways that race and racism are addressed and experienced within individuals' personal, professional, and social lives. The authors discuss how their silence or potential silence or their critiques about race and racism have served to control or perpetuate the silence of the "other." In addition, they consider how one's group membership affects the way one thinks and talks about race and racism. Finally, they address why it is imperative for this discussion to occur if the field of adult education is to develop a better understanding of how these factors have affected or will affect the field of practice.

Initially, when we (the five editors) discussed the idea of having a section of the book you are reading focus on Whiteness, White privilege, and White supremacy to be authored by White scholars, our reactions were mixed. At the same time, as editors of this book, we all thought it important that a major book dealing with race include White authors and focus on what Whiteness entails. We have witnessed and been personally involved in far too many conversations in which race was a topic expected to be raised by, or seen as only applying to, colleagues and learners of color. So for that reason alone we are glad to include the current section. In addition, it is impossible to talk about race without naming the ideology and practice of White supremacy as the central feature of contemporary racism; and as the White authors of Part Two discuss, when Whites become part of these conversations it is impossible for them to avoid acknowledging their own collusion in racism and how privileges accorded them because of their race have benefited them.

Chapter Six, the first chapter in this section, "White Whispers: Talking About Race in Adult Education," opens with an acknowledgment of these benefits. Chapter author Lisa Baumgartner explores the theoretical background to White privilege, the ways Whites develop racial identity, and Whites' development of discourses around questions of race. One of the subtle cruelties of racism is that many of the discourses that appear to challenge it or explain it actually end up perpetuating it. Baumgartner speaks to how she has fallen into this trap herself, and she builds an irrefutable case for building the White whispers about race into a loud conversation that engages the adult education field. One of the dangers of such a conversation is that it can easily remain in the head and never get to the gut—staying within the theoretical realm and refusing to confront the personal. One group that has worked to bring this conversation down to the concrete level of how Whites live out racial microaggressions in their daily lives is the European-American Collaborative Challenging Whiteness (ECCW). ECCW members are the authors of Chapter Nine.

Another focus of inquiry into Whiteness, White privilege, and White supremacy involves trying to understand the elements that make up the White perspective on the world. Although it is as dangerous to assume that there is a monolithical "White" view on anything as it is to assume that there is a "Black" perspective that all members of the African Diaspora share, there are nonetheless certain elements of the dominant ideology that reflect a Eurocentric tradition. In Chapter Seven, "Transforming White Consciousness," Doug Paxton (himself a member of the ECCW) develops an understanding of the dominant worldview—what he calls the *White paradigm*—in the United States. He explores this paradigm's ontology (views on the nature of reality), epistemology (ways of judging something as true), methodology (techniques for gathering information and expanding knowledge), and axiology (fundamental values that guide action). Through a case study of his involvement in an organizational task force on diversity, Paxton shows how his attempt to challenge institutional resistance to becoming more inclusive can be understood through the prism of the White paradigm. He problematizes his behavior as a *good White person* and shows how it was shaped by this paradigm.

Elaine Manglitz and Ron Cervero echo W.E.B. DuBois in their title for Chapter Eight—"Adult Education and the Problem of the Color (Power) Line: Views from the Whiter Side." In this chapter they explore the dynamics of racism in the particular field of adult education; they describe the different paths the two of them have traveled in coming to an awareness of their own racial identity; and they examine how they seek to work in antiracist ways on the White side of the color line. Although both acknowledge the progress the field of adult education has made in the last decade, they come to the same conclusion as the other section authors—that engaging in conversations with other Whites in order to comprehend how Whites learn and disseminate the ideology of White supremacy is truly a lifelong learning project.

In the final chapter in Part Two, "White on White: Developing Capacity to Communicate About Race with Critical Humility," the members of the European-American Collaborative Challenging Whiteness draw on their ten-year history of conversation to identify the problems they have run into when trying to engage other Whites on the issues of race and racism. They explore how proselytizing and disdaining shuts down dialogue and describe their struggle to develop a critical humility that stands for antiracist behavior while constantly acknowledging that such behavior won't ever be fully realized. Through a case study of one particular conversation, the ECCW members show how even after ten years they fall into the traps of seeking the approval of people of color and of exuding condescension as they "explain" racism to other Whites. As they point out, critical humility is a constant process of inquiry and not a destination they expect to reach.

6

White Whispers
Talking About Race in Adult Education

LISA M. BAUMGARTNER

A key feature of the social ontology of whiteness is that whites attempt to avoid discussing their own social, political, economic, and cultural investment in whiteness.

George Yancy (2004)

As a White female adult educator, I benefit daily from White privilege. Unlike some of my African American colleagues, I have never been stopped when taking a school laptop out of the building (Johnson-Bailey & Cervero, 2008). I can discuss race and White privilege without people assuming I have "an agenda." I can arrive at my office early in the morning and stay late without the campus police questioning me. My scholarship is not seen as "too White." My credibility as an instructor is not questioned because of my race. The adult education literature is replete with the accomplishments of White people. At adult education conferences, I see many people who look like me. However, my White privilege comes at a price paid by people of color, Whites, and the field of adult education.

This book's purpose is to create a dialogue about race among adult educators. A portion of that exploration centers on Whites' conceptualization of race and how Whites' discourse on race (or lack thereof) preserves White privilege. My chapter examines Whites' conceptualization and discourse of Whiteness, White privilege, and their effect on adult education. First, I delineate a brief history of White supremacy and racism in the United States. Next, using Helms's (1990) model of White identity development, I explore how Whites come to know their Whiteness. Third, through a delineation of Frankenberg's (1993) model, I discuss how Whites understand race and White racial privilege. Fourth, I present Hytten and Warren's recent work on White discourse on race. (Chapter Seven offers additional information on the White paradigm, including its ontology, epistemology, methodology, and axiology). Last, I discuss why it is important for adult educators to engage in a discussion of race and racism.

SEEDS OF RACISM

Racism and White supremacy have a long history in the United States. Rooted in religion, White supremacy arrived with the Puritans and is promoted by present-day intellectuals. Griffin (1999) writes, "The Puritans used the doctrines of sin, predestination, covenant, and creation to argue that God had favored them . . . placing them at the top of the hierarchy of humanity" (p. 17). The idea of White supremacy remained after the Civil War. Between 1865 and 1920, "scientific" ideas combined with bigoted theology to support racists' claims of White supremacy. Clergyman Josiah Strong and physician Josiah Nott used "God, nature, science, and history" to bolster their White supremacist claims (Griffin, 1999, p. 45). These racist ideas persisted as Ku Klux

Klan membership swelled in the 1920s and 1930s. During the Civil Rights movement of the 1950s and 1960s, White churches denounced racism, but later abandoned their commitment to racial equality. In the 1970s, President Nixon appointed Edward C. Banfield to determine the efficacy of the urban renewal program started under President Johnson. Banfield used psychology and sociology to demonstrate that Blacks were "lower class people" (Griffin, 1999, p. 75). More recently, Murray and Hernstein argued in *The Bell Curve* (1994) for the innate inferiority of Black intelligence. Well-publicized, racist remarks by comedian Michael Richards and talk show host Don Imus show that racism is alive and well.

Despite the continuous and tragic history of racism in the United States, the topic of race is often obfuscated in the adult education literature and classroom. When issues of race do surface, they most often concern discrimination against people of color, and Whites' perpetuation of racism on personal, social, and institutional levels is left unchallenged. Whites do not "see" race because it benefits them not to see it.

HOW WHITES CONCEPTUALIZE AND DISCUSS WHITENESS AND RACIAL PRIVILEGE

To understand the persistence of White privilege and racism, it is helpful to know how Whites learn their racial identity and privilege and how their discourses about Whiteness preserve White privilege. I delineate Helms's (1990) six-stage model of White racial identity development, Frankenberg's (1993) model of race consciousness, and studies that explore Whites' discourses about race (Hytten & Warren, 2003; Warren & Hytten, 2004).

Helms's Model

Helms's six-stage model delineates White racial identity development. Helms (1990) notes that during the *contact* stage, people of color are exoticized and Whites are oblivious to their own racism and to themselves as White. Generally, one or more incidents alert Whites to racism, and they then enter the *disintegration* stage, where they notice racism exists and they may distance themselves from Blacks and feel confused or guilty because they begin to recognize White privilege. During the *reintegration* stage, Whites believe there is an element of truth in the negative stereotypes of Blacks and may avoid associating with Blacks and may treat them poorly or act violently against them. During the *pseudo-independent* stage, Whites begin to understand that they are not superior but may still perpetuate that idea through their actions. For example, they may want to "help Blacks succeed by getting them to mimic Whites" (Thompson & Carter, 1997, p. 25). During the *immersion/emersion* stage, Whites start coming to terms with what it means to be White. They might join White consciousness-raising groups and talk to other Whites about racism (Helms, 1990; Thompson & Carter, 1997). Last, in the *autonomy* stage, people have a positive definition of Whiteness and understand that Whites perpetuate racism. However, they seek ways to eradicate racism on the personal and societal levels.

Frankenberg's Model

Frankenberg's (1993) model is based on interviews with thirty White women who were diverse in age (ranging from twenty to ninety-three years old), class, geographical location, sexuality, family situation, political orientation, and education. Frankenberg uncovered five phases of White racial consciousness. The first phase, *essentialist* racism, views Whites as superior based on biological difference. When White people say, "I am not racist," they usually mean they believe they are not essential racists. *Color blindness,* the second phase, is one of the most common discourses. Seeing race at all is considered prejudice. This perspective "preserves the power structure inherent in essentialist racism [because] ... [p]eople of color are 'good' only insofar as their coloredness can be bracketed and ignored, and this bracketing is contingent on the ability or decision—in fact the virtue of a ... white self" (Frankenberg, 1993, p. 147).

Women in the third phase, *power evasion,* recognize racial difference but do not acknowledge the power difference in relationships between Whites and people of color. They embrace relationships that make them feel good, such as talking about being friends with exchange students, but carefully avoid discussion of unequal power relationships with people of color. For example, a White woman raised by a Black domestic worker may try to create an equal power balance that does not exist by referring to the Black domestic worker in a discussion as Mrs. _____ when in reality, the White woman calls the Black woman by her first name.

Women in the *race cognizance: rethinking race and power* phase recognize how racial privilege shapes their daily life and understand institutional racism. They ponder "existential questions about the White complicity with racism and.... grapple with such questions in individual or collective ways" (Frankenberg 1993, p. 160). This stage focuses on internal thought rather than action.

In the final phase, *race cognizance: transforming silence into language and action,* women understand that they are racist. The term "my racism" is used (Frankenberg, 1993, p. 161). Sometimes, people do not act on this consciousness. However, many women see political activism as a way to do something about racism, and the focus becomes more collective than individual (Frankenberg, 1993).

How Whites Talk About Race

Many Whites do not reach the final phase of race consciousness (Frankenberg, 1993). The color-blind and the power-evasion stances are quite popular because they preserve White privilege and allow Whites to believe that they are fighting racism (Sullivan, 2006). As is shown in research conducted by Hytten and Warren, Whites' dialogue about race protects White privilege.

Hytten and Warren (2003) examined how White discourse about race protects racial privilege, asking these research questions: "How do students interact with the discourse of whiteness studies?" And, "How and why do students persist and/or resist engagements with whiteness?" (p. 68). Sixteen graduate students (fourteen Whites and two African

Americans) in a White studies course wrote reflection papers on "what it means to be White, how they engage racism in their lives and how they have experienced the culture of power" (p. 68).

Hytten and Warren (2003) found that the students used four techniques to preserve White privilege. The first technique, *appeals to the self*, can be used to empathize with others' oppression and to protect White privilege when the focus is only on the self. This appeal contains three discourses. In the *discourse of connections*, students believed that everyone "share[d] some core human experience" (p. 71). They foregrounded their experiences of oppression. For example, one White gay man always talked about his oppression as a gay man. This action "shift[ed] attention away from . . . race, allowing him to ignore his own whiteness and to construct himself always as a victim" (p. 71). The *discourse of self-absorption* allowed participants to focus obsessively on their feelings of White guilt, without seeing how White privilege affected the larger world. Using the *discourse of friends and family*, students compared how much more enlightened they were about racism than their friends or relatives were, but they did not examine their own racism or White privilege.

A second tactic, *appeals to progress*, involved three discourses. In the *fix-it discourse*, students proselytized about the danger of White privilege but eschewed continued reflection. Students suggested quick fixes that did not adequately address White privilege. The *mark-it discourse* concentrated on positive societal changes in race relations. Students cited their individual progress in their awareness of White privilege. The pitfall occurred when people's progress stopped. Third, students used the *enrich-me discourse* to "trivialize . . . racial issues and . . . to reduce exploring diversity to simply providing themselves with a broader enriching cultural experience" (Hytten & Warren, 2003, p. 78).

The *appeals to authenticity* technique was used when Whites asked people of color for their opinions and treated them as representative of their culture. Further, this perspective demanded that people of color be responsible for the work of understanding that Whites should do. In the *discourse of "yes, but . . . ,"* Whites understood others' experiences but "suggest[ed] that they do not match the way they experience the world" (Hytten & Warren, 2003, p. 79). In the *discourse of scholarly authority,* Whites used literature to discount the experiences of others.

Last, students *appealed to extremes* to protect the status quo. Using the *discourse of the real vs. the ideal,* students believed that the issues of White privilege and racism were too big to tackle and asked, "Why try?" Students using the *discourse of niceness vs. conflict* did not call each other to task for racist acts. Using the *discourse of voice vs. silence,* Whites believed they must remain silent while people of color talked, but they did not examine their White privilege.

Like my White colleagues writing in this handbook, I too have used several of Hytten and Warren's (2003) discourses to preserve my White privilege, including the discourses of connections. I foregrounded my position as a woman in a sexist society instead of focusing on my White privilege. I also used the discourses of niceness versus conflict and voice versus silence. I remained silent when people of color talked and did not use the opportunity to examine my White privilege. When I realized I had used these methods to preserve White privilege, I resolved to avoid these pitfalls. I understand that my knowledge of my Whiteness and racism is a lifelong process.

In a 2004 follow-up article, Warren and Hytten delineated five *masks,* or *faces,* from which Whites discussed race. A face is "a location, a position, a persona one takes, from time to time" (Warren & Hytten, 2004, p. 323). Students spoke from various positions at different times. Four of the five faces are seen as pitfalls for Whites when they work through White privilege. These four faces are situated on two intersecting poles. One pole has *active investigation* at one end and *static understanding* at the other. The other pole has *obsessive investment with self* at one end and *distanced engagement with self* at the other end. Active investigation types want to continue to engage with the Whiteness literature whereas static understanders rely on their current understandings about race. And those with an obsessive investment with self worry about their participation in racism whereas those on the other side of the continuum do not.

The *Torpefied* (active investigation and obsessive investment with self) realize that they oppress and do not know what to do about it. They are self-involved and worried about their actions toward people of color. They feel guilty and look to people of color for simple answers to White privilege and its manifestations. They want to talk and read about race, but they realize that "without the support of others they will not be able to continue to act against whiteness" (Warren & Hytten, 2004, p. 326). Guilt and obsession may paralyze them.

Missionaries (static understanding and obsessive investment with the self) believe that they "get" race and have the answers. They want action. They "desire to help those of color who suffer under the weight of racism" and to "save other white folks from racism" (Warren & Hytten, 2004, p. 327). For Missionaries, any action is better than just talking about racism. They act on their incomplete understanding of racism, which alienates others.

The *Cynics* (static understanding and distanced engagement with self) are true pessimists. They believe that racism is just a part of life. Conversation about racism is fruitless. This position is quite dangerous "since it denies hope [and] denies white folks' responsibility for racism" (Warren & Hytten, 2004, p. 328).

The *Intellectualizers* (active investigation and distanced engagement with self) find Whiteness fascinating but "they never locate the study and analysis of whiteness in their own experience" (Warren & Hytten, 2004, p. 329). Whiteness is an academic subject to be enjoyed, but daily life should not be affected.

Those who exhibit the fifth face, the Critical Democrats, occupy a position between the two intersecting poles. They examine their own and others' roles in racism. They understand Whiteness but realize that they need to understand more. They know action and reflection are a necessary part of dealing with White privilege and racism. They also realize that there needs to be a balance between listening and speaking on racism and White privilege. "Critical Democrats ... push toward a more reflexive social action that is built from the tension of guilt and agency, allowing the passion and energy that produces guilt to be put to productive use" (Warren & Hytten, 2004, p. 332).

In sum, most Whites' conceptualization and discussion of White privilege centers on denying its existence. Some Whites are stuck in the color-blind approach. Others become mired in their own guilt or they intellectualize White privilege so they do not have to grapple with its individual and social ramifications. This avoidance and denial not only affects individuals but, ironically, it also influences social movements aimed at the liberation of oppressed groups.

WHY ADULT EDUCATORS NEED TO DISCUSS RACE AND RACISM

Adult educators need to discuss the impact of race and racism on the field of adult education. First, Whites' color-blind approach to race allows them to ignore the contributions of people from other races (Sullivan, 2006). This has repeatedly occurred in the field of adult education. Although the work of Myles Horton and Malcolm Knowles is known, the contributions of Septima Clark, Alain Locke, and Nannie Burroughs are less recognized. Further, the predominantly White male view of White male accomplishments in adult education has been published (Jensen, Liveright, & Hallenbeck, 1964; Peters, Jarvis, & Associates, 1991), but the American Association for Adult and Continuing Education withdrew its support for a "source book . . . devoted to race and feminist concerns" (Cunningham, 2001, p. xi), which forced the book's editors to seek other venues for publication (Sheared & Sissel, 2001).

Second, racism sullies adult educators' history of engaging in social justice movements such as the women's movement. The women's rights movement began in 1848, as a call for universal suffrage. Shortly after the ratification of the Fourteenth Amendment in 1868, which granted Black men voting rights, Elizabeth Cady Stanton urged upper-class White women to fight for the vote so that "lower orders of Chinese, Africans, Germans and Irish" could not make laws for these upper-class, educated women (quoted in Andolsen, 1986, p. 31). White feminists remained silent during the late nineteenth and early twentieth century as Jim Crow laws eviscerated the rights of Black men and lynchings increased (Andolsen, 1986). This impoverished moral legacy continued in the second wave of feminism. White women in the mid-1960s compared the status of Blacks to the status of women as their predecessors had (Roth, 2004). The "White-women-as-Black" analogy infuriated some Black women, because "the actual situation of Black women was erased from view" (Roth, 2004, p. 199; see also Spelman, 1982). White women have continued to demonstrate their racism. In order to add the word *sex* to Title VII of the Civil Rights Act of 1964, which ultimately prohibited discrimination based on "race, color, religion, sex, or national origin," White women used the same tactics they had used when the Fourteenth Amendment passed. How, argued White women, could Blacks be protected above White women? (Griffin, 1999).

Third, racism affects adult education classrooms and scholarship. Racism affects classroom dynamics through the devaluation of Black professors and reification of White professors. Research shows that both Black and White students apply "more stringent credibility standards" to Black professors than to White professors (Hendrix, 1998, p. 748). Students see Black faculty as less competent than White faculty, and White faculty minimize the influence of White or male privilege in their classroom interactions (Harlow, 2003). Black female faculty are seen as overly aggressive when the same behavior in Whites is considered scholarly (Harlow, 2003). Last, Hendrix reported that in a survey of twenty-four Black researchers, nine had been asked if their race influenced their research. Black researchers believed it was more difficult to publish research on their race than it was for their White colleagues. White academicians dismiss their Black colleagues' research as less important, making tenure and promotion more difficult for people of color (Hendrix, 2002).

Racism remains an injustice that affects the individual, the field of adult education, institutions, and society. Ironically, a field that proclaims its commitment to social justice also engages in marginalizing the voices of people of color and has not, as a field, discussed the implications of racism. We need to have frank discussions about the impact of race on adult education in order to begin to understand how Whites' color blindness continues to privilege White students and affects the curriculum, student and teacher interactions, and our institutions. Talking about race in adult education is a start. It is a start to turning the White whispers about race into full-blown voices. It is a start for Whites to begin to peel back the layers of privilege that prevent us from working for the eradication of personal and institutional racism.

Sullivan (2006) considers racism an unconscious habit. Whites must work to bring their racist beliefs into consciousness through critical reflection and examination of their feelings. Through dialogue, these racist attitudes can be unearthed and examined and solutions can be implemented. Through dialogue, White adult educators can reflect on how they perpetuate racism through their discussions, thoughts, and actions. They can begin to ask themselves questions like these: How do I talk about race in my classroom? How does my dialogue about race (or lack thereof) perpetuate White privilege? How developed is my sense of racial identity? How does my institution perpetuate racism? What actions can I take to ameliorate that? How do I contribute to the perpetuation of a Eurocentric curriculum? Critical reflection on these questions will help Whites in their racial identity development and discourse about race.

In sum, racism, White supremacy, and White privilege have a long history. How Whites conceptualize and discuss race perpetuates White privilege. White privilege and racism affect adult education in a variety of contexts, including social justice movements and formal educational settings. It is imperative that the field of adult education begins to dialogue about race in order to begin to work toward the eradication of racism.

REFERENCES

Andolsen, B. H. (1986). *"Daughters of Jefferson, daughters of bootblacks": Racism and American feminism.* Macon, GA: Mercer University Press.

Cunningham, P. (2001). Foreword. In V. Sheared & P. Sissel (Eds.), *Making space: Merging theory and practice in adult education* (pp. xi–xvi). Westport, CT: Bergin & Garvey.

Frankenberg, R. (1993). *White women, race matters: The social construction of race.* Minneapolis: University of Minnesota Press.

Griffin, P. R. (1999). *Seeds of racism in the soul of America.* Cleveland, OH: Pilgrim Press.

Harlow, R. (2003). "Race doesn't matter, but . . . ": The effect of race on professors' experiences and emotion management in the undergraduate classroom. *Social Psychology Quarterly, 66*(4), 348–363.

Helms, J. E. (1990). *Black and White racial identity: Theory, research and practice.* Westport, CT: Greenwood Press.

Hendrix, K. G. (1998). Student perceptions of the influence of race on professor credibility. *Journal of Black Studies, 28*(6), 738–763.

Hendrix, K. G. (2002). "Did being Black introduce bias into your study?" Attempting to mute the race-related research of Black scholars. *Howard Journal of Communications, 13*, 153–171.

Hytten, K., & Warren, J. (2003). Engaging Whiteness: How racial power gets reified in education. *Qualitative Studies in Education, 16*(1), 65–89.

Jensen, G., Liveright, A., & Hallenbeck, W. (1964). *Adult education: Outlines of an emerging field of university study.* Washington, DC: Adult Education Association of the USA.

Johnson-Bailey, J., & Cervero, R. M. (2008). Different worlds and divergent paths: Academic careers defined by race and gender. *Harvard Educational Review, 78*(2), 311–332.

Murray, C., & Hernstein, R. (1994). *The bell curve: Intelligence and class structure in American life.* New York: Free Press.

Peters, J. M., Jarvis, P., & Associates. (1991). *Adult education: Evolution and achievements in a developing field of study.* San Francisco: Jossey-Bass.

Roth, B. (2004). *Separate roads to feminism: Black, Chicana, and White feminist movements in America's second wave.* New York: Cambridge University Press.

Sheared, V., & Sissel, P. A. (Eds.). (2001). *Making space: Merging theory and practice in adult education.* Westport, CT: Bergin & Garvey.

Spelman, E. V. (1982). Theories of race and gender: The erasure of Black women. *Quest: A Feminist Quarterly, 5*(4), 36–62.

Sullivan, S. (2006). *Revealing Whiteness: The unconscious habits of racial privilege.* Bloomington: Indiana University Press.

Thompson, C. E., & Carter, R. T. (1997). *Racial identity theory: Application to individual, group and organizational interventions.* Mahwah, NJ: Erlbaum.

Warren, J. T., & Hytten, K. (2004). The faces of Whiteness: Pitfalls and the Critical Democrat. *Communication Education, 53*(4), 321–339.

Yancy, G. (2004). *What White looks like: African American philosophers on the Whiteness question.* New York: Routledge.

7

Transforming White Consciousness

DOUG PAXTON

This chapter explores the water in which I swim as a White man in the United States. I begin with the idea that in order to transform the consciousness that creates racism, the structure and system of thought associated with that consciousness must also be examined. Building upon the foundation of critical race theory (Delgado, 1995), I see the White paradigm as a broader phenomenon than White racism, having an impact on all aspects of the ways White people know about and behave in the world. I begin by telling a story about my experience with race at work. I then consider White consciousness from a theoretical perspective, and conclude by applying the theoretical perspective back to my own story.

Ten years ago I began to learn new things about an old subject— racism. Prior to that time, I thought of myself as a *good White person* who was, naturally, against prejudice. I believed I was on the "right" side of issues, a defender of those who are marginalized in our society. Two parallel life experiences—my role at work and as a student in graduate school—conspired to shake the foundations of what I knew about myself and about racism, creating a "perfect storm" for learning.

Both my workplace and graduate school saw themselves as socially progressive institutions, and were going through significant change as they espoused the desire to build a culture more welcoming to people of diverse racial backgrounds. In both organizations, White people had historically predominated in positions of organizational leadership. Valuing diversity made sense to me as a gay man, as someone who had experienced the negative impacts of being different in America.

What increasingly caught my attention in the spring of 1998 was the heightened disenchantment that many people of color—at work and school—expressed as a direct consequence of what each institution was doing to address diversity issues. Both concerned and naive about race, I listened as people of color told me about their experiences.

The business trade association where I worked was dedicated to promoting corporate social responsibility and had made prior efforts to better "walk its talk" on the subject of racism and diversity. Paradoxically, the more attention we paid to race in the workplace, the worse people felt about the situation. People of color learned that their White colleagues knew less about race than they expected, and White people felt uncomfortable about how little they really knew about the racial lives of their colleagues of color. The more I heard, the more I realized that a racial reality gap existed between people of color and White people. With the CEO's blessing, I created a diversity task force at work, using action research to guide our process. The task force was charged with exploring and evaluating the organization's diversity climate. The timing of the task force was ideal, given the sobering news that eight of the eleven departing employees in the prior year were people of color.

The task force itself was quite diverse, and split its time between self-study—exploring the racial and cultural dynamics among members of the task force—and organizational study—conducting an all-staff survey on how employees felt about working at the organization.

Several months later the task force presented findings to the senior management team, findings that indicated the organization had a problem. According to a majority of the staff, it did not have a welcoming climate where people of diverse racial backgrounds could flourish. The predominantly White senior management team reacted defensively. Feeling a surge of righteous indignation, and knowing that no one else on the task force had the institutional position to challenge the top leaders, I gave an impassioned plea on behalf of the survey results and the task force recommendations for future work. It was the first time that I had spoken out publicly and directly on behalf of people of color and against racism, and taken an uncompromising stand against White people. I was angry, reacting to what I saw as the entrenched interests of the organization's leadership and the system that maintained the status quo. This moment of challenging my senior colleagues, who undoubtedly also saw themselves as good White people, was a watershed event in my professional life. I could for the first time detect the systemic resistance and denial pushing back against me, affirming what colleagues of color had been trying to explain to me. The experience of being a member of the task force was galvanizing for me, as issues of race seemed to be arising in many areas of my life.

On the face of it, my story may seem unproblematic or even noble—a personal account of resistance in the face of entrenched racism. Although I am glad I took this stand, my actions expose my unconsciousness about Whiteness and how I operate so thoroughly within the White paradigm.

A WHITE PARADIGM

It...is to history that we owe our frames of reference, our identities.... People who imagine that history flatters them...are impaled on their history like a butterfly on a pin and become incapable of seeing or changing themselves...and they suffer enormously from the resulting personal incoherence.

James Baldwin (1998, p. 321)

In 1962, White author and educator Thomas Kuhn published *The Structure of Scientific Revolutions,* which popularized the use of the word *paradigm.* According to Kuhn, a paradigm is not simply the current theory in fashion. A paradigm is the complete pattern of thought in which a particular worldview rests. Kuhn makes the point that until a new paradigm is understood, all science and conventional wisdom work to justify and defend the existing paradigm. Using the components of a worldview, or paradigm, identified by White authors Yvonna Lincoln and Egon Guba (2000), I explore the idea of a White paradigm as a functioning worldview, with its own ontology, epistemology, methodology, and axiology.

A few disclaimers are in order. I do not mean to conflate Western consciousness with White consciousness, though I do imagine they share similar roots and parallel ways of making meaning of the world. I also acknowledge that feminists might well comment that numerous qualities I attribute to Whiteness represent patriarchal behaviors of domination. I concur, and yet believe there is something about White skin privilege that White women share with me across the divide of gender. I also imagine that the White paradigm is not exclusive to White people. Perhaps it is more accurate to refer to Whiteness as the paradigm of the dominant culture, thereby explaining how people of color could also share such a paradigmatic orientation.

Ontology: The Nature of Reality

Ontology is the study of the form and nature of reality. For many of us who are White, our ontology springs from our history of deterministic, reductionist, rational, and objective ways of verifying what is real. Essentially, and admittedly oversimplistically, White people have come to believe the "real" world can be understood largely through the positivist application of science and hypothesis testing. We believe that time is linear, with past and future components that encourage us to reify "progress" as superior. We see logic and facts as synonymous with the truth. Knowledge and reality are largely assumed to be generalizable and universal—that is, not situated within a particular context. As White educator and author Peter Reason (1994) explains, "Western consciousness is characteristically dualist.... [T]he very notion of an individual self is at the root of our difficulties because it creates an ontology...in which the knower is detached from the world, rather than implicate within it" (p. 11).

Epistemology: The System of Knowing

Epistemology describes not just the way of knowing, but the system of knowing. How do White people know what they know? Elements in European-American systems of knowing include individualism, competition, positivism, rationality, logic, and objectivity; scientism; and dualism. Pan-African activist, author, and organizer Marimba Ani boils the European epistemological mode down to this: "Rob the universe of its richness, deny the significance of the symbolic, simplify phenomena until it becomes mere object, and you have a knowable quantity. Here begins and ends the European epistemological mode" (1994, p. 29). Without making an explicit connection to Whiteness, White educator and author Richard Tarnas (2002) frames the epistemological challenge of our time in a way that is consistent with Ani's view.

> [W]e need to radically expand our ways of knowing, our epistemology...to move beyond the very narrow empiricism and rationalism that were characteristic of the Enlightenment and still dominate mainstream science today. We need to draw on...the wider epistemologies of the heart [p. 9].

The emerging popularity of Eastern and indigenous spiritual traditions in Western society may well signal that many White people hunger for fulfillment with more diverse and expanded epistemologies.

Ani (1994) and Tarnas (2002) each allude to what is missing in the White epistemological view with terms like "richness of the universe" and "wider epistemologies of the heart." The White mind has shifted its consciousness from its original, more indigenous worldview to a view of the world as an object that is devoid of meaning and spirit. Author and shaman Malidoma Patrice Somé (1998) describes how difficult it was for him to move beyond the Western, literate consciousness that separated him from his African, indigenous roots.

> It was interesting to see the reaction of villagers who observed what literacy had done to me.... [W]hat I learned from my white teachers was considered poisonous, and even dangerous...[and] made me prone to doubt, incapable of trust, and subject to dangerous emotions such as anger and impatience.... Because of the Western consciousness...and its grandiose notions of superiority, I was slow to accept...intrusion from an indigenous worldview.... My Western-trained mind regarded [indigenous knowledge]...with hostile intention and therefore would fight against it with patriotic pride. I realize now that what I thought was my civilized mind was in fact a rather narrow mind [p. 8].

How can we facilitate the epistemological shift to a worldview that is not the opposite of dualism but transcends dualism? White systems theorist and author Gregory Bateson (1972) explained that being aware of the absence of a more expanded way of knowing is rare: "In the case of epistemological propositions, error is not easily detected and is not very quickly punished.... Epistemological error is often reinforced and therefore self-validating. You can get along all right in spite of the fact that you entertain at rather deep levels of the mind premises which are simply false" (pp. 479–480).

Methodology: Gathering Information

Methodology asks, how are data gathered for creating knowledge? White methodology is about how we discover and engage with the world to collect information and knowledge. The scientific process remains a central methodology of White culture, where hypothesis testing for quantitative results by objective and dispassionate researchers is the expected and reliable norm for finding answers that contribute to "valid" knowledge. The search for immutable laws that apply cause-and-effect understanding that can then be generalized to larger populations has long been bedrock for White methodology.

In many areas of White culture there is emphasis on direct verbal and written communication, content and task over process and relationship, timely adherence to agendas versus spontaneity, and considerable discomfort with nonrational ways of knowing, such as through our bodies or artistic expression. These methodological traits of Whiteness are often taken for granted as universal, and play an important role in screening and narrowing what is considered legitimate data for the White system of knowing.

Axiology: Ethics and Values

Axiology is the study of values and ethics—the realm where human societies make meaning of life's mysteries and question what is intrinsically valuable. White axiology represents the posture of ethics and values in relationship to the basic beliefs of European-American culture—the White paradigm described previously. When the Aristotelian value of knowledge itself as intrinsically worthwhile becomes the default value in White culture, we get "the modern propensity to educate the intellect in damaging dissociation from feeling, imagination, and action" (Heron & Reason, 1997, p. 287). This split was promoted by revolutions in European thought led by thinkers like Aristotle, Copernicus, Descartes, and Darwin, who made the values and mystery implicit in religion increasingly irrelevant to the ongoing scientific revolution (Tarnas, 2002). This revolution was pivotal for liberation from the limitations of religious and feudal societies; over time this compartmentalization has become central to how Whites see themselves in the world and how they prioritize what is important in their lives. Appreciation for one's ancestors and awe of and connection to the natural world are two indigenous values that get less attention in White culture, with potentially huge ramifications for the future.

For Whites, applying objectivity and rationality to the unknown reduces our level of uncertainty and discomfort. We assume that this removes us—through the application of reason—from the messy and value-laden arena of using religion and spirituality to address the unknown. White axiology is, then, less about what constitutes our values and more about what our values are disconnected from—broader and multiple ways of knowing.

It is the often unconscious universalization of the White worldview—ontology, epistemology, methodology, and axiology—coupled with the broad positions of power Whites hold in society that makes White consciousness simultaneously invisible and dominating. One implication of the White paradigm is clear—in order to transform and move beyond such a deeply ingrained system of thought, it will take far more than the election of one African American man to the presidency of the United States.

THE WHITENESS OF MY STORY

Reflecting back on my own story, I find many ways that illuminate how Whiteness was operating within me, even as I challenged the racial status quo in my organization.

The very language I used in telling my story exposes my Whiteness. When confronting senior management, I claimed to be speaking "on behalf of people of color." The paternalistic superiority was undisguised. What would it have meant to speak on behalf of White people? How might that stand have shifted the dynamics in the meeting?

The individualism wrought from the White ontology and epistemology described in the first part of this chapter left me unable to see myself as part of a White community of learners. In effect, I had separated myself from most other White people in the organization, and was unable to move from the perspective of an irate White do-gooder in order to ask the question, "What do *we* do, as a predominantly White organization, to create a more diverse culture?" As a White guy, living in the "we" is not something that comes easily to me.

The dualism of my worldview was clearly evident. I saw the office situation entirely in Black and White. I do see the necessity for righteous anger at times, where the force of an emotion can promote a breakthrough or direction for new inquiry. However, in the meeting with the senior leaders of the organization, my dualistic approach served to harden our positions of opposition, our inability to see one another as comrades in a shared struggle. Another casualty of my dualism were the staff members who did not fit neatly into the Black and White frames I brought to the struggle. One Asian/Pacific Islander on the staff explained that she felt more invisible than ever during my showdown with management. Given the polarizing atmosphere I helped to foster in the wake of the task force recommendations, how effective had I actually been as an advocate for change? Where were my heart and my compassion, for self and others?

In terms of the White paradigm, the self represented by my story is deeply embedded in the mind-set of rightness, superiority, and maintaining a precarious and overactive ego. The content of "right" as I defined it—in concert with the voices of people of color in the organization—may be laudable. However, through my experience with the diversity task force, I became more aware of how much my identity and ego are fueled by the need to be right, and I see this as connected to my Whiteness. How might I have been able to exert my rational thinking and education in the service of fostering relationship instead of being right? My righteous stance helped me better understand Somé's feedback from his indigenous elders, who worried about his focus on ego and the emotions of anger and impatience that came with the Western worldview that educated him.

White author and educator Edgar Schein (1995) links being right with one's identity: "In order to feel . . . anxiety or guilt, we must accept the disconfirming data as valid and relevant. What . . . prevents us from doing so . . . is a second kind of anxiety which we can call 'learning anxiety,' . . . if we admit to ourselves and others that something is wrong or imperfect, we will lose our effectiveness, our self-esteem and maybe even our identity" (p. 5). Schein's insight may help explain why the emotional stakes felt so high during this period for the White people in the organization. For a progressive good White person's identity and self-image, getting racism right feels fundamental and imperative. I believe our need to "get it right" left all of us on the senior management team in a fragile state where learning anxiety was high.

Learning from Experience

Without remarkable inspiration from colleagues of color at both school and work, I would easily have retreated from examining my Whiteness. The loving support from these colleagues was essential to hold me and keep me going. It then took working in groups with other White people on the subject of Whiteness (Paxton, 2003) to help me better understand the machinations of the White paradigm.

Another antidote to my individualism was my multicultural cohort from graduate school. Our group had been meeting together for two years and bore steady witness to the unfolding events in my workplace, encouraging me to stay in a mode of inquiry and, significantly, stay present to my emotions. In reflecting back on the diversity task force, I see how my preoccupation with the emotions of anger prevented me from listening for other voices in the room.

Over the years, I have slowly learned how diversity was something people in my organization were trying to "fix," so that we could move on to our admittedly stressful agendas. We were unprepared to simply sit with the truth of where we were in terms of racism. Perhaps there could have been a different frame, one that allowed us to honor the painful steps we were taking while acknowledging that we were not going to fix things. Ideally, we could have learned to practice better together and, through a strengthening of our relationships, to make more space for our inevitable mistakes.

In the end, it finally dawned on me that what needed to happen throughout the organization was what happened within the diversity task force. We needed an ongoing, relational group experience of exploring race and its associated dynamics. Action research met us paradigmatically where we were, and allowed for a communal opening to something new.

Whiteness and the Dilemma of Transformation

The dualism I associate with my Whiteness is still with me today as I write the final words to this chapter. I fear I have done a better job of being critical of the White paradigm than of providing much of a holistic or relational view of European-Americans as a people. I have alluded to transformation of consciousness with little mention of strategies that could better support a dialogue about race. In naming these strategies elsewhere (Paxton, 2003), I describe forming community to explore Whiteness, engaging affect and emotions more fully, increasing the capacity to hold paradox and ambiguity, honoring and utilizing more ways of knowing, and being more fully present to one another's experiences. In Chapter Nine, the European-American Collaborative for Challenging Whiteness presents another strategy— critical humility—that supports and encourages dialogue about race by White people.

Ultimately, healing racism may provide a painful but remarkable opportunity for White people to engage as individuals—and as a people—in transformation that brings greater congruence between their intentions for social justice and their actions in the world. Expanding my own consciousness about my racial position has paradoxically opened my heart and taught me about compassion and humility. As one White woman who attended a focus group about my dissertation put it, "Here [in the themes about whiteness] are the emotional patterns I've been living with my whole life because of how I was acculturated. And, they're wrecking my life. They're keeping me from loving people; they're keeping me from accepting love from other people" (Paxton, 2003).

Engaging in a dialogue about race is not just an exercise in White shame and guilt. A dialogue on race can help us heal our humanity and relationship with the world. How can love hold its rightful place in this dialogue when I am distracted by an overburden of rationality, dualism, scientism, narrow emotions, and intellectual rigor? What if the consciousness that allows racism to prevail in White culture is also responsible for how we treat one another, other countries, and the natural world? These other manifestations of the White paradigm raise the stakes even higher—we must come to better understand the paradigmatic water in which we swim.

REFERENCES

Ani, M. (1994). *Yurugu: An African-centered critique of European cultural thought and behavior.* Trenton, NJ: Africa World Press.

Baldwin, J. (1998). White man's guilt. In D. Roediger (Ed.), *Black on White: Black writers on what it means to be White* (pp. 320–325). New York: Schocken Books.

Bateson, G. (1972). *Steps to an ecology of mind.* New York: Ballantine.

Delgado, R. (Ed.). (1995). *Critical race theory: The cutting edge.* Philadelphia: Temple University Press.

Heron, J., & Reason, P. (1997). A participatory inquiry paradigm. *Qualitative Inquiry, 3*(3), 274–294.

Kuhn, T. (1962). *The Structure of Scientific Revolutions.* Chicago: University of Chicago Press.

Lincoln, Y., & Guba, E. (2000). Paradigmatic controversies, contradictions, and emerging confluences. In N. Denzin & Y. Lincoln (Eds.), *The handbook of qualitative research.* Thousand Oaks, CA: Sage.

Paxton, D. (2003). Facilitating transformation of White consciousness among European-American people: A case study of a cooperative inquiry. *Dissertation Abstracts International, 64*(01), 297A. (UMI No. AAT3078796)

Reason, P. (Ed.) (1994). *Participation in human inquiry.* Thousand Oaks, CA: Sage.

Schein, E. (1995). *Kurt Lewin's change theory in the field and in the classroom: Notes toward a model of managed learning.* Retrieved September 30, 2007, from http://64.233.179.104/scholar?hl= en&lr=&safe=off&q=cache:hmfgiH6RwokJ:https://hpds1.mit .edu/retrieve/2195/SWP-3821–32871445.pdf+%22kurt+ lewin%27s+change+theory+in+the+field+and+in+ the%22+author:e-schein.

Somé, M. P. (1998). *The healing wisdom of Africa: Finding life purpose through nature, ritual, and community.* New York: Tarcher/Putnam.

Tarnas, R. (2002). Is the modern psyche undergoing a rite of passage? *ReVision, Journal of Consciousness and Transformation, 24*(3), 2–10.

8

Adult Education and the Problem of the Color (Power) Line

Views from the Whiter Side

ELAINE MANGLITZ
RONALD M. CERVERO

O ur goal is to examine the intersections of Whiteness, privilege, and power from historical, sociological, and educational perspectives. The bases from which we operate both as a society and as individuals will be explored in an effort to examine some of the key questions of this book. A review of systems of privilege and White supremacy will elucidate both how the system works and how it can be challenged. The interplay among Whiteness, White supremacy, and power is highlighted, with particular attention to the work among adult educators that has the potential to effect change and transform lives.

The title of the chapter provides a framework to guide our approach to the content. Over one hundred years ago, W.E.B. DuBois (1900) said:

> The problem of the twentieth century is the problem of the color line, the question as to how far differences of race—which show themselves chiefly in the color of the skin and texture of hair—will hereafter be made the basis to denying over half the world the right of sharing to their utmost ability the opportunities and privileges of modern civilization [pp. 257–258].

Well into the first decade of the twenty-first century, we find that many life opportunities and especially true equity, including educational opportunities, are still distributed along the color (power) line. Lucas (2000) notes:

> [I]f we hope to avoid Jefferson's dire prediction of national self-destruction we need speak frankly about the issues of race. But a frank discussion of race, or any other dimension of oppression, cannot be had absent conversation concerning power—its material basis, its effort to legitimate itself, and its stubborn tendency to transform itself and remain in the same hands year after year. Thus, the problem of our time, with all its promise and danger, is the twentieth-century problem, writ large: the problem of the twenty-first century is the problem of the power divide—how will power be limited, how will power be shared, and how will power be used to nurture the capacities of all, or, instead, to stifle the potential of most [pp. 472–473].

As adult educators who profess tenets of inclusion, equity, and opportunity, it is incumbent on us to engage in a dialogue as one step toward the actions needed to move us as a society away from an outcome of self-destruction.

Racism has been defined by some historians and educators as White racism (Wellman, 1977; Bowser & Hunt, 1996). Although this definition does not exist in mainstream consciousness, it has been well articulated by some people of color and indeed some educators, including

White educators, across the years (Scheurich, 1993; Sleeter, 1996). It is incumbent upon White educators to explore what part they play in their personal and work lives in maintaining the systems of power and what part they can play in challenging those systems. As we proceed with our discussion, we will describe what we have learned in our own journeys as we have recognized and continue to come to terms with our own White privilege.

The historical and contextual examination of how others have advanced along the same journey will guide all of us to ever more effective ways to challenge racism and tip the balance of the color (power) line in our lives and in educational settings. The admonition that the "personal is political" is just as relevant now as it was when used during the 1960s and 1970s social movements. Without connecting the theory to our daily educational work and our lives, we risk engaging in just another academic exercise, written by and for other academics, without offering any strategies or tactics on how to address and, it is to be hoped, change the relations of power engendered by Whiteness and White privilege.

HOW WE CAME TO UNDERSTAND OURSELVES ON THE WHITER SIDE

Elaine

My initial recognition that something was not "right with the world" came not as recognition of my White privilege or Whiteness per se but rather as recognition of others' differences and oppression. This occurred for me during the late 1960s and early 1970s as I witnessed the unrest in the world related to the Vietnam War, the civil rights movement, and campus unrest. Although I was in my early teenage years, I was moved by the visual pictures I saw on television and the atrocities that were being portrayed. My initial recognition of what I now see as privilege was constructed first through social comparisons to those seen as less fortunate. I did not recognize then that White privilege was a problem or was even connected with the events unfolding around me. In fact, I did not understand that I had a racialized identity at all.

As I learned more about what was happening in the 1960s and early 1970s, I began to read everything I could, talk to others around me, and generally learn as much as I could from the milieu of my small, rural Georgia hometown. In my naivete at that time, I took people seriously when they said they believed in equality, believed in treating Blacks equally; I thought they really meant it. At the age of fifteen, when a Black male student and I became interested in each other, I was literally and figuratively slammed against the wall with the understanding that what people said and what people did were two different things. Although we were savvy enough to at least try to keep our relationship hidden, the fallout from my family, my friends, and the town when our relationship was discovered was a definite wake-up call for me as to what race meant in America. And although I do believe some things have changed, I still (perhaps jaded from my early experience) feel that for the most part racism or the outward signs of racism are just better hidden today. It does not help when educators, including adult educators, do not acknowledge, explore, and address the impact of racism on students' lives and on their own teaching, research, and curriculum.

My early reaction to my privilege parallels the experiences of other Whites and is congruent with an examination of racism from the perspective of people of color, rather than from the perspective of members of the group that continues to benefit from its existence. Whiteness or White privilege has made itself invisible by asserting its normalcy and transparency, in contrast to the marking of "others" on which that transparency depends (Frankenberg, 1997). Whites, including White activists in their early years, have begun the process of knowing themselves *racially* only through juxtaposition of their experiences with the experiences of people of color (Leonardo, 2004; Manglitz, Johnson-Bailey, & Cervero, 2005).

One of the most important factors for me has been to realize that my racial identity process and rearticulation of what it means to be White is an ongoing process that never ends; indeed, there are many times when the process is not linear, and depending on my life's current context and circumstances, I may not be as effective as I need to be in my efforts to challenge racism. Realizing that others have gone through this before and, indeed, working with other Whites and Blacks who work to challenge racism enables me to keep working. A sobering fact for me has been my understanding that my White privilege allows me to choose whether to work actively or to remain silent in any given situation.

Ron

I started my academic career in 1980, on a soft-money grant, as an assistant professor. I was hired to be the director of a literacy staff development program at a midwestern research university on the south side of Chicago. The fact that my mentor, a White female professor at the university, chaired the search committee likely increased my chances of obtaining the position. I was twenty-eight years old at the time. My mentor continued to work to move me onto a tenure track position. And two years later, in 1982, I was moved to the main campus on a tenure track position. There was no national search involved in this process. Three years after moving to the main campus and five years after my initial hire, I was promoted to associate with tenure in 1985. I think my letter said I was promoted a year early.

The next year I was recruited to my present institution, another research university. Even though I was hired as an associate professor without tenure, I didn't worry about giving up tenure. In 1988, two years later, I went through the tenure process. Two years after that, in 1990, I was promoted to full professor, and I don't remember any big deal about it. It was just the time to go up. I just assumed all of this would happen. I suppose the main point of my story is that there were no major turning points, no angst about the promotion process, and nobody doubting that I didn't deserve my successes. In fact, I remember saying that I wasn't worried about giving up a tenured position for an untenured one because I felt that I would have the record to be given tenure.

Initially, it didn't occur to me that my race benefited me or that all of the professors around me were also White. My own mentor, Phyllis

Cunningham, a famous American adult educator, and I worked together for over ten years in Chicago in exciting, though sometimes very difficult, multiracial work environments. I learned a lot about power relationships from Phyllis. She continues to be a beacon for me in my own work as an adult educator (Cervero & Merriam, 2007). What I had learned in my earlier life helped me to be in this relationship. My parents showed me that every person was a human being and thus deserved to be treated with dignity and respect. I am sure that the basis of their beliefs was their own experience as immigrants who came to the United States in the 1930s and who suffered discrimination as both Italian immigrants (Guglielmo & Salerno, 2003) and as members of working-class America.

Racial privilege afforded me the luxury of moving through life without a critical examination of Whiteness (Frankenberg, 1993). I have come to see Whiteness as a type of passport that allows me to move freely through the world. The President's Initiative on Race produced a wonderful report that put this concept succinctly. It defined this currency as follows: "institutional advantages based on historic factors have given an advantage to white Americans . . . . We as a nation need to understand that whites tend to benefit, either unknowingly or consciously, from this country's history of white privilege" (Advisory Board to the President's Initiative on Race, 1998, p. 46).

Only years later, as I engaged in researching and writing about race, did I come to develop a more complete understanding of my White racial identity as being socially constructed for my benefit and for the detriment of the "others" (Frankenberg, 1993; Helms, 1990). Although learning about this was a gradual process, the jolt that made it crystal clear was reading McIntosh's (1995) chapter on White privilege. I know that I have a psychological freedom that is derived from belonging, and I now realize that this is a privilege not extended to women and Blacks and academics who are members of disenfranchised groups. This freedom is ever present, although it is easy not to see all its manifestations in every context. Juanita Johnson-Bailey and I have written extensively since then (for example, Johnson-Bailey & Cervero, 2008) about these manifestations in our common and divergent experiences in higher education, as a way to illuminate how academic careers are shaped by racism and sexism.

HOW WE CAME TO ACT ON THE WHITER SIDE

Elaine

One of the most difficult challenges for me has been to discern when to act and how to act in any particular context to make a change for the better. As Whites, we always have a choice whether or not to *actively* engage in challenging White privilege, unlike people of color who confront it every day in many different areas of their lives. These differing experiences based on race have been brought home to me many times, but none more poignantly than in a conversation I had with a Black activist who described the daily, even though small, aggressions he experienced as being like paper cuts that occur in the same place repeatedly. He described them as being not that painful singly, other than the initial insult at first, but as building up over time as they happen again and again. I know that as I choose to work against racism I do not have to experience this daily pain based on my race.

Being White and working to challenge racism is in many ways a contradiction, as I will always be seen as White and be able to trade on the privilege it brings to me. This sentiment has been echoed by White activists and educators who have worked for many years in various arenas to challenge racism (Manglitz et al., 2005). In addition, I can cite the example of several close, White friends who have become in some sense pariahs and alienated in their educational lives and departments because other Whites view everything they do and say as suspect or radical. They have spoken about their lack of effectiveness in their current settings. Yet even though they may have lost some of their effectiveness in specific settings, they can still carry on with their own lives, choose to speak up or not, and be in some ways unaffected by the work they do for social justice.

However, the question remains as to what to do and how to act if our goal is to advance social justice and challenge the inequities engendered by a racist society. Several strategies have been advanced by work that has examined the lives and histories of Whites who have intentionally addressed these issues. Most often White educators and activists talk about the importance of relationships with other Whites and with people of color. They emphasize the quality of these relationships, which must not be superficial and exploitive but rather respectful and sincere, and they emphasize the significance of being mindful of racism's impact on all of us and of the different internal and external manifestations of racism we all experience (Manglitz et al., 2005; O'Brien, 2003). O'Brien (2003) emphasizes the importance of authentic relationships and accountability, suggesting that when we can survive discussions that confront racism head-on, authentic relationships are established. She continues on to say, "it is in interpersonal relationships that accountability is sustained. The personal is indeed political, as one's political action is inspired and adjusted by the personal connection of authentic relationships" (p. 260). Although it is sometimes difficult to stay in relationships when conflict arises, the trust that makes this possible can lead to more effective actions, and more important, the relationships can become sustenance for sites of social change. Through ongoing and authentic relationships, I have a better sense of when to step forward, when to listen and take a backseat, and when to adjust my own interpretation of racism in any specific context. I have learned to act *with* others rather than *for* others.

Ron

It was particularly easy for me to see how privilege operated in an incident that occurred when Juanita Johnson-Bailey and I were copresenting in Vancouver, British Columbia, in 1999. This was an important marker in my coming to understand race work on a concrete rather than abstract level. The title of our presentation was "The Invisible Politics of Race in Adult Education," and the reception Juanita and I received was less than enthusiastic. It felt as though we were, metaphorically, in battle together, because we had to struggle with a fairly hostile audience who disagreed with the idea that race and racism were present in our world and work as adult educators. As a White man I had experienced this feeling of being outside the White power structure before when I stood against my White neighbors who wanted district schools zoned to conform to segregated housing patterns. Vancouver provided a moment of clarity for me as I realized that, as a White person, I have the privilege of choosing whose side I will be on in the struggle against racism. Juanita does not have that privilege. Perhaps that is the most important lesson I have learned from working with Juanita. Of course, in that situation I was clearly on her side, but my dilemma was with the more practical issue of how to be supportive when Juanita's remarks were being critiqued. I wanted to be supportive and to respond to the critique while at the same time not appearing to be a White man who thought she needed rescuing.

CONNECTING THEORY WITH LIVED EXPERIENCE

Several common themes emerged from the exercise of writing this chapter and communicating with others who have done the same. These themes point us to our initial goals of connecting theories to our daily lives and examining what part we can play in challenging the racism that exists in our society. As White adult educators we do have a choice in acting and in choosing how we act to challenge racism This has ramifications for the work we do as we decide how we work *with* others in authentic relationships and for the importance of having an analysis of racism that guides our work within the context of our daily lived experiences and not just as an academic exercise. In addition, we believe it is important to continually reflect and refine our analysis of racism, on both the personal and societal levels, as we move forward.

We know that our journeys to understand our White, racialized identities and the effects those identities will have on our lives and others will always evolve as we learn and grow. We also know that the texts and messages that mainstream and academic discourses use to discuss or deny the effects of race in this country will continue to change. We all must refine our analyses and actions to maintain our resolve, commitment, and effectiveness. How we understand our racialized identities and how we work with others always occurs against the backdrop of a social and historical context that changes over time, calling for increasingly intentional understandings and actions.

Although we believe adult education teaching, research, and practice have made advances toward equity and inclusion over the years, and especially since Colin III and Preciphs's (1991) clarion call to action and statement that "almost nowhere in adult education literature and research is racism recognized as an integral and influential part of American life that requires our immediate attention" (p. 62), we know adult educators still have a long journey ahead. A frank discussion of race, and in particular one that explores how the power relationships in society affect the lives and work of all of us in adult education, can only move us in a direction where we learn our way out of the morass and toward a more just society. As Johnson-Bailey and Cervero (2008) assert, it is by acknowledging that barriers and differences do exist and choosing to address them on a regular basis that we can at least have a chance to challenge them "or defy their ability to define us" (p. 313). It is by connecting our theories to our lived experiences and continuing to reflect and act in concert with others that we will move forward.

REFERENCES

Advisory Board to the President's Initiative on Race. (1998). *One America in the 21st century: Forging a new future* (The Advisory Board's Report to the President). Washington, DC: U.S. Government Printing Office.

Bowser, B. P., & Hunt, R. G. (Eds.). (1996). *Impacts of racism on White Americans* (2nd ed.). Thousand Oaks, CA: Sage.

Cervero, R. M., & Merriam, S. B. (2007). Dr. Phyllis M. Cunningham, spacemaker. In K. B. Armstrong, L. W. Nabb, & A. P. Czech (Eds.), *North American adult educators: Phyllis M. Cunningham archive of quintessential autobiographies* (pp. iii–v). Chicago: Discovery Association.

Colin, S.A.J., III, & Preciphs, T. (1991). Perceptual patterns and the learning environment: Confronting White racism. In R. Hiemstra (Ed.), *Creating environments for effective adult learning* (New Directions for Adult and Continuing Education, No. 50, pp. 61–70). San Francisco: Jossey-Bass.

DuBois, W.E.B. (1900). *Address to the nations of the world.* Presentation to the first Pan African Conference, London, England. Retrieved January 14, 2010, from http://docsouth.unc.edu/neh/walters/walters.html#walt257.

Frankenberg, R. (1993). *White women, race matters: The social construction of Whiteness.* Minneapolis: University of Minnesota Press.

Frankenberg, R. (Ed.). (1997). *Displacing Whiteness: Essays in social and cultural criticism.* Durham, NC: Duke University Press.

Guglielmo, J., & Salerno, S. (2003). *Are Italians White? How race is made in America.* New York: Routledge.

Helms, J. (1990). *Black and White racial identity: Theory, research, and practice.* Westport, CT: Greenwood Press.

Johnson-Bailey, J., & Cervero, R. M. (2008). Different worlds and divergent paths: Academic careers defined by race and gender. *Harvard Educational Review, 78*(2), 311–332.

Leonardo, Z. (2004). The souls of White folk: Critical pedagogy, Whiteness studies, and globalization discourse. In G. Ladson-Billings & D. Gillborn (Eds.), *The Routledge Falmer reader in multicultural education* (pp. 118–136). New York: Routledge.

Lucas, S. R. (2000). Hope, anguish, and the problems of our time: An essay on the publication of "The Black-White Test Score Gap." *Teachers College Record, 102*(2), 461–473.

Manglitz, E., Johnson-Bailey, J., & Cervero, R. M. (2005). Struggles of hope: How White adult educators challenge racism. *Teachers College Record, 107*(6), 1245–1274.

McIntosh, P. (1995). White privilege and male privilege: A personal accounting of coming to see correspondences through work in women's studies. In M. L. Anderson & P. H. Collins (Eds.), *Race, class, and gender* (pp. 76–87). Belmont, CA: Wadsworth.

O'Brien, E. (2003). The political is personal: The influence of White supremacy on White antiracists' personal relationships. In A.W. Doane & E. Bonilla-Silva (Eds.), *White out: The continuing significance of racism* (pp. 253–267). New York: Routledge.

Scheurich, J. J. (1993). Toward a White discourse on White racism. *Educational Researcher, 22*(8), 5–10.

Sleeter, C. (1996). Multicultural education as a form of resistance to racism. In C. Sleeter (Ed.), *Multicultural education as social activism* (pp. 1–16). Albany: State University of New York Press.

Wellman, D. T. (1977). *Portraits of White racism.* New York: Cambridge University Press.

9

White on White

Developing Capacity to Communicate About Race with Critical Humility

EUROPEAN-AMERICAN COLLABORATIVE CHALLENGING WHITENESS

Our intent in this chapter is to explore how White people might avoid putting each other on the defensive when talking about race, racism, and White privilege. We describe a dialogic practice called critical humility that helps us have more fruitful conversations about these issues.

The European-American Collaborative Challenging Whiteness fosters research and learning about the subject of racism and White privilege. Using a group name to designate collective authorship reflects the collaborative members' understanding of the way in which knowledge is constructed. The members of the collaborative came together originally through a cultural consciousness project at the California Institute of Integral Studies in San Francisco; members are Carole Barlas, Elizabeth Kasl, Alec MacLeod, Doug Paxton, Penny Rosenwasser, and Linda Sartor. Inquiries about the collaborative's work may be addressed to any member via e-mail: collaborative@eccw.org. Find further information at our Web site: http://www.iconoclastic.net/eccw.

We are a group of White adult educators who have been meeting monthly since 1998 to support each other in our mutual efforts to challenge hegemony and institutionalized racism. Others at times have viewed as problematic our decision to create a White-only inquiry group, with its echoes of segregation and the separate-but-equal policies that dominated the United States for the century following the Civil War. Questions are raised about whether members of a dominant group can learn about themselves in isolation, whether oppressive behaviors will remain invisible, or worse, be reinforced. Yet we have found that working together as White people on these issues has been intrinsic to our learning.

We hold the assumption that we who benefit from White skin privilege have a responsibility to confront racism in ourselves and in society. We also feel that White people need to find ways to engage questions about race with one another. Rather than relying solely on people of color to inform us about racism, we need to accept responsibility for and direct our own learning about racism as well. At the same time, each of us sees participating in our all-White group as a complement to, not a replacement for, learning in multicultural settings.

SHUTTING DOWN DIALOGUE BY PROSELYTIZING AND DISDAINING

By examining our own development as well-meaning, White adult educators, we have noticed behaviors that not only impede dialogue but also perpetuate White privilege. Two of these behaviors are proselytizing and disdaining. By *proselytizing* we mean exhorting in an officious and tiresome way. By *disdaining* we mean treating as less worthy and rejecting with aloof contempt or scorn. Our ideas about proselytizing and disdaining have been shaped by our experience of wanting both to be and to be perceived as being *good White people*—White people who act as effective allies to people of color by challenging the injustices of White hegemony and privilege. The irony is that this desire to be and to be seen as being a good White person often leads each of us to behaviors that have the opposite effect of what we intend. Several things happen. At times we start thinking of ourselves as superior to other White people who "just don't get it." In our zeal to enlighten them, we end up proselytizing in ways that put them on the defensive or close down conversation altogether. At other times our desire to distance ourselves from the unenlightened White person can manifest as disdain. We are then blind to the ways in which we are similar to those to whom we feel superior.

Under such circumstances, we find that we are less open to new learning. Proselytizing and disdaining can be subtle. We may intend to communicate gentle compassion and sincere respect. However, if our words spring from the attitudes just described, the person(s) with whom we are interacting will probably feel patronized or defensive, or both.

CRITICAL HUMILITY AS A HABIT OF BEING THAT SUPPORTS REFLECTIVE PRACTICE

Seeking an antidote to our own proselytizing and disdaining, our group evolved a concept that we call *critical humility,* which we see as a habit of being to which we aspire. Critical humility embodies a delicate and demanding balance of *speaking out* for social justice while at the same time *remaining aware that our knowledge is partial and evolving.* The two parts of this definition capture the paradox with which we struggle. If we are to hold ourselves accountable for speaking up, we must have confidence that our knowledge is sufficiently valid to support what we say. At the same time, we need to be constantly alert to how the validity of our knowledge is limited by the distortion of hegemony and self-deception. In other words, we hold ourselves accountable for striving toward being the good White person, while trying not to fall into the trap of thinking we have actually become that person.

We devised questions that help us reflect on what is underneath the ways we communicate (European-American Collaborative Challenging Whiteness, 2005). The questions, which appear in Exhibit 9.1, focus on three areas that can shed light on our efforts to embody critical humility: self-identity and values, role of privilege, and purpose. A fourth set of questions helps us sharpen critical self-reflection. Ideally, the questions in Exhibit 9.1, which appears on pages 150–152, would be used to guide reflection-*in*-action. However ideal this goal, we typically use the questions to guide our reflection-*on*-action, either prospectively when we plan for a difficult conversation or retrospectively when we analyze how a conversation went astray. (We credit our use of the terms *reflection-in-action* and *reflection-on-action* to Donald Schön, 1987.) The questions are derived from our experiences of helping each other unravel what went wrong when efforts to engage in dialogue about race or privilege did not have the outcome we intended.

TRYING TO REFLECT-IN-ACTION USING CRITICAL HUMILITY

We now illustrate how we have applied the questions in Exhibit 9.1, using the example of a group experience that we describe in three parts. First, Victoria tells the group about an occurrence in which she believes she failed her commitment to action. Instead of speaking up when she thought another White woman's comment was offensive to people of color in the room, she was silent. Second, we describe a role play in which Andrew and Daniel fail to get a satisfactory result when they try to model how Victoria might have embodied critical humility. Third, we show how our group used some of the guiding questions from Exhibit 9.1 to better understand why our communications came across the way they did.

Victoria Describes Her Perceived Failure

One of our group's practices is to reserve time at our monthly meetings for members to bring up issues or incidents for group reflection and feedback. Victoria was eager to seek the group's reflection regarding an incident at a professional conference she had recently attended. She explained it this way:

> I attended a roundtable about race and racism convened by three colleagues of color. About twenty people came, mostly women, evenly divided as people of color and White people. During the

introductions, a White woman smiled brightly as she swept her eyes around the circle, saying, ''I have always believed that I was meant to have been born Black.''

I was thrown into one of those moments of confusion when, as a White person, I thought I should say something. I was embarrassed by what I thought was her lack of sensitivity—she spoke so lightly about giving up White skin privilege.

I noticed that the White woman had turned away from the circle so that she now spoke directly to the African American woman sitting next to her, apparently seeking approval or connection. I was struggling to figure out what I should say when the introduction process moved on and the moment passed.

Andrew and Daniel Attempt to Apply Critical Humility

Our group decided to role-play how Victoria might have responded. Victoria would play the White woman who said she should have been born Black. Andrew and Daniel would experiment with what Victoria might have said. Andrew now takes up the narrative:

Before we started the role play with Victoria, Daniel and I talked it over. We agreed that it would probably be best to approach the woman privately after the roundtable adjourned. We did not want to put her on the spot publicly and we also wanted to be sensitive about not disrupting the event. I tried first.

I tapped Victoria on the shoulder and said, ''Excuse me. Could we talk a moment about the roundtable?'' When she agreed, I went on, ''When I heard you introduce yourself, saying that you felt you were meant to be born Black, I have to confess that I felt uncomfortable. I know I have said that kind of thing out of the best intentions, but over the years I have found that the impact on people of color hasn't always been very positive. Would you be open to talking about another interpretation?''

While I tried to engage Victoria in discussion, I found myself feeling less and less effective. The more I said, the more she seemed to withdraw. Finally, looking for help, I turned to Daniel. I don't remember what he said, though I can vividly recall the response. Although his tone was compassionate, Victoria became increasingly silent. Clearly, our strategies had silenced Victoria rather than opening up dialogue.

REFLECTING ON THE ATTEMPTS TO APPLY CRITICAL HUMILITY

After the role play, group members reentered the conversation as themselves as we all tried to learn how to improve our communication with other White people about racism and privilege. Louise had been witnessing the interaction, and she reflected on it to Andrew and Daniel:

I felt that instead of staying with your own experience and struggle, you had your attention on trying to change Victoria. Even though you were trying to be humble, you still seemed to be trying to show her how she was wrong. It sounded patronizing to me.

We all acknowledged how ironic it seemed that we had entered this role play in order to try out our ideas about critical humility, and instead, we created another example of being critical without humility. To help us understand what happened, we used our guiding questions displayed in Exhibit 9.1 to probe the experience.

EXHIBIT 9.1. QUESTIONS TO GUIDE THE PRACTICE OF CRITICAL HUMILITY

1. Self-Identity and Values
- What are all the self-identities that might be operating and at risk in this situation (for example, competent teacher, understanding parent, good person, antiracist ally, and so forth)? Are there competing or contradicting values or identities involved?

- Where do I feel threatened? What am I scared about?

- What attracts me in this situation?

- What is the identity label I seek to avoid? How do I see myself as different from others in this situation?

- What are the costs and benefits of changing self-identity? How are these costs related to feelings of self-worth?

2. Role of Privilege

- What privilege is operating in the situation? Acknowledging that we all have multiple identities, which ones are salient here?

- In what ways am I resisting perceiving myself as in a dominant position?

- Is the context indifferent to my identity? Does it reinforce or reject my identity?

3. Purpose

- What is the phenomenon I wish to change?

- To what extent is my purpose aligning with or threatening one or more of my self-identities?

- How might I be perpetuating the phenomenon I wish to change in this situation?

4. Self-Reflective Process

- To what extent have I disclosed myself, allowed myself to be vulnerable to new learning?

- How am I similar to that which I am criticizing?

- Can I catch a glimpse of what I didn't know that I didn't know?

(continued)

- Do I truly believe that I don't hold all the answers? How is my information incomplete?

- How patient am I with myself about being wrong? How compassionate?

Source: Adapted from European-American Collaborative Challenging Whiteness, 2005.

Beginning with the questions that appear in section 1 of Exhibit 9.1, we asked Andrew to reflect on what aspects of his self-identity and values he felt were important to him in the interaction. He noted that being a good White person who is a strong ally to people of color was the most important identity he had at stake. In situations like the one we role-played, his fear is that he will silence himself and not speak up. He explained: "In most areas of my life, I don't tend to think that being right is all that important. But in this area, I cling to the hope of being right. In fact, I have a strong *need* to be right." Victoria asked, "Why is that?" and Andrew continued:

> I think I feel the need to speak up because the stakes are so high. Learning how our society can better communicate across difference is one of our most crucial questions and I cannot be neutral on this. I need to take a position even if I may not be right. I have to counteract the silence that perpetuates the issue. Throughout history, horrible things have happened because the people who have the power to change things don't speak up. Silence is collusion.

This example illustrates critical humility's dual challenge. Victoria had not spoken in the roundtable situation because she lacked confidence about saying the right thing. Andrew took action, but fell into the trap of proselytizing. Both reactions impoverish dialogue and impede relationship.

Our group then queried Daniel on the identities he had at stake. He offered a general reflection about relationships.

You know how African Americans often refer to each other as "brother" or "sister"? It's a way of saying something about their connection and what they have in common. I realize that when I get into a situation like the one in the role play, I'm not thinking that person is my brother or my sister. I find myself wanting to correct them and to show them what is right, not build a relationship with them.

We sighed in mutual recognition of how caught we can get in being right and how that distances us from others, especially people whom we see as being less conscious of White hegemony than we perceive ourselves to be. *Good White person* is a label we have used over the years as a sort of verbal shorthand that testifies to a moment of recognition, "Oh, there I go again, being the good White person." Even though we have all gotten better at seeing that we have fallen into this trap, we still struggle with how to get out of it. In the role play, Andrew's and Daniel's encounters with Victoria left her feeling confused and defensive. If her character in the role play learned anything from the interactions, it might have been to take fewer risks and be more guarded in her discussions of race. In our real lives that is not what we want to evoke through our communications.

Continuing with our examination of the role play, we used our guiding questions for the self-reflective process (Exhibit 9.1, section 4). Asking, "To what extent have I disclosed myself?" Andrew described how he often engages in false disclosure:

I realize I often try to make a connection with someone by telling a story on myself. I might say something like, "I realize that sometimes I've said something very similar to what you just said." I create what amounts to a false Socratic dialogue, trying to set someone up to see my point of view. I'm invested in being a nice guy, so I fall into a strategy of false disclosure and do it all in the guise of "helping." My approach is actually a false humility, calculated to demonstrate my superiority. It would be more honest to say, "I'm really offended by what you said. Would you like to know why?" But even if she said yes, I might still go on in a way that is patronizing. Whichever way I acted, either as I did in the role play or telling her straight out that I was offended, the main thing that is missing is my own genuine vulnerability.

Andrew's failure to reveal the limits of his own knowledge reflects his investment both in knowing what is right and in his identity as a teacher. He feels compelled to teach others what he believes he knows, and he is not open and vulnerable to new learning because he has cast himself as the expert rather than embracing an identity as a learner.

Daniel used the question, "How am I similar to that which I am criticizing?" to discover a need that had been unconscious. He notices:

In a situation like this, I am more likely to put my attention on protecting the feelings of people of color than to focus on the White woman. I guess what I really want is to get the approval of people of color for being on their side. I see that tendency as a reenactment of what the White woman in this scenario did when she looked only at the Black woman next to her after she said she wanted to be Black, which we interpreted as *her* desire for approval.

In this way, Daniel saw how he perpetuates the very phenomenon he wants to change—a White person looking to a person of color for approval.

One important element that becomes apparent in Daniel's and Andrew's reflections is that multiple identities can be operating at any given moment. Another is that noticing what we desire to change in others can help us discover what we do not accept about ourselves. As we concluded our discussion, Victoria observed:

I don't remember what Andrew and Daniel said to me, but I can still feel the condescension. I felt terribly misunderstood, and quite affronted that they were making unfair assumptions about me.

They never asked me why I said that I thought I should have been born Black.

With this comment about Andrew and Daniel, Victoria saw herself. In the original situation she had assumed she knew why the woman said what she said, and did not even consider asking her why she said that. After playing the part of that person and feeling what it was like to be judged harshly based on someone else's assumption, that mistake was painfully obvious. Victoria then reflected on how *White* it is to believe one's assumptions to be the truth, and thus she experienced a new insight about humility.

REACHING FOR A NEW WAY OF BEING

As White people confronted with issues of race and racism, we must not collude with silence. We need to speak up and challenge racism, and still acknowledge the limits of our own perspectives and consciousness. To engage another with criticality, we need to find a place of genuine care and compassion for that other person and ourselves, remembering we have something to learn. To engage with humility, we need to be emotionally authentic and actively promote dialogue. The example in this chapter reminds us how easily we fall back on polarizing bad habits. Though critical humility can be seen as a difficult paradox, we see the power and possibility of integrating this less dualistic practice into our lives. Although there is no formula for what to say, there is an attitude to cultivate. There are also ways to prepare for challenging moments of interaction.

Critical humility is not a destination. It is the process of reaching for a new way of being, a work in progress, a practice. Striving on a daily basis to take actions that challenge racism and White hegemony, we also strive to remember that even as we challenge White privilege, we are still immersed in it. Remaining open to discovering the insidiousness of our *un*consciousness is an ongoing challenge. Over our years of working together, we have struggled to stay in an inquiry mode that avoids the smug sense of confidence that we have "done the work" and therefore achieved the "right" perceptions about Whiteness, race, and dominating systems of power. Yet each of us still slips easily.

Our intent here has been to demonstrate how we have used a set of guiding questions to learn from our experience as we attempt to act from a place of critical humility. In this context, we often focus on analyzing what went wrong when our efforts to practice critical humility fell short. Lest it appear that we see ourselves as failures or that engaging in this practice is too difficult, we point to the success we felt recently when we led an all-day institute at an annual conference on White privilege. After spending the day with us and learning about the practice of critical humility, our workshop participants remarked that we consistently seemed able to walk our talk. Because the program indicated the workshop was designed for White people, almost all of the participants were White. Their feedback reassured us that to some extent we are learning how to talk to other White people about issues of race from a place of critical humility.

Our discussion in this chapter was limited to our talking about applying critical humility to racism and White privilege. We are mindful that there are also issues of gender and class at play in our example that we did not have the space to discuss. Furthermore, we perceive the practice of critical humility to be useful beyond the challenges of avoiding proselytizing and disdaining—the two behaviors explored here. The guiding questions that support the practice of critical humility may be relevant for a variety of other applications, particularly for engaging with multicultural groups and in cross-difference interactions. Wherever we apply it, striving to develop our capacity to embody critical humility helps us to discover the chasms between our espoused values and our actual communications and to move toward more congruent communication.

In reflecting on how our chapter interfaces with others in this section, we see several connections. Our description of proselytizing and disdaining illustrates the "need to be right" that Doug identifies as part of the dualism in White epistemology. We often use Frankenberg's model, described by Lisa, to explain that critical humility helps deepen capacities for race cognizance. We join Elaine Manglitz and Ronald Cervero in trying to learn from reflecting critically on our lived experience.

REFERENCES

European-American Collaborative Challenging Whiteness. (2005). Critical humility in transformative learning when self-identity is at stake. In D. Vlosak, G. Kielbaso, & J. Radford (Eds.), *Appreciating the best of what is: Envisioning what could be* (Proceedings of the Sixth International Conference on Transformative Learning, pp.121–126). East Lansing: Michigan State University.

Schön, D. (1987). *Educating the reflective practitioner.* San Francisco: Jossey-Bass.

Struggling
A Journey of Comfort and Discomfort

One of the recurrent conversational themes that arose as we (the Part Two chapter authors and the section editor, Stephen Brookfield) discussed this Whiteness and White privilege section was the crucial beneficial role played by colleagues of color in the development of our own racial awareness. However, we also recognized that some conversations must occur among same racial group members. In addition we struggled with the questions of at what point and how often the section editor (chosen for the arduous task of leading these conversations on White privilege because he is the only White individual among the editors) should enter into a dialogue with and between the authors. So in these reflections you will often see us less as a group with one thematic voice and more as a set of individuals grappling with White privilege.

Each of us came to these conversations with an understanding that we had an obligation to engage in conversations about race and our roles in either perpetuating or ending racism and racist acts in our lives and or practices. More important, we recognized that we had to examine these factors in connection with our own White privilege and the ways in which we had come to rely on our colleagues of color for shaping the discourse on race and racism in people's professional and personal lives.

We could all point to examples of colleagues who, while dealing with the onslaught of the racist White power structure on them, nevertheless found time and space to share resources with us and to offer guidance and support as we struggled to understand the effects of an ideology and practice that was so much a part of who we all are as Whites. As we offered different examples from our own histories of these supportive colleagues of color a nagging dilemma constantly asserted itself. On the one hand, we felt that these colleagues were our teachers, who were generous enough to spend time with us naive learners as we struggled to understand what they lived with and clearly understood every day of their lives. On the other hand, to some of us, casting ourselves in the role of learners felt uncomfortable.

What was the source of this discomfort? Partly, it came from our feeling yet another layer of an all too familiar friend—liberal White guilt—at expecting colleagues of color to take on the job of teaching us about our own racism. It was because we recognized that we needed to take on this task ourselves that we ended up writing for this book. But our discomfort also came from hearing ourselves, and seeing other White colleagues, give earnest thanks, pay earnest witness, to these colleagues who have taught us. It is hard to put a finger on the nature of this discomfort. The best we could come up with was that we felt we had given these thanks in a patronizing way—that there was a whiff (or maybe a full-blown stench) of condescension in how our heartfelt thanks were offered.

Whites often struggle with how to thank colleagues of color in ways that feel authentic. Not giving acknowledgment, recognition, and thanks was not an option that we considered for long. As we talked about this, three possible responses suggested themselves to us. The first was to offer these thanks privately and individually to the colleagues and friends concerned. This can help to sidestep the feeling some may have that giving thanks to colleagues in public may come across as self-congratulatory, as the declarations of Whites trying to be *good White people,* which we and some others are always trying to guard against. Second, we felt that the most authentic way a White person could give thanks was through action, through doing his or her best to live out a commitment to naming and challenging racism. Third, and connected to this, were our attempts to honor different racial group traditions in our practice and scholarship. We felt it important to do this as matter of factly as possible, rather than in a dramatic public flourish, so that people would interpret it as being so obviously the appropriate thing to do that calling attention to it was almost superfluous.

The discussions about how to thank colleagues of color took us in several promising, and also frustrating, directions. One of these concerned the ways Whites use scholarship of color. In their analysis of Black intellectual life, bell hooks and Cornel West (1991) discuss the ways in which, according to hooks, "White theorists draw upon our work and our ideas, and get forms of recognition that are denied Black thinkers" (p. 36). She speaks of how "there is a feeling now that a White academic might take your idea, write about it, and you'll never be cited" (p. 36). In the same conversation West observes, "White scholars are bringing certain baggage with them when they look at Black culture, no matter how subtle and sophisticated the formulations" (p. 36).

As I, in my capacity of section editor, listened to my colleagues' stories, I began to reflect more acutely on some of my own practices. Their stories were and are the stories of so many White scholars engaged in antiracist work or practices. Just how do we as White scholars demonstrate appreciation for the willingness and need of our colleagues of color to explore issues of race and racism in this society? My own way of dealing with the problematic nature of this practice contains two rationalizations that to me seem credible but that to others may well appear self-serving. The first has to do with the broader issue of conducting racial dialogue and touches on the dilemma already mentioned of how we thank colleagues of color for their work with us. When White scholars ignore the contributions of colleagues of color, they often invoke the argument that only a person of color can truly understand the work a colleague of color produces. This seems respectful but is actually, in my opinion, a racist double standard. Those same Whites would feel no compunction critiquing a colleague of color who misrepresents or in their view does not seem to properly interpret the work of a European scholar. We expect as a matter of course that colleagues of color are able to speak and write knowledgeably about critical theory or postmodernism and to know the debates both within and between these paradigms. We do not hold White scholars to the same standard of being able to write and speak knowledgeably about Africentrism and critical race theory and to know the debates within and between them.

In their discussions, the authors in this section (all Whites of European descent) found that this double standard is plain, for example, when Whites include a book by a colleague of color in a syllabus reading list and therefore assume that the Black, Hispanic, or Asian perspective is addressed, showing no awareness of the multiple positions and differences extant in any racially grounded body of scholarship. So if Whites assume as a matter of course that their colleagues of color should be au fait with Eurocentric scholarship, simple fairness means that Whites have to be equally au fait with Latino scholarship, indigenous people's scholarship, scholarship of the African or Asian Diasporas, and so on. The chapter authors also determined that when White educators, who dominate mainstream discourses and serve as academic gatekeepers, say that the ideas or practices of educators of color should be written about only by colleagues of color, they are trying to excuse themselves from seriously engaging with other racially grounded scholarship. This risks playing into the hands of White racists who maintain that nothing of value is produced outside the Eurocentric mainstream and that the only scholars whose work counts are White.

As Whites begin to draw upon the works and contributions of their colleagues of color, it is important that they use these colleagues' words as written, rather than offering reinterpretations of these words based on White views of the world and word. How should Whites use the scholarship of colleagues of color and at the same time avoid acts of paternalism? For the authors in this section the answer is to rely as much as possible on using the words of scholars of color in the form of multiple direct quotes and clear citations, never assuming to speak for these scholars. A problem can arise if the White scholar slips into an authorial mode that suggests he or she has logocentrically divined the essence of what educators, activists and scholars of color are *really* saying. Parenthetically, this has always seemed a good general rule of scholarship, irrespective of the racial identity of the author or of the subject of scholarship, but it seems doubly important when White majority scholars publish about scholarship of color.

The tortuous rationalizations and justifications Whites tend to offer for their practice—as described in the preceding paragraphs—lead us to the final theme of the conversations among the authors in Part Two. This theme is evident in Doug Paxton's essay on the characteristics of White epistemology when he writes of the White person's need to be correct, to get things right. This need is rooted in a dualistic epistemology that holds that complex problems contain unitary, monolithically appropriate solutions that can be discovered through diligent research, whether that be qualitative or quantitative. One of the things the authors in the section talked about in our conversations was how Whites with similar beliefs constantly strive to do the right thing and how often that is equated with doing something that pleases everybody. Rightness here is sometimes spoken of as a *win-win* solution, or an action that carries with it no adverse effects. White educators and activists who struggle with their own racism or who try to get colleagues to treat this struggle as a matter of common urgency obviously want to take actions that somehow address this evil. Bitter experience has taught these educators and activists that when one is confronting racism no action is innocent if by innocent we mean that it has only desirable consequences.

Our stories as educators and activists are infused with the constant reality of error, of trying something out and seeing it backfire horribly, so that we end up accused of the very racism we profess to combat. Sometimes we feel we have stumbled onto the Holy Grail of antiracist work, an exercise that forces White people to recognize how deeply the ideology of White supremacy is embedded within them, only to find that what worked just as we'd hoped with one group is highly problematic with another.

For example, you might want to institute ground rules that keep students from committing one of the many racial microaggressions that critical race theorists frequently identify, dismissing other students' experiences with counterexamples that negate those students' personal truths. Students should learn that this is not allowed. As teachers, we know that as Whites become more engaged in this work, this is just one of the things we must do. Put it out on the table and let students work their way through it. Do not attempt to shelter or move people away from what is quite obviously a microaggression, an aggression that if ignored could fester and cause a huge chasm in the group members' willingness to work with race and racism in their own lives.

As you move forward with conversations on race, remember that there is no perfect or scientific response that works for all. All the authors in this section have had myriad similar experiences that illustrate the futility of the hope of discovering ways of confronting racism that are always clear, successful, and transferable. Throughout our conversations, the authors also spoke about how they had reached a point of acknowledging that it was usually better to try something out than to be paralyzed with fear. The more we come out to each other about the times we have tried something and failed, the more we normalize failure or, perhaps more accurately, the more we reconceptualize failure as an unanticipated but necessary corollary to any attempts to focus on race. I personally long ago got used to the feeling that plagued me every time I tried to address race with students or colleagues of wishing I could just run the videotape back to the beginning of the conversation and try again.

Finally, as the authors and I talked and they read each other's chapters, we realized that we felt we were implicated in and had colluded in perpetuating racism and White supremacy. None of us felt we had escaped its clutches or that we had successfully slain the dragon of our own internalized racism. We believe the more White adult educators talk publicly about that fact, the more likely they are to recognize and step back from the dangers of preaching and disdaining that the members of the European-American Collective Challenging Whiteness so accurately name.

We recognize that, as the stories, perspectives, and ideas shared in this portion of this book's dialogue suggest, determining how educators should carry out the task of leading tough conversations about race and racism is not easy. One never knows when one might step on that proverbial toe or put one's foot in one's mouth. We suggest that you be willing to ask yourself the following questions:

1. Why should I become engaged in the dialogue on race and racism?

2. What is my role in perpetuating the myths of race and racism in my practice and life? And what can I do to make the realities of race and racism visible?

3. In what ways will maintaining White privilege benefit or hurt Whites? And what will be the impacts on others?

4. How might these conversations lead to changes in my personal life, my professional life, and my social life? What changes might occur in my work, my community, and my institution?

These are just a few of the questions that we as Whites, and other people as well, must be willing to engage if we are going to make a difference with and between all peoples of color—Whites included.

REFERENCE

hooks, b., & West, C. (1991). *Breaking bread: Insurgent black intellectual life*. Boston: South End Press.

Theoretical Responses to Race and Racism

Part Three, "Theoretical Responses to Race and Racism," offers a discussion on the diffusive nature of power and positionality and on the ways in which systems of oppression have produced and structured the inequalities in our society and our educational system. The chapters in this section will focus on how particular theoretical perspectives—critical race theory, Latino and Latina critical theories, or postmodernist, structuralist, or constructivist theories—have attempted to assess and reflect on race and racism within the field of adult education. They will examine the use of these multiple and varied theoretical perspectives to analyze and assess how race and racism affect the ways in which we in adult education live, communicate, and operate within our learning, work, and personal spaces.

Race and racism are provocative topics in our American society. Typical responses to this subject matter are avoidance, denial, and the politically correct response of acknowledgment and then redirecting the conversation. However, in academia one can often find scholarly or theoretical responses to race and racism that are offered not to avoid an honest or practical dialogue but as a means of deepening or structuring the analysis.

In true academic tradition the six authors in this section have reached for theory to guide their efforts to explore and dissect racial issues. Although they focus on critical race theory (CRT), these authors are not bound by that theory; they use it as a base from which to launch their work but are not restricted by its tenets. CRT sets forth the concept that racism is endemic to American life—a critique that emerges from the interstices of the writings of civil rights movement and legal scholars who embrace reformist civil rights ideas combined with activist, analytical political engagement (Bell, 1992; Crenshaw, Gotanda, Peller, & Thomas; 1995; Ladson-Billings & Tate, 1995; Wing, 1997; Williams, 1991). Two primary tenets of critical race theory are that the nature of race and racism are ever-changing and that racism is not necessarily the product of biased actions but can be the artifact of seemingly liberal, neutral, or normed rules and actions. Five components of a critical race perspective, as asserted by Ladson-Billings & Tate (1995), are (1) a central focus on race and racism, (2) a direct and overt challenge to hegemonic discourse, (3) a commitment to social justice, (4) an honoring of the experiential base of marginalized people, and (5) a multifaceted disciplinary viewpoint.

Further, critical race theory embraces subjectivity and a political standpoint as acceptable and appropriate stances for analysis, believing that scholarship is never neutral. Using their personal and academically honed perspectives, the six authors challenge, agree with, disagree with, and expand the concept of CRT.

Rosemary Closson opens Part Three with the thought-provoking Chapter Ten, "An Exploration of Critical Race Theory," wherein this African American scholar sounds a hopeful note by declaring that she will not subscribe to the belief that racism is eternal, stating, "While I believe that racism is endemic I do not agree that it is permanent," which represents a key departure from CRT. According to Closson, she has embraced the legacy of her family members who were civil rights activists and in doing so has taken on their religious and spiritually grounded beliefs that adopt the idea of redemption. And so Closson, after stepping the reader through the evolution of CRT, offers a firm position that CRT holds the seeds for change.

In Chapter Eleven, Mitsunori Misawa agrees with CRT, and seeks to expand the dialogue by examining the intersection of race and sexual orientation. In this chapter, "Musings on Controversial Intersections of Positionality: A Queer Crit Perspective in Adult and Continuing Education Pedagogy," Misawa warns against the folly of looking only at race and urges that racism will be understood only when it is examined in its full context, as it interlocks with other positionalities. He writes that an impediment to a more open examination of race has been a reluctance of race scholars to make such connections, particularly around the issue of homosexuality. Misawa sets forth the idea that including sexual orientation in the conversation will strengthen the broadening of the debate and the modeling of true democracy. By enlisting all, it will bring newly formed strong forces to the multifaceted fight to end racism.

While Misawa uses CRT as a tool for augmenting the fight against racism, Mary Alfred, in Chapter Twelve, "Challenging Racism Through Postcolonial Discourse: A Critical Approach to Adult Education Pedagogy," wants to refocus theory and use it as a tool to look inward. In asking this question about racism, "Are you part of the problem or part of the solution?" she offers a new perspective by asking it of people of color. As a West Indian American, Alfred cautions against seeing racial categories as monolithic and uses her own experiences of growing up in St. Lucia and her difficult transition to life in the United States as a lens for comparing the various ways race functions within the African Diaspora. She asserts that she has too often observed those Blacks who have internalized racism using the colonizers' tools to subjugate other Blacks, acting as agents of the oppressors. In her view, although racism is endemic, as CRT states, it is also not confined to Whites, and she suggests that any successful campaign to end racism must also involve the insiders who operate in disguise.

In Chapter Thirteen, "Black Skins, No Mask," Taj Johns, an African American woman, continues what Mary Alfred began and examines her own adult education practice, confessing that she has often unconsciously demoralized her Black students because she was mimicking the educational system that trained her. Through much struggle and personal introspection, she has developed a program that promotes self-healing, Self Affirming Soul Healing Africans (SASHA), to help other educators avoid the mistakes that she has made in the classroom. Although admitting that SASHA is influenced by CRT, especially in its use of personal stories and counterstories, Johns points out that this learning tool she offers is emancipatory in nature and based on African-centered principles. Furthermore, she feels that in order to heal there must be movement to directly connect the body and mind to theory-influenced learning.

Luis Kong uses his personal experiences in a different way in Chapter Fourteen, "Immigration, Racial Identity, and Adult Education: Reflections on a Transnational Paradigm of Resistance," moving away from Johns's look inward to heal and instead embracing his memories and experiences of growing up as a Peruvian Chinese American to travel within and across boundaries, challenging the notion of a fixed racial identity. He writes of situational racism and uses his shifting immigrant's perspective to examine ways of surviving and thriving in a society where race and racism are always present. Kong feels that avoiding the process and language of inclusion and exclusion can lead the way to throwing out the ideas that offer false notions about people from different cultures, nationalities, and ethnicities and can put the focus on building a world where similarities are emphasized more than differences.

In the final chapter in Part Three, "A River Runs Through It: Building Bridges Across Racial Divisions in Urban Graduate Education," authors Catherine Monaghan and Catherine Hansman, fully accept all the tenets of CRT and describe how they work to disassemble racism and examine their own White privilege. Challenging themselves to "practice what we preach," Hansman and Monaghan risk being vulnerable to their students by revealing their personal struggles around race and racism, refusing to shy away from the difficult conversations that expose their frailties. In an attempt to find common ground for the Black and the White students who share their urban classroom, these two White women educators constructively ask the White students to move beyond their comfort zones of examining race from the sidelines, requiring instead that these students delve into their Whiteness. And these educators also try to avoid centering the responsibility for race discussions and telling about race on their Black students. They conclude that while their CRT perspective informs their worldview on the intransience of race (and racism) as a fixture in our society, their classroom practices renew them so that their battle against this hegemonic monster can be ongoing.

REFERENCES

Bell, D. (1992). *Faces at the bottom of the well: The permanence of racism.* New York: Basic Books.

Crenshaw, K., Gotanda, N., Peller, G., & Thomas, K. (Eds.). (1995). *Critical race theory: The key writings that formed the movement.* New York: New Press.

Ladson-Billings, G., & Tate, W. (1995). Toward a critical race theory of education. *Teachers College Record, 97*(1), 41–62.

Williams, P. (1991). *The alchemy of race and rights: Diary of a law professor.* Cambridge, MA: Harvard University Press.

Wing, A. K. (Ed.). (1997). *Critical race feminism: A reader.* New York: New York University Press.

10

An Exploration of Critical Race Theory

ROSEMARY B. CLOSSON

As an African American woman, I have developed an epistemology grounded in my family's history—one that contains a recurring humanist vision and an African American feminist epistemology. These form the nexus of my spiritual beliefs. A persistent humanist perspective is evident across a wide span of African American women intellectuals, ranging from Fannie Lou Hamer to Anna Julia Cooper (Collins, 1990), who engaged in "a process of self-conscious struggle that empowers women and men to actualize a humanist vision of community" (Collins, 1990, p. 39). My humanist perspective is not absent God but reflects universal spiritual principles that I believe are embedded throughout all religious teachings.

My life as a Black woman has not been filled with overt racist acts, but my parents and grandparents, who were affected significantly by

American racism, passed on their legacy of struggle in the face of overt racist acts and oppression. I carry an appreciation of the sacrifices they made. Having grown up in a family that was active in civil rights organizations, I regularly heard race and racism being discussed. So even as a child I was aware of the systemic ways in which African Americans continued to be subordinated in society through the schooling systems (in which my mother worked) and through the denial of opportunities available to others from labor unions as well as colleges and universities. For example, part of my family lore is my mother's story of wanting to be a writer but, while attending a historically White university, being told by one of her professors, "You write well. I suggest you go to Latin America and return to the U.S. as a South American citizen." Instead, she became a teacher and later a school counselor.

ORIGINS OF CRITICAL RACE THEORY

Critical race theory (CRT), which has been referred to as a framework and also as a movement (West, 1995; Monaghan, 1993), draws together a set of premises and strategies derived in large part from critical theory but related directly to racism and is being increasingly used by educational scholars to analyze the educational enterprise (see Ladson-Billings, 1998; Ladson-Billings & Tate, 1995; Dixson & Rousseau, 2005). Like critical theory, CRT, as conceived by legal scholars of color, critiques society and social structures (for example, the legal system and schooling systems), opposes the wrongs and ills of modern societies, and seeks to change society by critiquing the forms of theorizing that legitimize those societies and systems (Bernstein, 1995, p. 11). Although CRT is a derivative of critical theory, its central construct is racism.

CRT was conceived as an oppositional scholarship within mainstream legal scholars' discourse (Crenshaw, Gotanda, Peller, & Thomas, 1995, p. xvii), but the genesis of CRT stems back to a group known as *critical legal scholars* (CLS)—a mix of leftist law faculty, students, and practitioners. A small number of legal scholars of color, active among the CLS, found themselves increasingly distanced from the members of the primary group who, at the same time that they "challenged the way American law served to legitimize an oppressive social order" (p. xviii), conceptualized race in a postmodernist frame as a social construction and therefore not a category for analysis.

Derrick Bell could be considered the father of critical race theory. His book *Faces at the Bottom of the Well: The Permanence of Racism* (1992) combined allegories with actual legal findings to sketch the outlines of an American society in which liberalism is a facade and a place where racial inequalities will never be rectified and only addressed to the extent that the White citizenry sees itself as threatened by the status quo. Bell, an experienced civil rights attorney prior to his academic career, resigned from Harvard University's law school in 1992 in protest that no African American female law faculty had been hired during his twenty-three-year tenure. Bell's legacy to CRT is skepticism about the civil rights discourse, an activist orientation, and counterstory telling—all of which remain integral parts of CRT today.

DESCRIPTION AND DISCUSSION OF CRT

As CRT has evolved and made its way from legal scholarship to education, one can see eddies and shifts in the descriptions of its core principles, which can make it difficult to grasp the essential constructs in the framework (see, for example, DeCuir & Dixson, 2004; Solórzano & Yosso, 2002; Ladson-Billings & Tate, 1995). A defining work in CRT scholarship is *Critical Race Theory: The Key Writings That Formed the Movement* (Crenshaw et al., 1995). The editors of this work used two common interests to characterize CRT: (1) an understanding of how *White supremacy* in America was created through an examination of "professed ideals," such as "the rule of law" and "equal protection"; and (2) "[a desire] to change the existing relationship between racial power and the law" (p. xiii).

The most cogent presentation of critical race theory as it is understood in the educational field is provided by DeCuir and Dixson (2004, p. 27) in their identification of five tenets that constitute critical race theory and their attempt to ground CRT with examples from a schooling case study. The tenets are (1) the use of counterstory telling; (2) the permanence of racism; (3) Whiteness as property; (4) interest convergence—the status quo will change only when the interests of Blacks and Whites converge—and (5) a critique of liberalism that challenges three assumptions about race and the law: that the law is color-blind, that the law is neutral, and that change must be incremental so that it is palatable to those in power.

Counterstory Telling

Throughout educational scholarly literature, counterstory telling is arguably the most widely used element of CRT. Some may question its utility, because narrative research in education is not new. However, one has to keep in mind that the original purposes of CRT are grounded in issues of race representation in legal scholarship. Thus the aim of counterstory telling within CRT is to restructure legal scholarship; counterstories are intended to illuminate, by setting up a contrast, the majoritarian, race-neutral, and liberal meta-story in the law. Counterstories are used to demonstrate that color blindness, from a CRT perspective, serves principally to obscure the ways in which African Americans and other people of color are being disadvantaged.

Racism as Endemic to American Society

The permanence of racism is another way of stating a basic assumption in CRT: that racism is normal, not aberrant, in the United States (Ladson-Billings, 1998; Dixson & Rousseau, 2005) and that this calls for different strategies in addressing racism—strategies that target conditions of our society and not just "the isolated redneck" (Delgado, 1995). Like Frantz Fanon, Bell believes that racist structures are embedded in the "psychology, economy, society and culture of the modern world" (Bell, 1992, p. xiv). In *Faces at the Bottom of the Well*, Bell supported his premise with quantitative measures to show that strides once made by African Americans had been lost by the 1990s.

Whiteness as Property

The concept of Whiteness as property is thought provoking. Harris (1995) explains the origins of this concept best when she states:

> Slavery produced a peculiar, mixed category of property and humanity—a hybrid with inherent instabilities that were reflected in its treatment and ratification by the law. The dual and contradictory character of slaves as property and persons was exemplified in the Representation Clause of the Constitution [p. 278].

Turning the historical use of Black humans as property on its head, Harris now positions Whiteness as property: "Whiteness fits the broad historical concept of property described by classical theorists" (p. 279). She considers the three rights of all legally defined property as they might (and in many cases have in the courts) related to Whiteness: the rights of use, disposition, and possession. The right of possession extends to a provision for exclusion rights. Ladson-Billings and Tate (1995) apply the White property right of possession to an educational setting so that we may see how it could serve to explain, for example, the segregation of schools—functioning as an absolute right to exclude used to deny Black children access to education.

Interest Convergence

Dixson and Rousseau (2005) explain Bell's concept of interest convergence succinctly. From a CRT perspective it is an explanation of a racial reality as well as a strategy for surmounting racial obstacles. Interest convergence holds that racial injustice will decline only when White policymakers believe that decline is in their best interest; further, any policy to benefit Blacks and other people of color will be declared unnecessary when White superior standing is threatened (p. 18). Bell (1995) derives his position at least in part from his experience during the civil rights era when *Brown* v. *Board of Education* was decided. He strongly believes that the decision in this case was based more on an effort to boost the international prestige of the United States among so-called Third World countries during the Cold War than on moral arguments for racial justice. Donnor (2005) applies the interest convergence principle to good effect in demonstrating how commercialism more than racial altruism was responsible for the integration of college sports.

Critique of Liberalism

Bell (1992) explains that civil rights laws in America have become "deified" in the following way: "The worship of equality rules as having absolute power benefits whites by preserving a benevolent but fictional self-image, and such worship benefits blacks by preserving hope" (p. 101). From a CRT perspective, in order for civil rights legislation to be passed the majority of White Americans needed to *not* see themselves as racists; thus racism was construed by the legal system as aberrant, intentional behavior, perpetrated by a conscious wrongdoer (Crenshaw et al., 1995, p. xiv). Once mainstream legal discourse used this "perpetrator perspective" (Freeman, 1995, p. 29) in construing racism as discrete acts of racial discrimination based on the "irrelevant" attribute of race, it was but a short step for legal scholars to embrace the ideal of color blindness as the guide to racial enlightenment (Crenshaw et al., 1995, p. xv). Liberalists also could support their position by using Martin Luther King Jr.'s rejoinder that a person should be judged "by the content of his character not by the color of his skin" (p. xv). Shifting the critique of liberalism from civil rights law to education, Ladson-Billings and Tate (1995) paralleled the multicultural movement in education with the liberal approach taken in civil rights law, leveling a CRT critique at the multicultural paradigm and calling it "a liberal ideology offering no radical change in the current order" (p. 56). A hallmark of critical race theorists is their respectful critique of the civil rights movement's incremental approach to racial reform, when what has really been needed is restructuring of institutions and systems. What have infrequently been heard are solutions. We turn now to a discussion of critiques of CRT.

ADULT EDUCATION AND CRT

Critical race theory posits that racism is endemic in our society, and I agree. Because of that, I believe all professions and fields need to continue the dialogue on how to heal racism with an eye toward the creation of conditions that help to eradicate the spread of the disease while also creating opportunities to create a rich environment for growth among all members of all races in our field. My question continues to be how to do this while building the appreciation for differences that I believe truly enriches our society and our profession.

The CRT tenets and explications that I discussed earlier can assist in the conceptual unveiling of color blindness, which I believe has become "sloganized" in our society. Critical race theory is a relatively recent and, in adult education, infrequently used framework for examining and responding to racism. In this part of this chapter, I situate CRT in an intellectual context and summarize some of the major critiques (from both legal and nonlegal scholars); of particular concern are those that signal caveats when translating CRT into other fields, such as adult education. Additionally, I build upon the respiritualization discourse in the social sciences regarding the significance of spirituality, particularly as it applies to racism. I raise the question, what are the implications of both CRT and respiritualization for our field and our practice? A persistent critique of CRT charges that it offers no solutions for the problem of racism in society or in schools (Dixson & Rousseau, 2005); however, I believe that respiritualization provides spiritually grounded possibilities for positive race and racism research and practice.

Among the few who have addressed the CRT framework within adult education are Peterson (1999) and Rocco and Gallagher (2004). Peterson (1999) drew on critical race theory to describe the ways in which a culturally relevant dialogue within adult education could be created. She suggested that adult educators reevaluate curriculum, instruction, assessment, and funding (pp. 86–87) to determine the effectiveness in these areas. She pointed particularly to the funding of adult basic education (ABE) programs as an area of marked inequality that was arguably influenced by racial inequity. For many programs in adult education, CRT provides a framework that centers race as the prime organizing construct and shows how legislation as a mirror of values and beliefs has contributed to the inadequacy of those programs.

Rocco and Gallagher (2004) discuss how the perpetrator perspective mentioned earlier allows White faculty to escape responsibility and accountability; once racism is defined as an overt act, faculty can exempt themselves as having committed no such act. Rocco and Gallagher emphasize that when faculty assume no accountability they are continuously at risk of performing discriminatory acts.

At one time I had serious doubts about the power of critical theory to promote the individual and societal changes I desire that would lead to the eradication of racism; this doubt arose because one of critical theory's leading proponents held deep racist beliefs: "Antonio Gramsci (1971), the otherwise radical Italian theorist, may as well have been speaking for Western civilization when he digressed from his thoughts on traditional and organic intellectuals to refer to 'negro' intellectuals as a dangerous element with only one positive function: to lead 'their people' back to Africa" (Stanfield, 1988, p. 291).

Starting with the publication of the Bronze Booklets in the 1930s (see Johnson-Bailey, 2006, for a discussion of these), scholars in adult education have sporadically addressed the effects of racism and raised concerns about our field's collective response. Now we have the bounty of Afri-centric analyses of Garvey's "selfethnic reflectors" (Colin III, 1996), and concepts such as "polyrhythmic realities" (Sheared, 1999), which begin to explain the complexity of the learning environments in which non-dominant persons participate. We are developing evidence of the significant historical efforts made by Black adult educators concerning race and adult education (see, for example, Peterson's *Freedom Road,* 1996, and Denton's *Booker T. Washington and the Adult Education Movement,* 1993). As social scientists have begun to theorize Whiteness, adult educators have explored and challenged White privilege (Manglitz, 2003) and begun to reexamine the extent to which critical theory can effectively address racism (Brookfield, 2003). Although, clearly, these contributions are constructs in the knowledge base of our field, I retain the sense that these perspectives have yet to fully penetrate the epistemology of the field of adult education. To put a fine point on it, the 2000 *Handbook of Adult and Continuing Education* was the first edition of this handbook in which a chapter was devoted to the examination of the issue of race and racism (Johnson-Bailey & Cervero, 2000)—as opposed to the discussion of racial groups in terms of, for example, education for the Negro or Native American—and to discussing the ways that race and racism might be presented during the preparation of adult education practitioners.

Critical race theorists posit that in the field of education the concept of race is undertheorized (Ladson-Billings & Tate, 1995), that gender and class theories alone fail to explain the lack of achievement and academic success of African American children and thus of Black adults. Critical race theory is not the same as racializing criticality (Brookfield, 2003) and is different from Africentrism, although it is related to both these conceptual camps. CRT is related to Africentrism to the extent that critical race theorists believe that the African American experience is distinct enough in its phenomenology to merit a framework that uses that experience as the basis for analyzing the law, policies, and institutions in the United States. CRT situates itself in the African American intellectual tradition of scholars and activists such as W.E.B. DuBois, Frederick Douglass, and Marcus Garvey (Ladson-Billings & Tate, 1995).

A WAY FORWARD: RESPIRITUALIZATION AND COMMUNITY

At the outset of this project I thought that one important contribution I would like to make to the discourse was to introduce the idea of spirituality and its import for helping us find solutions to racist ideologies and racism in our societal and institutional systems, because a CRT framework alone does not provide a vision of the future. Although I believe that racism is endemic, I do not agree that it is permanent, and this view represents a key departure from CRT.

So the question for me becomes, what does reconstruction look like in adult education? M. L. Perry's challenge to social scientists (2005) is to understand humanity as essentially spiritual, and therefore he posits that social science must be dual, exploring both scientific *and* spiritual values. Perry (2005) traces the roots of racism to the despiritualization of Western religious traditions and offers a future vision for the social sciences based on the respiritualization of social science research. The goal of Perry's work is to outline the ways in which corruption and ultimately schisms within Western Christianity contributed to the emergence of a society that looks to social science rather than spiritual values for moral confirmation and guidance. It is this historical deterioration of what we know as Christianity, beginning in the early Middle Ages, that Perry demonstrates led to a societal moral collapse that in turn was a key factor in the rise of slavery and racism (p. 15). Perry goes on to explain—through a deeply detailed analysis of the history of racism, the church, and social science—that what we as a society now know of Christianity (and religion) is in fact distinct from spirituality and the original message and intent of Christ.

Like Perry, I wonder what would happen if in our professional field of adult education we used a metaphor of family (Perry, 2005, p. 248). If we think of our colleagues as family, then how would we handle them if we believed they were color-blind and if we believed racism was an endemic disease—a disease that our entire family suffered from and that all our systems had been affected by? Perry suggests a vision in which resources are available to all, not limited to those with privilege by virtue of race, wealth, or power. Moreover, he envisions a community where those who are more qualified assist those who may be less so. As Perry notes, in a family it would be absurd for senior family members to withhold assistance from junior members. A spiritual approach posits a belief, and actions built on this belief, that all are endowed with infinite talents and skills. He notes that racist societies have always feared the *success* of minorities, not their inadequacy (p. 248). So this community is one where policies privilege the underrepresented—so that, for example, when there is an electoral tie between a member of an underrepresented group and an overrepresented one, the vote goes to the underrepresented—a community in which the oneness of humanity is acknowledged as a fundamental truth and therefore infused throughout its learning and policy-making systems.

REFERENCES

Bell, D. (1992). *Faces at the bottom of the well: The permanence of racism.* New York: Basic Books.

Bell, D. (1995). Brown v. board of education and the interest convergence dilemma. In K. Crenshaw, N. Gotanda, G. Peller, & K. Thomas (Eds.), *Critical race theory: The key writings that formed the movement* (pp. 20–29). New York: New Press.

Bernstein, J. (1995). *Recovering ethical life: Jürgen Habermas and the future of critical theory.* New York: Routledge.

Brookfield, S. (2003). Racializing criticality. *Adult Education Quarterly, 53*(3), 154–169.

Colin, S.A.J., III. (1996). Marcus Garvey: Africentric adult education for selfethnic reliance. In E. Peterson (Ed.), *Freedom Road: Adult education of African Americans* (pp. 41–66). Malabar, FL: Krieger.

Collins, P. (1990). *Black feminist thought.* New York: Routledge.

Crenshaw, K., Gotanda, N., Peller, G., & Thomas, K. (Eds.). (1995). *Critical race theory: The key writings that formed the movement.* New York: New Press.

DeCuir, A., & Dixson, A. (2004, June/July). So when it comes out, they aren't that surprised that it is there: Using critical race theory as a tool of analysis of race and racism in education. *Educational Researcher,* pp. 26–31.

Delgado, R. (1995). The imperial scholar. In K. Crenshaw, N. Gotanda, G. Peller, & K. Thomas (Eds.), *Critical race theory: The key writings that formed the movement* (pp. 46–57). New York: New Press.

Denton, V. L. (1993). *Booker T. Washington and the adult education movement.* Gainesville, FL: University Press of Florida.

Dixson, A., & Rousseau, C. (2005). And we are still not saved: critical race theory in education ten years later. *Race, Ethnicity and Education, 8*(1), 7–27.

Donnor, J. (2005). Towards an interest convergence in the education of African-American student athletes in major college sports. *Race, Ethnicity and Education, 8*(1), 45–67.

Freeman, A. (1995). Legitimizing racial discrimination through antidiscrimination law: A critical review of Supreme Court doctrine. In K. Crenshaw, N. Gotanda, G. Peller, & K. Thomas (Eds.), *Critical race theory: The key writings that formed the movement* (pp. 29–45). New York: New Press.

Harris, C. (1995). Whiteness as property. In K. Crenshaw, N. Gotanda, G. Peller, & K. Thomas (Eds.), *Critical race theory: The key writings that formed the movement* (pp. 276–291). New York: New Press.

Johnson-Bailey, J. (2006). African Americans in adult education: The Harlem Renaissance revisited. *Adult Education Quarterly, 56*(2), 102–118.

Johnson-Bailey, J., & Cervero, R. (2000). The invisible politics of race. In A. Wilson & E. Hayes (Eds.), *Handbook of adult and continuing education* (new ed., pp. 147–160). San Francisco: Jossey-Bass.

Ladson-Billings, G. (1998). Just what is critical race theory and what is it doing in a nice field like education? *Qualitative Studies in Education, 11*(1), 7–24.

Ladson-Billings, G., & Tate, W. (1995). Toward a critical race theory of education. *Teachers College Record, 97*(1), 41–62.

Manglitz, E. (2003). Challenging White privilege in adult education: A critical review of the literature. *Adult Education Quarterly, 3*(2), 119–134.

Monaghan, P. (1993). Critical race theory: Some startling analyses. *Chronicle of Higher Education.* Retrieved July 28, 2006, from http://chronicle.com.

Perry, M. L. (2005). *The last war.* Kidlington, U.K.: George Ronald.

Peterson, E. (Ed.). (1996). *Freedom road: Adult education of African Americans.* Malabar, FL: Krieger.

Peterson, E. (1999). Creating a culturally relevant dialogue for African American adult educators. In T. C. Guy (Ed.), *Providing culturally relevant adult education: A challenge for the twenty-first century* (New Directions for Adult and Continuing Education, No. 82, pp. 79–91). San Francisco: Jossey-Bass.

Rocco, T., & Gallagher, S. (2004). Discriminative justice: Can discrimination be just? In L. G. Martin & E. Rogers (Eds.), *Adult education in an urban context: Problems, practices, and programming for inner-city communities* (New Directions for Adult and Continuing Education, No. 101, pp. 29–41). San Francisco: Jossey-Bass.

Sheared, V. (1999). Giving voice: Inclusion of African American student's polyrhythmic realities. In T. C. Guy (Ed.), *Providing culturally relevant adult education: A challenge for the twenty-first century* (New Directions for Adult and Continuing Education, No. 82, pp. 33–48). San Francisco: Jossey-Bass.

Solórzano, D., & Yosso, T. (2002). Critical race methodology: Counter-storytelling as an analytical framework for education research. *Qualitative Inquiry, 8*(1), 23–44.

Stanfield, J. (1988, Winter). Not quite in the club. *American Sociologist,* pp. 291–300.

West, C. (1995). Foreword. In K. Crenshaw, N. Gotanda, G. Peller, & K. Thomas (Eds.), *Critical race theory: The key writings that formed the movement* (pp. xi–xiii). New York: New Press.

11

Musings on Controversial Intersections of Positionality

A Queer Crit Perspective in Adult and Continuing Education

MITSUNORI MISAWA

As a gay adult educator of color, I think it is important for educators to ask questions like, "What happens to queer students of color when they come into an environment where the majority of students are White heterosexuals?" and, "How can we understand diversity and multicultural education at all without looking at the intersection of the most oppressed identities?" Although these questions are a good start, one could go even further and ask, "How does the intersection of race and sexual orientation play out in adult and continuing education?" Race matters in education (Johnson-Bailey, 2002; Ladson-Billings & Tate, 1995; Maher & Tetreault, 2001), and so does sexual orientation (Grace, 2001; Hill, 2004). The question is then, when both these elements are combined, can we still have dialogues about both without discounting one or the other? Although these questions are difficult to answer, they are questions we must ask. One way to find answers to these questions is by looking through a queer crit perspective.

Understandings of various types of inequity, discrimination, and marginalization based on individual positional markers like race, gender, and class have been extensively disseminated by social scientists including educators and scholars in adult and continuing education, but significant intellectual discourses on the positional markers of sexuality and sexual orientation are lacking (Grace, 2001; Hill, 2004). Also, although studies of the intersection of positional markers, like race and gender, race and class, and sexual orientation and gender, exist in the field of adult and continuing education, discourse on the intersection of race and sexual orientation is still scarce (Misawa, 2006).

In his book *Troubling Intersections of Race and Sexuality: Queer Students of Color and Anti-Oppressive Education,* Kumashiro (2001) asserted that although many educators have tried to combat racism and homophobia in educational settings, they have not explored the intersection of the two positions. Each person is born into socioculturally predestined positions—such as race, sexual orientation, and gender—that influence his or her life. Martin and Van Gunten (2002) have stated that "we are all raced, classed, and gendered and...these identities are relational, complex, and fluid positions rather than essential qualities" (p. 46). The human world is bound by a web of positionality that entangles everyone in power differences based on socially constructed positional markers (Johnson-Bailey & Cervero, 2000). This is a place we must negotiate in our daily interactions with other people (Tisdell, 2001). The way we treat others, and how we are treated by others, greatly influences our positions in society. Although discussion of race is becoming prominent in academia, especially through the multicultural aspect of adult and continuing education, talk about sexual orientation still lags behind. Dialogue about both race and sexual orientation is almost nonexistent. This chapter will initiate such a dialogue.

Because positionality is diffused throughout society, the environments of adult and continuing education programs are not devoid of it. The concept of positionality implies that people do not belong to one group, rather they belong to multiple identity groups (Martin & Van Gunten, 2002). Educators and practitioners in the social science fields critically examined how positionality affected their own careers as educators and practitioners and how it affected their students in postsecondary education over the course of twenty-five years (Johnson-Bailey & Lee, 2005; Maher & Tetreault, 2001). Adult learners and teachers still enter educational institutions with sociocultural positional markers (Johnson-Bailey & Cervero, 2000; Misawa, 2006; Tisdell, 2001).

Educators and learners share their time and space with each other in educational contexts that are affected by positionality. The teaching-learning transaction emphasizes pursuit of social justice and equality in educational careers. Even though educators and scholars in adult and continuing education understand the impact of positionality on the teaching-learning transaction, there is a gap between what they know about their practice and what they actually do in their practice (Cervero, 2001; Tisdell, 2001). Even now, educators and practitioners in adult and continuing education are challenged with reconciling this gap.

CRITICAL RACE THEORY AND QUEER CRIT

Race is an important factor in the United States, and it usually refers to a person's skin color (Johnson-Bailey, 2002). As a gay male born in Japan, a largely homogeneous society, I am amazed at how socially constructed categories and sociocultural positions determine how people live; what they can purchase; and what kinds of property rights, civil rights, and other basic human rights they have in the United States (Haney Lopez, 2007). Skin color is a major factor in power disparities and (un)equal rights in the United States.

Rose's (1964) description of racial struggle in the United States shows how historical perspectives greatly influence the concept of race in this country. People of color struggled to become first-class citizens at the time of the civil rights movement in the 1960s.

> The movements for desegregation have gained legal support in the Supreme Court decisions of 1954, 1955, and 1963 pertaining to school desegregation, and that of 1962 regarding the desegregation of both intra- and interstate transportation facilities. The Justice Department...has helped to facilitate integration.... The road, however, has been exceedingly rough, the costs extremely high. In spite of measurable gains, the color line continues to exist *de facto*, if not *de jure*, maintained by the pressures of social conformity and the economic and social advantages accruing to those who maintain it [Rose, 1964, pp. 113–114].

Scholars such as Derrick Bell and Richard Delgado and their students in the legal field witnessed these slow-paced changes in racial inequalities. Then Delgado and Stefancic watched as the 1960s civil rights gained by people of color were "stalled and...rolled back" (2001, p. 4). It was in such conditions that critical race theory was developed through the legal field in the 1970s (Delgado & Stefancic, 2001). Critical race theory sprang from critical legal studies but then diverged because it focused more on legal perspectives on race. One of the critiques of critical legal study was that it had not focused enough on race because the field of legal studies consisted predominantly of White scholars, whereas people of color in the field of law needed perspectives of social justice for their own lenses (Lawrence, Matsuda, Delgado, & Crenshaw, 1993).

Although critical race theory originated in the legal field, it was quickly applied to the social sciences such as education, women's studies, and sociology (Dixson & Rousseau, 2005). In contemporary academia, critical race theory has been widely used to analyze race and racism. The first time critical race theory appeared in education was in the mid-1990s, when it was used by Ladson-Billings and Tate, according to Dixson and Rousseau (2005). Ladson-Billings and Tate (1995) published groundbreaking work in the field of education in their article titled "Toward a Critical Race Theory of Education." It was the first publication calling for critical race theory, and it indicated that critical race theory would be a useful tool in examining inequities involving race and poverty in the field of education. This essay was admired by many scholars of color in education because a tool had finally been acquired that could critically analyze inequities based on race and racism through the lens of minorities in academia (Dixson & Rousseau, 2005). Subsequently, positionality-oriented research on race, critical race analysis, and narratives of people of color in the field of adult and continuing education have been published (Hayes & Colin III, 1994; Johnson-Bailey, 2002; Peterson, 1996; Sheared & Sissel, 2001).

Critical race theory continues to gain adoption for use in various fields and perspectives including the queer crit perspective, which is being integrated into six themes of critical race theory, as discussed in the next section of this chapter.

A QUEER CRIT PERSPECTIVE

In recent years, some minority scholars in the legal field injected the queer perspective into critical race theory. These queer crit theorists emphasized critical examinations of both race and sexual orientation in society through the perspectives of gay and lesbian scholarship (Delgado & Stefancic, 2001). Delgado and Stefancic (2000) stated that gay and lesbian scholars in critical race theory began "to create a body of queer jurisprudence that examines whether antiracist literature and movements incorporate a heterosexist bias that marginalizes and excludes the concerns, perspectives, and voices of gay and lesbians" (p. 321).

At present, in 2009, there is no official queer crit group in adult and higher education. However, I find that I personally identify with queer crit theory and not queer theory because the former does not discount my racial identity and the latter does. Given where we are today, I believe that we will make significant headway if during this year we can establish a body that can employ the queer crit perspective in education. Here are the six contributions of queer crit (QC) to critical race theory.

QC1: The Centrality of the Intersection of Race and Racism with Sexual Orientation and Homophobia

Scholars of critical race theory in education and law recognize that race matters in contemporary U.S. society. In this politically correct society, all racial factors—all skin colors—are supposed to carry equal weight, but this has inevitably led to the promulgation of *color blindness*, which emphasizes that "one should treat all persons equally, without regard to their race" (Delgado & Stefancic, 2001, p. 144); hence discrimination based on race is socially prohibited. But this push for color blindness has created another dimension of racial discrimination; because people do not explicitly talk about race or skin color, racial discrimination has become implicit. Racism or race-based crimes used to be explicit, but now these crimes are subtle, invisible, and oftentimes even more damaging to people of color than explicit crimes (Haney Lopez, 2007).

The United States is a society where heterosexual perspectives dominate; homosexuality has been thought of as a form of mental illness and many Christian religious beliefs still consider same-sex attraction to be a disdainful novelty. Like race, sexual orientation is not viewed as a polite topic of conversation, but heterosexist aspects are strongly encouraged, both implicitly and explicitly, and heterosexuality is aggressively labeled "normal." For queer people of color, oppression and marginalization occur on two fronts; they have to face both racial discrimination and homophobic violence. These experiences are ones lesbians and gays encounter every day (Grace, 2001).

QC2: The Challenge to Mainstream Ideologies

Critical race theory challenges the conventional norms that were created by Whites and that have led to racism and power disparities in the United States. It takes on an important role in this White supremacist society because it centers people of color's perspectives (Ladson-Billings, 1999). As people of color, we can use critical race theory to create our own knowledge about race and critically examine how non-White races are affected by conventional laws and public goods in the United States (Haney Lopez, 2007).

Solórzano (1998) tells us that a "critical race theory in education challenges the traditional claims of the educational system and its institutions to objectivity, meritocracy, and color and gender blindness, race and gender neutrality, and equal opportunity" (p. 122). In addition to this, queer crit asks whether the conventional norms and standards that are created and sustained by White heterosexual males are applicable to queer people of color. Queer people of color often face a situation where they have to choose between an array of these stereotypes to navigate through different social contexts (Misawa, 2007). When challenging mainstream ideologies, queer people of color are empowered with experiences that enable them to criticize and understand both racial and sexual stereotypes.

QC3: The Confrontation with Ahistoricism

According to Lawrence et al. (1993), "Critical race theory challenges ahistoricism and insists on a contextual/historical analysis of the law" (p. 6). Critical race theorists believe that conventional knowledge and norms are perpetuated by majorities in the United States as strategies to sustain powerful social positions. Queer perspectives also need to be examined through the historical context. People who grew up in the pre-1980s were taught that homosexuality was illness and queer people were deviant. Although the notion that homosexuality is de facto a mental illness started to crumble in the 1970s, many people and religious groups in contemporary society still stigmatize queer people as deviants (Fone, 2000), in what amounts to sustaining the ideology of the higher sociocultural status of heterosexuals (Hill, 2004). An analysis based on contextual/historical analysis of queer people of color is needed to combat the intersection of racism and homophobia.

QC4: The Centrality of Experiential Knowledge

According to Valdes (1995), the perspectives of people of color are central to understanding their everyday realities; this idea also applies to queer people of color because critical race theory centers on individual experiential knowledge. Life experiences are valid and appropriate for examining and challenging oppression (Delgado & Stefancic, 2001). Solórzano (1998) has emphasized critical race theory's recognition of personal narratives. Subjective aspects are important because they empower queer people of color to create their own knowledge. Because conventional knowledge and norms are created and perpetuated by a dominant majority, there is not much occasion for queer people of color to create their own knowledge (Valdes, 1995). Emphasizing the lives of queer people of color provides a more complete understanding that enables educators and scholars in adult and higher education to effectively combat racism, heterosexism, and homophobia. Knowledge is power, and it empowers those who have been silenced in American culture (Kumashiro, 2001).

QC5: The Multidisciplinary Aspects

Queer crit challenges the unidisciplinary focus of most analyses and insists on examining the multiple positions and oppressions experienced by queer people of color (Valdes, 1995). This enables queer crit to explain the effects of multiple oppressions on queer people of color, thus enabling educators and scholars to develop more thorough understandings of how positionality affects queer people of color and how sociocultural positions in adult and continuing education are connected (Misawa, 2006). Additionally, educators and scholars acknowledge that the history of queer people of color is diverse and powerful in terms of revealing the ways in which stereotypes based on the perpetuation of White supremacist and heterosexist understandings influence positionality, and the ways in which the conventional academic focus creates hegemonic understandings in the educational field and prevents the achievement of equality in educational settings (Kumashiro, 2001).

QC6: The Social Justice Perspective

Critical race theory works toward eliminating racial oppression as part of the broader goal of ending all forms of oppression. Lawrence et al. (1993) state: "Racial oppression is experienced by many in tandem with oppression on grounds of gender, class, or sexual orientation" (p. 6).

When educators and scholars in adult and continuing education focus on creating safe learning environments, they need to consider how interlocking positionalities affect the educational context. They also need to examine how a person's race and sexual orientation have an impact on his or her experiences in the learning environment. The educational context is a system that disseminates knowledge and behavior from the larger society (Johnson-Bailey & Cervero, 2000). Educators and scholars in adult and continuing education can start practicing educational equality in their own classrooms and, eventually, their commitment to social justice will spread beyond these classrooms. This aspect is significant in the queer crit perspective. An integrative and collaborative perspective for combating racism and homophobia will help queer people of color attain better social justice. Because adult and continuing education emphasizes social justice and educational equality for learners, this perspective should be put into practice.

PRACTICING EDUCATIONAL EQUALITY

The following short story, summarized from a February 2004 personal journal entry, briefly describes one of my experiences as a queer person of color. Perhaps it indicates the need for a lively conversation about race and sexual orientation.

> While gaining information sources for my master's thesis, I made contact with the director of Student Services through a colleague in multicultural education. We spent intellectual time discussing racial issues, but when I brought up the issue of sexual orientation, he suddenly reversed his attitude and behavior toward me from warm and friendly to cold and hostile. He said, "We don't talk about it [sexual orientation] in our daily conversation. I do not want to talk about it at all and do not want to deal with it. Our meeting is over now, so leave. Good day." I was stunned by what happened and questioned how he could work with his students effectively while being so oppressing toward an integral aspect of diversity.

Valdes (1995) experienced a similar situation as a panel speaker about lesbian legal theory. The audience, White lesbians, questioned the inclusion of a gay Latino man in the panel. At least in my experience and Valdes's experience, there is easily exacerbated tension between minority sociocultural groups. It seems obvious that many minority rights groups perpetuate one-dimensional identities (Hutchinson, 1997). They focus on only one sociocultural dimension and mute other important perspectives because they try to work one perspective at a time. Also, their members tend to be rallied by a prominent and visible identity (Misawa, 2009).

Positionality both positively and negatively influences our practice and our students' learning experiences. Educators and learners treat each other differently depending on their sociocultural identities. There are at least two reasons why positionality influences educational settings for adults. First, positionality locates adults as either privileged or underprivileged, according to a weighted sum of their multiple sociocultural markers. White males are located at the top of the U.S. social hierarchical pyramid in almost all social contexts (Johnson-Bailey, 2002). Second, certain sociocultural positions are unseen and invisible. Because positionality involves the sociocultural positions of all people in the educational context, oftentimes educators and learners look for only visible factors like race and gender to determine how they will interact with others (Misawa, 2006). However, invisible sociocultural positions, such as sexual orientations often are, exist even if they are not obvious. It is not possible for educators in adult and continuing education to create safe environments or achieve social justice in practice without thinking about the hidden aspects of positionality. So a queer crit perspective that addresses race and sexual orientation together as a valid identity is crucial in educational settings.

A queer crit perspective in adult and continuing education can help educators achieve real institutional democracy for learners. A major first step is to address race and sexual orientation not in contention but in harmony.

REFERENCES

Cervero, R. M. (2001). Continuing professional education in transition, 1981–2000. *International Journal of Lifelong Education, 20*(1–2), 16–30.

Delgado, R., & Stefancic, J. (2000). *Critical race theory: The cutting edge* (2nd ed.). Philadelphia: Temple University Press.

Delgado, R., & Stefancic, J. (2001). *Critical race theory: An introduction.* New York: New York University Press.

Dixson, A., & Rousseau, C. (2005). And we are still not saved: Critical race theory in education ten years later. *Race, Ethnicity and Education, 8*(1), 7–27.

Fone, B.R.S. (2000). *Homophobia: A history.* New York: Metropolitan Books.

Grace, A. P. (2001). Using queer cultural studies to transgress adult educational space. In V. Sheared & P. A. Sissel (Eds.), *Making space: Merging theory and practice in adult education.* Westport, CT: Bergin & Garvey.

Haney Lopez, I. (2007). Introduction. In I. Haney Lopez (Ed.), *Race, law and society.* Burlington, VT: Ashgate.

Hayes, E., & Colin, S.A.J., III. (1994). Racism and sexism in the United States: Fundamental issues. In E. Hayes & S.A.J. Scipio III (Eds.), *Confronting racism and sexism* (New Directions for Adult and Continuing Education, No. 61, pp. 5–16). San Francisco: Jossey-Bass.

Hill, R. J. (2004). Activism as practice: Some queer considerations. In R. St. Clair & J. A. Sandlin (Eds.), *Promoting critical practice in adult education* (New Directions for Adult and Continuing Education, No. 102, pp. 85–94). San Francisco: Jossey-Bass.

Hutchinson, D. L. (1997). Out yet unseen: A racial critique of gay and lesbian legal theory and political discourse. *Connecticut Law Review, 29*(2), 561–646.

Johnson-Bailey, J. (2002). Race matters: The unspoken variable in the teaching-learning transaction. In J. M. Ross-Gordon (Ed.), *Contemporary viewpoints on teaching adults effectively* (New Directions for Adult and Continuing Education, No. 93, pp. 39–49). San Francisco: Jossey-Bass.

Johnson-Bailey, J., & Cervero, R. M. (2000). The invisible politics of race in adult education. In A. L. Wilson & E. Hayes (Eds.), *Handbook of adult and continuing education* (new ed., pp. 147–160). San Francisco: Jossey-Bass.

Johnson-Bailey, J., & Lee, M. (2005). Women of color in the academy: Where's our authority in the classroom? *Feminist Teacher, 15*(2), 111–122.

Kumashiro, K. K. (2001). *Troubling intersections of race and sexuality: Queer students of color and anti-oppressive education.* Lanham, MD: Rowman & Littlefield.

Ladson-Billings, G. (1999). Preparing teachers for diverse student populations: A critical race theory perspective. *Review of Research in Education, 24,* 211–247.

Ladson-Billings, G., & Tate, W. (1995). Toward a critical race theory of education. *Teachers College Record, 97*(1), 47–68.

Lawrence, C., Matsuda, M., Delgado, R., & Crenshaw, K. (1993). Introduction. In M. Matsuda, C. Lawrence, R. Delgado, & K. Crenshaw (Eds.), *Words that wound: Critical race theory, assaultive speech, and the First Amendment* (pp. 1–15). Boulder, CO: Westview Press.

Maher, F. A., & Tetreault, M.K.T. (2001). *The feminist classroom: Dynamics of gender, race, and privilege* (expanded ed.). Lanham, MD: Rowman & Littlefield.

Martin, M. J., & Van Gunten, D. M. (2002). Reflected identities: Applying positionality and multicultural social reconstructionism in teacher education. *Journal of Teacher Education, 53*(1), 44–54.

Misawa, M. (2006). Queer race pedagogy in adult higher education: Dealing with power dynamics and positionality of gay students of color. In M. Hagen & E. Goff (Eds.), *Proceedings of the 47th annual adult education research conference* (pp. 257–262). St. Paul: University of Minnesota.

Misawa, M. (2007). Political aspects of the intersection of sexual orientation and race in higher education in the United States: A queer scholar of color's perspective. *Journal of Curriculum and Pedagogy, 4*(2), 78–83.

Misawa, M. (2009). The intersection of homophobic bullying and racism in adulthood: A graduate school experience. *Journal of LGBT Youth, 6*(1), 47–60.

Peterson, E. (1996). *Freedom road: Adult education of African Americans.* Malabar, FL: Krieger.

Rose, P. I. (1964). *They and we: Racial and ethnic relations in the United States.* New York: Random House.

Sheared, V., & Sissel, P. A. (2001). *Making space: Merging theory and practice in adult education.* Westport, CT: Bergin & Garvey.

Solórzano, D. (1998). Critical race theory, race and gender microaggressions, and the experience of Chicana and Chicano scholars. *Journal of Qualitative Studies in Education, 11*(1), 121–136.

Tisdell, E. J. (2001). The politics of positionality: Teaching for social change in higher education. In R. M. Cervero & A. L. Wilson, *Power in practice: Adult education and the struggle for knowledge and power in society* (pp. 145–163). San Francisco: Jossey-Bass.

Valdes, F. (1995). Sex and race in queer legal culture: Ruminations on identities and interconnectivities. *Southern California Review of Law and Women's Studies, 5*(1), 25–74.

12

Challenging Racism Through Postcolonial Discourse

A Critical Approach to Adult Education Pedagogy

MARY V. ALFRED

I have struggled for many years to see how race affects my life in America. It was difficult for me to see the color of racism. During my interactions with Black Americans, they were quickly able to identify vestiges of racism in restaurants, educational institutions, and other public spaces, but I often failed to see the racist acts that my colleagues identified. Why couldn't I see race in its many manifestations? As a Black person, my early recollection of life in America was that I was an outsider even among American Blacks. I was a Black woman who did not have the experience of being overtly racialized in my own country;

therefore understanding race and its impact on Black life in America has been a lifelong learning process.

I am descendant of slavery, born into a lower-class family in St. Lucia, British West Indies, where I spent the first twenty-two years of my life. My parents were sharecroppers who worked the land of people whom I could consider *elitist Blacks of mixed heritage.* It is clear to me now that the arrangement between my parents and this family were that of servant and master. My father worked the land, marketed the crops, and delivered to these people the financial proceeds. Although we resided on our own property, they lived in the big house and we in the little house. Therefore, when I was a child growing up, effects of slavery and colonialism influenced my worldviews. I lived under colonial rule, and I had my early schooling socialization under British colonialism, a system that objectified Black people and their experiences while placing White Europeans and their cultural forms as the dominant regime for human representation. Because of the ideological doctrine of subject and object, in order to carry on the work of the colonizers after their physical departure, a very small number of individuals were allowed into the halls of secondary and postsecondary education to be rigorously indoctrinated with ideologies of power, superiority, and subordination.

For Black Caribbean immigrants, their arrival into the United States is often the first time they are asked to socially categorize themselves based on their physical characteristics and cultural heritage. Additionally, it is the first time that they are forced to view themselves as a Black minority and to internalize the stereotypical images that accompany that identification. Racism has a systematic impact on people of the African Diaspora that is experienced personally, collectively, and culturally (Jones, 1997). As Black people, we all have experienced enslavement, personal racism, and various forms of institutional racism. However, even though Blacks living in the United States are often assumed to be a homogeneous group, owing to their shared physical characteristics, there is considerable variation in their ethnic origins and cultural orientations. Despite the common legacy of slavery, Blacks throughout the Diaspora have been affected by differing sociopolitical histories (Hall & Carter, 2006; Helms & Cook, 1999; Hintzen, 2001), which may influence their views of race and its impact on everyday life. Moreover, findings from research on Caribbean Blacks in the United States suggest that they have different views of racism from other Black Americans and that these different views enable them to achieve academically and financially (Helms & Cook, 1999; Hunter, 2006; Waters, 1994, 1999). Waters has theorized that West Indian Black immigrants' low perception of personal discrimination enables them to persevere whereas African Americans' perception of discrimination hinders them from achieving in many areas. Similarly, evidence from the literature suggests that West Indians in general do not want to be viewed from the same perspectives as American Blacks and that they identify themselves through their ethnicity rather than through race (Hall & Carter, 2006; Waters, 1994, 1999). Many identify as Afro-Caribbean or in terms of their island of birth (thinking of themselves as Jamaican, Grenadian, Trinidadian, or St. Lucian, for example) rather than identifying as African American. Hintzen (2001) and Waters (1999) theorize that knowledge of the low social status of African Americans in their home country influences the importance that West Indians give to their own ethnic group membership by minimizing race and stressing ethnicity.

This ethnic identification is significant in understanding intergroup perceptions of racism. In fact, El Nasser (2003) quotes Robert Hall, a professor of African American studies, as saying, "Some West Indian families tell their kids not to associate with Black Americans." Indeed, while I was living in Florida, I had several conversations with a very well-known African American scholar who lamented the fact that her daughter was not invited into the homes of West Indian Black families. We lived in an upper-middle-class community, consisting of primarily West Indian and Latin American families and a small number of African American families. As a teenager, the daughter of my African American colleague and friend yearned for friendship among her Black (Afro-Caribbean) student peers only to experience alienation from that cultural group. The mother's perception supported that cited by

El Nasser (2003). In my own research with Anglophone Caribbean immigrant women on their learning and development in the United States, I found similar attitudes among some of the participants I interviewed. Several of the group members portrayed an attitude of British West Indian superiority and African American inferiority in terms of cultural values and self-identity. This attitude, however, was less pronounced among the women with more advanced degrees and professional careers.

Overall, evidence from the literature suggests that West Indians have different perceptions of racism and racial discrimination as a result of their cultural orientations. Hunter (2006), in her dissertation study on perceptions of racial discrimination and collective self-esteem among African Americans and West Indian Americans, therefore suggests that "for African Americans, race may be the salient group identification because African Americans are usually unable to identify with strong ethnic ties to a specific nation in Africa. Thus, African Americans' and West Indian Americans' perception of racial discriminations may differ and result in differing feelings that are derived from their racial and ethnic groups" (p. 3). Hunter cautions that such a claim had not been investigated in the psychological literature. However, the findings of her study support evidence in the social sciences literature that suggests there are differences in perceptions of race and racism among Caribbean Black immigrants and among American Blacks, resulting from these groups' differing racial and ethnic identities. Similarly, Gaines, Ramkissoon, and Matthies (2003) conducted a study of Jamaicans in the United States and found that the participants negotiated their understandings of race and racial discrimination based on their cultural orientations. These authors therefore theorized that differences in cultural socialization deriving from ethnic or racial group shape cultural orientation, which in turn influences perceptions of discrimination and feelings.

Confronting issues of race and racism is an important aspect of Black life for people of the African Diaspora because of the history of institutional, personal, and cultural racism that exists in the United States. There is no doubt that all Blacks in America are affected by racism, because racist ideologies rest on the assumption of shared internal attributes based on physical characteristics (Helms & Cook, 1999). However, Hunter (2006) suggests that for West Indian Blacks who originate from countries where they were in the majority and were the primary holders of positions of power, confronting issues of discrimination in the United States is a very complex issue.

ENGAGING IN AUTHENTIC DIALOGUE

Using this forum, I seek here to open a dialogue, an exploration, on the subjects of race and racism within the context of colonial hegemony. I, as a subject in this dialogue, must situate my position. As Hall (1994) writes, "We all write and speak from a particular place and time, from a history and a culture which is specific. What we say is always in 'context,' *positioned*" (p. 392). My positionality as first a colonial and later a postcolonial subject, colonized by British imperialism, and later still a naturalized Black citizen of the United States frames the experience for this dialogue.

Today most Whites do not see racial discrimination as a widespread or deeply entrenched problem in predominantly White workplaces, schools, and public service agencies. As a result, Blacks and Whites have different views about racial inequity and injustice. According to Feagin and Sikes (1994), Whites look at matters of racial discrimination with detachment, whereas Blacks view racism in terms of their and their relatives' experiences in past and present encounters with White people. These oppositional views of White and Black individuals about racism make it difficult, if not impossible, for Black and White adult educators to have authentic dialogues about race and its impact on adult learning and teaching. Moreover, issues of race go beyond discourses between Blacks and Whites; they are found among all races and also within racial groups. As many postcolonial scholars have found, there is a distinct relationship between racial identity, ethnic identity, and perceptions of racial discrimination among people of the African Diaspora (Hall & Carter, 2006; Hunter, 2006; Waters, 1994).

Perceptions of racial discrimination are determined by one's views of one's race and ethnic identity. Even among Blacks in America, notions of race and racial discrimination vary within ethnic groups. Therefore, all of us who are adult educators must be inclusive in our dialogue and understanding of race and race relations. It is incumbent upon us to broaden the discourse to include intergroup perceptions of race and racism as shaped by ethnic group identity and affiliations. Accordingly, as Colin III and Preciphs (1991) put it:

> As adult educators develop greater tools and resources for dealing with a multiracial society and world, we are challenged to engage our understanding of the influence of racism on perceptual patterns and the teaching-learning process. Therefore, an understanding of the role and importance of perceptual patterns must become an integral part of the educational process [p. 62].

Colin III and Preciphs further define *perceptual patterns* as "one's views of the world based on mental images formulated from the standards and ideals of the individual's social reference group" (p. 63). The acquisition of perceptual patterns, therefore, must be understood as shaped by historical, cultural, and geographical contexts. Similarly, any attempts at addressing racist ideologies and practices must begin with an understanding of how history and the politics of location work in the interests of privilege and power to transcend cultural, political, and textual borders in the practice of colonial hegemony (McLaren, 1995).

The United States and its founding documents stand for democracy, liberty, and justice for all. Yet the founding documents, especially the U.S. Constitution, supported the long-term enslavement of African American people, which was overt and cruel and produced a lasting physical and psychosocial impact. The civil rights movement of the 1950s and 1960s brought an end to legal segregation, and the federal and state governments, along with corporate America, began the task of dismantling the structures that created a separate and unequal nation (Feagin & Sikes, 1994). It appeared, on the surface, that the ideology and practice of racism were under attack. However, as Feagin and Sikes (1994) reported, that appearance was short lived, for as early as the mid-1970s, programs developed to rectify racial discrimination came under siege, with the result that group superiority and inferiority based on racial characterizations remain at the heart of U.S. society.

UNDERSTANDING AFRO-CARIBBEAN IDENTITY AND PERCEPTIONS OF RACISM

As Hickling-Hudson (2006) has observed, some of the researchers who explore postcolonial theory in education studies are scholars whose lives have been shaped by postcolonialism, either in the sense of having lived in a former colony and having experienced its decolonizing process or of having lived in a metropolitan center and being beneficiaries of the gains of the empire. I represent the former, one whose life has been shaped by colonial imperialism and later postcolonialism. In Spivak's (1995) view, the colonial subject, or the subaltern, has often been denied voice by elitist theorists who have chosen to write her out of the literary text or, when she is included, have chosen to speak for her. In this forum, I, the postcolonial subject, speak from my own authentic voice. What I say here and the views I share are mine at this moment in time. My views stem from my being the product of the global currents of colonialism, decolonization, and postcolonialism and influenced by an imperialist education indoctrination. As I continue to think, to reflect, and to transform ideologies and self, these views may later change.

As Hickling-Hudson (2004) has observed:

> The Caribbean education system still remains an elitist examination system that tends to privilege a small percentage of the Caribbean eligible population, while hegemonizing the majority. Indeed, in the absence of the colonial masters, it was necessary for a few of the colonial citizens to be socialized to become the colonist in the name of colonial progress. Systems of inclusion and exclusion were in place to make sure that neo-colonial doctrines were transmitted to the promising few to take on the role of keepers of imperialism [p. 297].

I was one of the promising few, identified at age nine, placed in a special class with eleven other students, and socialized through an exclusionary, elitist educational system to carry on the work of imperialism. Later, as a teacher in St. Lucia, I taught the canons of Western ideologies and worldviews to my indigenous peoples, knowledge that served only to reinforce their implied inferiority to Western imperialists. I became a keeper of the culture and perpetuated the exclusionary practices of superiority and inferiority through the imperialist educational system without question. I had been groomed to take on the role of keeper of imperialism. As a result, I was so steeped in the culture that I could not identify practices of hegemony within the educational system. Is it possible, then, for the colonized to later become the colonizer and, similarly, for those who have been racialized to hold racist views, thus becoming the oppressor?

I have lived most of my adult years in the United States, straddling the borders of White America and the Black Diaspora, a place that Hall (1994) calls "in the belly of the beast" (p. 392). Yet through this hybrid existence, I have acquired the roles of associate professor and associate head, head of a large department and not associate dean, in a major research university. To an outsider, these positions are semblances of privilege, positions that grant me much power to dominate my subordinates while I continue to experience domination by virtue of my race. Is it possible for me, a Black woman, while being colonized in academe to be a colonizer of those within and across the races whose locations are perceived as subordinate to mine? Indeed, we must also consider intergroup relations in the discourse on race and race relations. If our perceptual patterns are our mental images of our world—historical and cultural—and our experiences within that world, then it is incumbent upon us to engage in this dialogue with an authentic assessment of the ways by which we acquired our perceptions of self and others. In so doing, we can begin to understand how we acquire our views about race and racism. One place to start is with our educational system.

Racism in education is a process of cultural, intellectual, and physical violence that strips its targets of their dignity and dispossesses them of their culture and resources (Hickling-Hudson, 2004) while showering the colonists with endowments of superiority and power over their captives. Such endowments are internalized and are later manifested in oppressive, racist behaviors. Neocolonial Caribbean education, through its majority exclusionary practices and the indoctrination of a minority to carry on the practices of imperialism, contributes to such a devaluation of humankind. There is no question that a neocolonial education contributes to low self-esteem among students by attacking their self-image and their identities. For example, Hickling-Hudson (2006) has written about the Caribbean history curriculum with its textbooks and examination questions that reflected a colonial interpretation. She cited an incident in which Black Caribbean students were asked to imagine that they were slave traders, and to write essays describing how they would organize the African slave trade.

Such scenarios represent my socialization within a Caribbean system of education. As a result of such indoctrination, the colonial subject learns to internalize success and human value with White identification. A typical thought process goes like this:

> If I acquire the behaviors of my White colonists, then I will escape the negative stereotypes of the typical Black. I will be seen as better than the other Blacks. Being better than most of the other Blacks affords me a place among the minority Black elites and hence a position of power.

This cruel and inhumane curriculum strategy was inflicted not only by Whites but also by the colonial subjects who had been indoctrinated to carry out the works of imperialism. For Black Caribbeans, it was the world we lived in and accepted. As James (1969) reflected:

> It was only long years after that I understood the limitation on spirit, vision and self-respect which was imposed on us by the fact that our masters, our curriculum, our code of morals, everything began from the basis that Britain was the source of all light and leading, and our business was to admire, wonder, imitate, learn;

our criterion for success was to have succeeded in approaching that distant ideal [p. 30].

With such a perspective, is it not possible for the colonized to later become the colonizer? I believe that it is possible.

USING POSTCOLONIAL THEORY AND DIALOGUES ON RACE

Using a postcolonial framework, one can experience how the stereotypes of the non-European "other" were constructed in the imperial literature and the impact of imperial socialization on perceptions of race and racism. Additionally, this framework is relevant not only for understanding the impact of racist constructions on the colonized but also for identifying how these constructions profoundly influenced the learning experiences of children in the imperial center (Tikly, 1999). It draws from the knowledges of indigenous and colonized peoples (Spivak, 1995). As a result, Western educators must be privy to the knowledges and experiences of the postcolonial subject in order to have authentic dialogues about race.

Most important, we must enter this dialogue with the knowledge that postcolonial subjects do not constitute a monolithic group. Therefore our dialogues should not be limited to Europe's colonization and exploitation of its captives. Tikly reminds us, "If we are to take account of the complexities of the postcolonial condition, then attention also needs to be given to how non-European elites defined by ethnicity, cast, class, and gender also legitimize their dominance over other groups through their control over education systems" (p. 612). Therefore any discussion on race is incomplete without an exploration of ethnic group perspectives.

According to Young (2003), "post-colonialism seeks to change the way people think, the way they behave, to produce a more just and equitable relation between different peoples of the world" (p. 7). Using a postcolonial framework to conceptualize racism in adult education discourse is significant in helping students and researchers explore education in a way that recognizes and situates colonized frames of thinking and behaving, thus advancing alternative ways of theorizing race. This method has the potential to disrupt internalized binary notions of race, allowing individuals to move beyond them.

The difficult journey of writing this chapter helped me to identify racism and my own racist behaviors and crystallized my understanding about how colonialism and postcolonial educational systems failed to give me an authentic education. I am a product of imperialist ideologies in West Indian education, but I had not formerly developed the critical lens to understand the damage done by that kind of racialized neocolonial discourse, nor had I acquired such a lens in my bachelor's or master's degree programs in U.S. academe. My doctoral program in adult education and human resource development was no exception. Race was invisible in program courses and classroom discussions, as it still is in adult education curricula across the United States (Johnson-Bailey & Cervero, 2000). Only in my first exposure to race and ethnicity in an anthropology course did I begin to develop a critical lens to observe, not yet to contest, the hegemonic ideologies of White imperialism that had dominated my worldview.

As I sharpened the focus of that lens, I learned to identify neocolonial interpretations and name them in public discourse. At first I could not see racism as my Black American colleagues did. Now, through learning and reflecting and by keeping constant vigilance over my actions and those of others, I am better able to name the enemy. However, my naming the enemy is not restricted to a Black-White dichotomy, as I share Tikly's view that people of color whom society has placed in positions of power and control can be racist to those whom society has deemed to be in minority positions. These persons can be agents of the colonial powers and, as such, can possess internalized racist beliefs. Because this is the case, we adult educators, a multiethnic, multicultural, and multiracial group, must broaden our authentic dialogue about race.

EMBRACING A PRACTICE OF CRITICAL PROFESSIONALISM

As adult educators we cannot afford the luxury of ignoring the colonizing effects of globalization and imperialism and the ways that they inform race and race relations. Similarly, in order to understand the significance of perceptual patterns, how they originate, and their impact on our worldview, we require a curriculum for educational practice that is steeped in reflexivity and critical inquiry—what Lavia (2006) calls a *practice of critical professionalism.* We must have serious professional development efforts that include a strong focus on social justice. Professional development cannot be divorced from social justice issues (Lavia, 2006), and we must come closer to living out the democratic values and committing to social justice (Walker, 1997). The professional development proposed is a deliberate practice in critical professionalism and critical pedagogy.

Thus it is not enough to identify problems of racism in adult education discourse; we must also connect our theoretical understanding of racism with the practical approaches to addressing racist ideologies that have historically framed our profession. Adult education therefore requires professionals who have the courage to challenge imperialistic ideologies and worldviews as well as Eurocentric theories, curricula, and practices within the profession.

I propose that we move away from mere pedagogical techniques or methods in addressing race and race relations to a more postcolonial and revolutionary pedagogical discourse, one that will allow us to evoke the historical and cultural representations that shape our worldviews. To be engaged in an authentic dialogue on race requires adult educators to take an exile from *home* (Giroux, 1992), their place of safety, power, privilege, and comfort. I call on each adult educator to move away from the comfort of that home and become a *border intellectual* (Freire, 1985) so we can collectively engage in dialogues that lead to a more critical *revolutionary pedagogy* (McLaren & Farahmandpur, 2001) in adult education. It is important for adult educators to take a border-crossing journey in order to reconstruct home and to create the culturally relevant classroom.

REFERENCES

Colin, S.A.J., III, & Preciphs, T. K. (1991). Perceptual patterns and the learning environment: Confronting White racism. In R. Hiemstra (Ed.), *Creating environments for effective adult learning* (New Directions for Adult and Continuing Education, No. 50, pp. 61–70). San Francisco: Jossey-Bass.

El Nasser, H. (2003, February 16). Black America's new diversity. *USA Today.* Retrieved April 18, 2007, from http://www.usatoday.com/news/nation/2003–02–16-black-america-diversity-usat_x.htm.

Feagin, J. R., & Sikes, M. P. (1994). *Living with racism: The Black middle-class experience.* Boston: Beacon Press.

Freire, P. (1985). *The politics of education.* Westport, CT: Bergin & Garvey.

Gaines, S. O., Ramkissoon, M., & Matthies, B. K. (2003). Cultural value orientations and accommodation among heterosexual relationships in Jamaica. *Journal of Black Psychology, 29*(2), 187–209.

Giroux, H. A. (1992). *Paulo Freire and the politics of postcolonialism.* Retrieved June 5, 2007, from http://jac.gsu.edu/jac/12/1/Articles/2.htm.

Hall, S. (1994). Cultural identity and Diaspora. In P. Williams & L. Chrisman (Eds.), *Colonial discourse and post-colonial theory: A reader* (pp. 376–390). New York: Columbia University Press.

Hall, S. P., & Carter, R. T. (2006). The relationship between racial identity, ethnic identity, and perceptions of racial discrimination in an Afro Caribbean descent sample. *Journal of Black Psychology, 32*(2), 155–175.

Helms, J. E., & Cook, D. A. (1999). *Using race and culture in counseling and psychotherapy.* Westport, CT: Greenwood Press.

Hickling-Hudson, A. (2004). Towards Caribbean "knowledge societies": Dismantling neo-colonial barriers in the age of globalization. *Compare, 34*(3), 293–300.

Hickling-Hudson, A. (2006). Cultural complexity, post-colonialism and educational change: Challenges for comparative educators. *Review of Education, 52,* 201–218.

Hintzen, P. C. (2001). *West Indians in the west.* New York: New York University Press.

Hunter, C. D. (2006). *Cultural orientation, perceptions of racial discrimination and collective self-esteem among African Americans and West Indian Americans.* Unpublished doctoral dissertation, Columbia University.

James, C.L.R. (1969). *Beyond a boundary* London: Stanley Paul.

Johnson-Bailey, J., & Cervero, R. M. (2000). The invisible politics of race in adult education. In A. Wilson & E. Hayes (Eds.), *Handbook of adult and continuing education* (new ed., pp. 147–160). San Francisco: Jossey-Bass.

Jones, J. M. (1997). *Prejudice and racism* (2nd ed.). New York: McGraw-Hill.

Lavia, J. (2006). The practice of postcoloniality: Pedagogy of hope. *Pedagogy, Culture, and Society, 14*(3), 279–293.

McLaren, P. (1995). Introduction: Postmodernism, post-colonialism and pedagogy. In P. McLaren (Ed.), *Postmodernism, postcolonialism, and pedagogy* (pp. 3–36). Alberta Park, Australia: James Nicolas.

McLaren, P., & Farahmandpur, R. (2001). Teaching against globalization and the new imperialism: Toward a revolutionary pedagogy. *Journal of Teacher Education, 52*(2), 136–150.

Spivak, G. C. (1995). Can the subaltern speak? In B. Ashcroft, G. Griffiths, & H. Tiffin (Eds.), *The post colonial studies reader* (pp. 28–37). New York: Routledge.

Tikly, L. (1999). Postcolonialism and comparative education. *International Review of Education, 45*(5–6), 603–621.

Walker, M. (1997). Subaltern professionals: Acting in pursuit of social justice. *Educational Action Research, 4*(3), 407–425.

Waters, M. C. (1994). Ethnic and racial identities and second-generation black immigrants in New York. *International Migration Review, 28*, 795–820.

Waters, M. C. (1999). *Black identities: West Indian immigrant dreams and American realities.* Cambridge, MA: Harvard University Press.

Young, R. (2003). *Postcolonialism: A very short introduction.* New York: Oxford University Press.

13

Black Skins, No Mask

TAJ JOHNS

I have been a professional adult educator, lecturer, and assistant city manager for years. I realize that in order to establish and maintain my credibility in the adult education arena, it is necessary to publish. Most recently, a group of friends were talking when another educator, who had read some of my published work, spoke highly of a chapter I was writing and asked if I had shared it with anyone in my circle. I said no, dismissing my accomplishment and my friend's honoring of my work. Someone asked me, "Why do you do that? Why are you minimizing yourself?" I had to think: "Am I minimizing myself?" Then I saw how internalized racism remained a thirsty fiend inside me, eager to swallow my self-confidence and consume my esteem. I don't want to appear too proud, too assimilated, or not Black enough. Thinking about my response, I felt a truth in my stomach: I was finding ways to make myself invisible—just as I have been made to feel invisible all these years by the dominant culture. This was my internalized oppression as a woman and as a person of African descent.

After this experience, I began to look at my life as an adult educator. How many times have I minimized a Black student's experience when the student has told me that another instructor was treating him or her unfairly? How many times have I tightened my body in anticipation of being embarrassed by Black students' speech patterns or their loudness, wanting to make them invisible? How many times have I expected less because they were Black? How many times have they expected more because I am Black? How many other educators have not questioned their actions, not examined how internalized racism has made them disconnect from our community, be overly critical, or discredit students' experiences or our own?

Although I have done years of work addressing my internalized issues, they continue to be revealed. These questions led me to write this chapter so that, as educators, we can begin to understand the impact of internalized racism on our struggle to work together and on our patterns of helping one another fail.

> Internalized racism has been the primary means by which we have been forced to perpetuate and "agree" to our own oppression. It has been a major factor preventing us, as Black people, from realizing and putting into action the tremendous intelligence and power which in reality we possess [Lipsky, 1995, p. 1].

DEFINING INTERNALIZED RACISM

In order to open a meaningful dialogue capable of influencing the current pedagogy, it is essential for African Americans to understand how internalized racism has affected their daily lives. "In spite of our vigilant rejection of racism on political, social, psychological and institutional levels, people of African descent have nonetheless internalized racism to a varying degree" (Watts-Jones, 2002, p. 592). Internalized racism has a hold on all African Americans; no Black person has been spared (Lipsky, 1995). And so from a critical race theoretical perspective, a discussion of internalized oppression seems an important and missing component of an examination of racism in the United States.

In any discussion of internalized racism, we must first understand the enormous complexity inherent in this issue. Current thought recognizes that there are psychological and systemic dimensions to internalized racism. The psychological dimension describes internalized racism as a group of behaviors and attitudes that are the results of repeated racial psychological assaults. These assaults, in the form of myths and stereotypes, were created by the dominant culture. Yet the members of the oppressed group incorporate these myths and stereotypes into their belief system, and individuals begin to view and judge themselves and other members of the racial group through this distorted lens (hooks, 2003; Lipsky, 1995; Tatum, 1997; Bivens, 1995). These psychological attacks can result in a mental state that produces behaviors such as isolation, alienation, low or poor self-esteem, shame, and self-hatred.

Shame is a consequence of internalized racism that is often overlooked yet remains a powerful tool used by the dominant culture to control and regulate our behaviors. According to Watts-Jones (2002), there are two sources of shame which can be associated with internalized racism. Shame occurs as a result of Blacks viewing their African-ness only through the lens of slavery or racism and the impending shame that comes from that association. Shame of being shamed keeps the system of internalized racism in place, because we keep our feelings and experiences a secret. Our shame can disconnect us from our internal experiences— muting our feelings, needs, and drives. An overall feeling of "not being good enough" or worthy of some aspiration invades our lifeworld.

Internalized racism described as low self-esteem, color prejudice, stereotyping, shame, or self-hatred is "frequently used to explain or describe 'dysfunctions' or inadequacy among Black people" (Bivens, 1995, p. 2). For this reason alone, it is important that we understand internalized racism as a reaction to systemic oppression that we have internalized. Both psychological and systemic internalized racism sentence us to live in a state of mental, bodily, and spiritual uncertainty, resulting in our fragmenting and disconnecting ourselves from our personal life forces.

Bivens (1995, 2005) suggests that systemic internalized racism causes the real harm to African Americans, but because it is caused and maintained by external factors, we have power to change the impact. Clearly there are some limitations to overemphasizing or applying psychological terms or explanations to issues of race and racism, for in so doing there is a greater likelihood of obfuscating how these factors affect the lived experiences of individuals suffering from racism on a daily basis.

Systemic internalized racism is expressed in the way we people of color support the oppression of one another while upholding White supremacist ideologies. One of my primary findings in my research with the Self Affirming Soul Healing Africans (SASHA) community was our difficulty in embracing the fact that there are as many different ways of being Black as there are Black people (Johns, 2008). Our narrow definition of Black culture leads us to proclaim that a person is not Black enough or, worse, is "trying to be White." Our failure to see our differences is testimony to our systemic internalized racism, just as Whites' failure to see us as individuals is a testament to their racism. We are seeing ourselves as Whites have seen us, invisible as individuals and stereotyped as a group.

I put forward that how we express our internalized racism is connected to our personal developmental histories, which have been shaped by both personal and systemic influences. Therefore liberation from internalized racism must be addressed on the personal level (psychological components) and on the social justice level (systemic internalized racism) if we are to no longer be vulnerable to this type of manipulation.

In the following pages I present findings from a case study with the Self Affirming Soul Healing Africans (SASHA), a group of African Americans who, for over ten years, worked together to unravel the complexities of internalized racism. The exercises and techniques we developed are known as the *SASHA process*.

Figure 13.1 shows the seven steps of the SASHA process; space does not permit a detailed explanation of each step. What Figure 13.1 delineates is that the seven steps are divided into two sections—Self Affirming and Soul Healing. In the Self Affirming section it is essential

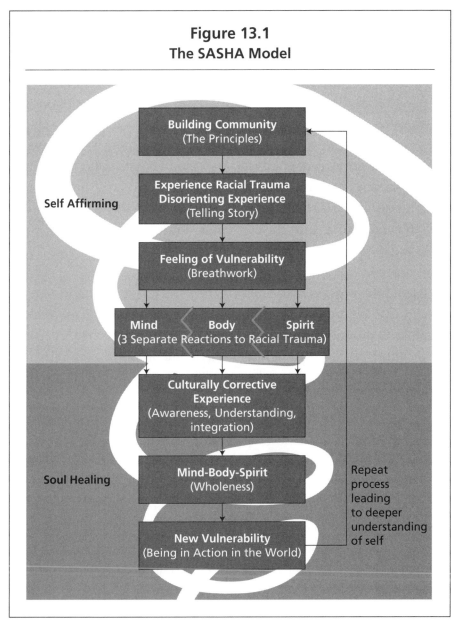

Figure 13.1
The SASHA Model

Building Community
(The Principles)

**Experience Racial Trauma
Disorienting Experience**
(Telling Story)

Feeling of Vulnerability
(Breathwork)

Mind   Body   Spirit
(3 Separate Reactions to Racial Trauma)

**Culturally Corrective
Experience**
(Awareness, Understanding,
integration)

Mind-Body-Spirit
(Wholeness)

New Vulnerability
(Being in Action in the World)

Self Affirming

Soul Healing

Repeat process leading to deeper understanding of self

Source: Design by Jeanette Madden

that a trusting community is established. This allows each person to have a safe place to feel the experiences of racial trauma and to come to terms with old emotional vulnerabilities. Often we do not allow ourselves to feel a racial act; we only defend ourselves or ignore the impact.

The Soul Healing section of the process encompasses three steps through which participants integrate their learning and become vulnerable to life in a new way. They understand when their body is out of harmony and develop methods for maintaining their internal balance. They realize that they are open to choices, to alternatives, and hence to new opportunities. Thomas Parham (1993) put it this way: "You are now vulnerable to a different conceptual understanding of both your predicament, as well as your choices to be (as Spike Lee would say) 'mo betta'" (p. 3).

The SASHA process is an emancipatory learning tool, meaning that participants "are presented with an alternative way of interpreting feeling and patterns of action; the old meaning scheme or perspective is negated and is either replaced or reorganized to incorporate new insights" (Mezirow, 1991, p. 88). Through storytelling and reliving racial incidents in the course of a series of exercises and breathing techniques, individuals are supported while they explore and understand how internalized racism has resulted in the development of distorted meaning schemes.

From our work, the SASHA participants and I learned that internalized racism is a way in which African Americans obstruct their personal and community growth while shaping their racial identity. It stands to reason that in order for African Americans to be effective adult educators and open the conversation of race within the current structures, it is imperative for us to understand how our internalized racism perpetuates the system that works to constrict our expansion.

POSITIONING SASHA PEDAGOGY IN ACADEMIC DISCOURSE

The SASHA process incorporates principles and theories of an African-centered worldview, or paradigm. SASHA as a new pedagogy is a departure from most Eurocentric models of academic knowledge, created under critical race, postmodern, constructivist, or structuralist philosophies. These models are mental constructs of ontological and epistemological philosophies that promote European hegemony, thus White supremacist thought. These are the models saturating the academy. The SASHA process, while influenced by some or all of these philosophies, is positioned in an African-centered philosophy and an Afrocentric paradigm.

The terms *Afrocentric* and *African-centered* are "interchangeable . . . representing the concepts that categorize a quality of thought and practice . . . rooted in the . . . interest of African people" (Wade W. Nobles, quoted in Hill, 1995). These views are "polyrhythmic . . . with simultaneously intersecting realities" (Sheared, 1999); therefore our experiences cannot be situated in a cognitive one-dimensional Eurocentric paradigm nor in a paradigm where individualism is honored. As Colin III (2005) notes, an Afrocentric paradigm reflects a particular value system, out of which emerges philosophical frames, conceptual constructs, and theoretical formations.

Mazama (2001) illustrates the concerns that SASHA addresses when she states, "Afrocentricity contends that our main problem as African [American] people is our usually unconscious adoption of [the] Western worldview . . . and conceptual frameworks" (p. 387). There are many features of the Afrocentric worldview; here I am selecting only a few that best describe the experiences of the SASHA participants. First, for example, an Afrocentric approach to research suggests that the outcome should be the production of emancipatory knowledge focusing on African Americans' experiences from an African perspective. As mentioned earlier, SASHA was developed for African Americans to liberate themselves from issues associated with internalized oppression. Second, Afrocentric ideology suggests learning should awaken a "consciousness that focuses on our victories, not our oppressions" (Asante, 1988). This ideal is supported in the New Vulnerability (phase 7 of the SASHA model), where the individual no longer reacts to the oppressive actions of the dominant culture but instead comes to realize his or her choices, living "in action" with the world as opposed to reacting to negative stimuli that historically have affected African Americans' health and well-being. Third, an Afrocentric paradigm holds an epistemology that dictates interconnectedness, a practice suggested in phases 4 and 6 of the SASHA model, where participants begin to understand and work to maintain a harmony of mind, body, and spirit during racial incidents. Finally, with an African-centered worldview, individual action is also a community action: "Whatever happen[s] to the individual impact[s] . . . the corporate body, the tribe, and whatever happen[s] to the tribe reverberate[s] into the individual" (Akbar, 2004, p. 68).

SASHA builds a community of support and trust so previously denied experiences can be addressed.

Bringing Our Experiences into the Academy

Asante (2006) offers the idea that "the real test for the academy is to see if it can accommodate those whose views are clearly different and perhaps whose aims are to dispel myths, breakdown hegemonic rules, and introduce pluralism without hierarchy" (p. 650). To meet the challenges of bringing the experiences of those from the Diaspora into the halls of academia, thereby developing a racialized pedagogy, we need to establish educator cohorts in which issues particular to our community can be discussed and in which our experiences are acknowledged and our personal issues addressed. If we are to construct a new paradigm, we must examine how internalizing White supremacist ideology has affected our lifeworld. Our work should not be limited to merely exploring the impacts of racism; it should also include a design in which our continued encounters with racism can be explored and those subtle encounters we experience are reframed to support a new consciousness of victories. Our work should be about Afrocentric research that adds emancipatory knowledge to our community (Asante, 2006; Mazama, 2001).

The SASHA model is cyclical; we go through the phases, cycling back to the beginning in order to strengthen our relationship with self and community. As Figure 13.1 communicates, the first phase of SASHA is building a safe community where we, as African Americans, can collectively examine the effects of internalized racism on our abilities to trust each other. As our relationships begin to penetrate our distrust, we can take risks to fully explore our African-ness, using our cultural cosmology, ontology, and axiology to develop meaningful knowledge about our experiences as African Americans.

Offering Community Support Within the Academy

There are three components that are essential for establishing communities where this type of interaction can safely occur. These elements are: continuity of membership, location, and meeting times (Johns, 2008). These three elements enhanced participants' faith in the process and reliability of SASHA. These elements allowed individuals to reframe internalized racial experiences.

Many of us have either heard stories about or have personally suffered racial ignominies in educational, employment, and social settings. This humiliation often precipitates an internal monologue where questions of self-worth, blame, and shame begin to occupy our thoughts. Racial remarks and actions will continue to be present in the ideologies that reflect White supremacy. This form of "[i]nstitutionalized racism and the internalized racism which results from it have given rise to patterns which cause us to mistrust our own thinking" (Lipsky, 1995, p. 8). The face of racism is changing, and one of its new expressions is called *unaware/unintentional racism* (Yamato, 1998, p. 90). This form of racism allows Whites to practice racial acts and then claim, "That was not my intention." Thus an unconscious act can be lightly explained away, with no responsibility taken to alter the behavior. Consequently, it is imperative that we African Americans guard against such attacks by doing our internal work, ensuring that we increase our consciousness of internalized racism so we deem acts or remarks from the oppressor powerless.

If African American learners are to begin to feel safe in an adult education environment, supportive cohorts or communities must be established where those with similar learning experiences, social issues, and encounters with racism can be supported and their experiences validated (Tatum, 1997). When I compare my learning experience doing undergraduate work with my experience in the doctoral program after five years in the SASHA community, the results are remarkable. The difference is that my doctoral experience was approached with the support of community and knowledge of the power of my internalized racism to silence my voice and deny me access to resources.

As African Americans we expend such large amounts of energy repressing racial acts toward our person, explaining racial politics, or taking care of Whites that we lose synchronization with our basic life force. My work in the SASHA community provided a space where I could contemplate healing my life, a loving, nurturing place to slow down, reflect, and create. It is in these slow, reflective moments that I began to hear the whispering of a new dream.

ALLOWING MEANINGFUL DIALOGUE TO OCCUR

Internalized racism makes one "feel intolerant of, irritated by, impatient with, embarrassed by, ashamed of, not as Black as, blacker than, better than, not as good as, fearful of, not safe with, isolated from, mistrustful of, not cared about by, unable to support, or not supported by another Black person" (Lipsky, 1995, p. 7). How can adult educators begin to bring the discourse of race into the halls of academia without addressing the obstacles that prevent us from viewing each other and ourselves in a humanistic way?

Allowing ourselves a venue to explore these issues is paramount for our healing and our community healing. Offering an arena where meaningful dialogue can occur—by developing an intragroup community, for example—is one solution to this concern. In these communities we can have meaningful dialogue, be transparent, and be willing to express our feelings, even through such emotions as fear and shame. Through meaningful dialogue we will develop compassion for ourselves and for group members, allowing our personal triggers to expand our self-awareness. In SASHA there was a conscious intention and a structure established for participants to feel safe. This safety allowed us to remain present with our feelings without projecting these feelings onto group members. We created a venue where we could address "[p]atterns of internalized racism [that] caused us to accept many of the stereotypes of Blacks created by the oppressive majority society" (Lipsky, 1995, p. 8). We deconstructed our feeling of "being angry at, ashamed of, anything that differs too much from a mythical ideal of the middle class of the majority culture" (Lipsky, 1995, p. 8). We began to realize, as one participant said, "What we did to survive racism is okay"(Self Affirming Soul Healing Africans, 1999). We found our bodies, stayed in our bodies, and developed self-love of our total self. As Self Affirming Soul Healing Africans we began to love and respect our body, mind, and spirit. Another SASHA participant serves as a voice for all the community members in this statement:

> With SASHA I feel part of a community. Our community provides for me idealism and hope to make those leaps of faith. Being in community is a real spiritual process. SASHA is not snake oil; that's magic. The commodity we are selling is community in which we can be seen, tender, human and Black in a fuller way. Thank God for community [Self Affirming Soul Healing Africans, 1998].

REFERENCES

Akbar, N. (2004) Akbar paper in African psychology. Tallahassee, FL: Mind Productions.

Asante, M. K. (1988). *Afrocentricity.* Trenton, NJ: African World Press.

Asante, M. K. (2006). A discourse on Black studies: Liberating the study of African people in the western academy. *Journal of Black Studies, 36*(5), 646–662.

Bivens, D. (1995). *Internalized racism: A definition.* Women's Theological Center. Retrieved February 9, 2009, from www.Thewtc .org/Internalized_Racism.pdf.

Bivens, D. (2005). What is internalized? In M. Potapchuk & S. Leiderman (Eds.), *Flipping the script: White privilege and community building.* MP Associates and the Center for Assessment and Policy Development (CAPD). Retrieved February 9, 2009, from www.capd.org/pubfiles/pub-2005–01–01.pdf.

Colin, S.A.J., III. (2005). *Racializing the discourse of adult education.* Symposium paper presented at the annual Adult Education Research Conference, Athens, GA, University of Georgia.

Hill, P., Jr. (1995, Spring). African centered paradigm. *The Drum.* Retrieved December 7, 2009, from http://www.ritesofpassage.org/ds95–1.htm.

hooks, b. (2003). *Rock my soul: Black people and self-esteem.* New York: Atria Books.

Johns, T. (2008). *SASHA case study.* Unpublished doctoral dissertation, California Institute of Integral Studies.

Lipsky, S. (1995). Internalized racism. *Black Re-emergence,* No. 2. Retrieved December 7, 2009, from http://www.rc.org/publications/journals/black_reemergence/br2/br2_5_sl.html.

Mazama, A. (2001). The Afrocentric paradigm: Contours and definitions. *Journal of Black Studies, 31,* 387–405.

Mezirow, J. (1991). *Transformative dimensions of adult learning.* San Francisco: Jossey-Bass.

Parham, T. (1993). *Psychological storms: The African American struggle for identity.* Chicago: African American Images.

Self Affirming Soul Healing Africans. (1998). SASHA archives. Unpublished data.

Self Affirming Soul Healing Africans. (1999). SASHA archives. Unpublished data.

Sheared, V. (1999). Giving voice: Inclusion of African American students' polyrhythmic realities in adult basic education. In T. Guy, (Ed.), *Providing culturally relevant adult education: A challenge for the twenty first century* (New Directions for Adult and Continuing

Education, No. 82, pp. 33–48). San Francisco: Jossey-Bass. Also available from, http://vnweb.hwwilsonweb.com.

Tatum, B. (1997). *Why are all the Black kids sitting together in the cafeteria?* New York: Basic Books.

Watts-Jones, D. (2002). Healing internalized racism: The role of a within-group sanctuary among people of African descent. *Family Process, 41*(4), 591–601.

Yamato, G. (1998). Something about the subject makes it hard to name. In M. Andersen & P. H. Collins (Eds.), *Race, class, and gender: An anthology* (3rd ed.). Belmont, CA: Wadsworth.

14

Immigration, Racial Identity, and Adult Education

Reflections on a Transnational Paradigm of Resistance

LUIS KONG

My personal experience as a Latin American immigrant of Chinese descent has played a role in my understanding of the dynamic of a racialized immigrant experience. Although racism and racial inequality do exist in Peruvian society, as a consequence of colonialism and social and economic rank, most Peruvians see themselves as citizens of a diverse nation, with the rights and privileges provided to active members of a developing nation. In Peru, I was confronted with class issues much stronger than race issues. My behavior and worldview originated from my middle-class upbringing and were linked to my identification with being Chinese.

A CHINOTINO STORY

The historical memory of the vanishing Chinese community in my hometown of Pisco surrounded me with a protective cocoon woven from the indentured servitude of early immigrants and from the Chinotino (Chinese-Latino) cultural and racial mix common in coastal Peru. The Kuomintang and Communist China were part of my grandparents' history. China was a distant country that lived in the minds of Cantonese immigrants who came to Peru to work the cotton and sugar cane fields starting in the mid-1800s (Fukumoto, 1994) and who eventually became Catholics with Spanish names and undistinguishable from the rest of the population (Stewart, 1970). They married Negros (Blacks) and Indios (Amerindians), who shared their class status as laborers and who lived near the bottom of the colonial and postcolonial social order.

I have never felt more Chinese than I did once I came to the United States. As a Peruvian immigrant of Chinese descent, I grew up with complex and dualistic racial signifiers that at times pounded racism and prejudice against Asians (or Chinos—people of any Asian origin) and racially mixed Blacks (or Zambos—people of African and Amerindian descent) and Cholos (or Amerindians). At other times these terms could be used as nicknames without racially hateful connotations. Chinese became conditionally White, with a social status based on class more than race. The famous Peruvian Chinese restaurants, Chifas, became symbols of cultural acceptance and an integral part of Peruvian cuisine (Rodríguez Pastor, 1996). My awareness and experience of race and racism here in the United States and in Peru sensitized me to racial identity and to differing notions of ethnicity and nationality and concepts of race. My identity as an immigrant of Chinese ancestry is something I live with every day, whether I am in Peru or the United States.

As an immigrant I formulated a reality of fear that kept me in the shadows. I did not want to stand out. I felt like a fugitive even though I had not broken any laws. This feeling of not deserving a voice reinforced my invisibility as well as created barriers to social participation in the United States. Although deportation is a real concern among immigrants, the mental construction I created was far more damaging to my social participation than the consequences of the law were. My resistance to this social and generational conditioning came about through a slow process of gaining self-awareness and self-definition, influenced by mentors and organizations working in community projects. I began to see myself in a different light—as someone capable of contributing to a larger common cause and someone whose fear and invisibility were shared by many others.

I am a global immigrant. My awareness of my immigrant legacy, as a descendant of Chinese grandparents, as a third-generation Peruvian Chinese, as a first-generation Peruvian Chinese American, and as a Latin American national, was a result of researching my family's history and the history of Chinese immigration in Peru. Subsequently, I gained an understanding of historical and environmental events that dispersed thousands of Chinese nationals all over the world, creating an extensive racially diverse and complex Diaspora. Again, the product of this complexity is an amalgamation of overlapping realities over time.

My discussion of race opens up the category by viewing the notion of race through the lens of self-identity. My multiple perspectives serve as a foundation to claim an identity that allows a sense of hope and freedom of expression, no matter how different from the mainstream cultural norms. This perspective provides an openness to belong to a cultural group of choice whereby racial identity and formation are integrated into a multiracial and multilingual self as well as being a part of a larger cultural center.

Race identity can be situational in that it can reflect where the racialization of our identity takes place. We can be more or less from here and from there depending on whom we are talking to and where we are presently located (Kong, 2008). We can have a situational racial identity depending on where and with whom we interact. For example, as a Peruvian of Chinese descent, my identity is more grounded in the Latin American experience than in any other experience. I have a greater affinity to South America and Peru. However, after living in the United States more years than in Peru, how I behave, speak, and act has changed.

When I travel back to Peru, I find myself becoming more Peruvian as I reconnect with people and places and participate in the local pulse over time. Even when I look different, I can act like other people around me. Conversely, I can look the same but act differently. For instance on a trip to China, while walking down a street in Guangzhou, in southern China, completely absorbed by the sights and rhythms of the place, for a few moments I became a part of the place as if I were just another Chinese citizen in the eyes of the people around me. However, on the inside I realized that I had very little in common with those who lived in Communist China. Although I am part of the more than thirty-four generations of the Kong family who lived in a village near Guangzhou, I remained a social and cultural island in those crowded streets. I was separated by my divergent experience, language, and political and social beliefs. I was not from there.

In the United States, I become Chinese by the way others see me. I become the perpetual immigrant, not from Peru but, on first sight, from China or Asia. I become part of the polyglot term, Asian American. I become more Chinese than in Peru. The force of racial identity shaped by others reduces how I view the sum of my entire personal life experience. Racial identity is the friction between how I choose to identify myself and how others, including the larger historical narratives, describe me, construct a picture of who I am. To what degree another person sees me as Chinese or Latin American depends on the circumstance, language, institutions, and location where interactions with that person take place. Racial identity is situational and changeable. The changes result in inclusion or exclusion; they reflect how people have viewed racial identity over time and how this perception has influenced the beliefs and therefore the responses to privilege and oppression among people of different racial identities. The definition of race is grounded in inequality and power relationships. Even though biologically there are more similarities among people than differences, what one sees is often how one defines a person's racial identity.

Race lives with me every moment of every day, and it can be peeled away only as I begin to understand and build the places in which I feel comfortable, honored, and heard, places in which being from Latin America and being Chinese, North American, citizen, and immigrant become part of my personal narrative and part of a common dialogue, not part of a system of oppression and conflict. The task is to build institutions and social movements able to construct viral narratives that perpetuate a relational society where dialogue, reflection, and knowledge (social capital) are gathered and distributed without racial identity becoming a barrier. I think that critical race theory offers those of us involved in teaching immigrant learners some useful strategies. My story is their story, and their story is my story.

EXPANDING CRITICAL RACE THEORY

Viewed within a social constructionist framework, immigrants are the recipients of a socially constructed set of codes serving a racialized system of privilege. By resisting and in turn socially constructing their own set of codes and language through dialogue and action and through the creation of their own social and cultural institutions, immigrants can promote a sustainable self-identity, manage a more complex view of race and racial relations, and participate as active citizens in social change. Their challenge is to be able to generate new meanings that can mobilize and support their beliefs and hopes for a better life for themselves and their families.

The importance of seeing immigration and immigrant rights from a social constructionist framework has relevant implications for adult education and adult educators. Social construction offers an opportunity to build a new set of language codes and transform the future. The opportunity of validating the self-definition of a people without *essentializing* their inner qualities as a unique characteristic of a group allows a reconstruction of political and social classifications (Gergen, 1999). We can begin to interpret the world in which we live with a new awareness of our conditions and challenges. This generative dialogue can, for example, guide immigrants toward resisting racial profiling and toward acting in a way that is authentic to their culture and social needs by valuing what works in their community and building a preferred future (Cooperrider, Whitney, & Stavros, 2003).

In the remainder of this chapter, I provide an expanded discussion of race as a socially constructed concept and expand on the usual examination of critical race theory while reflecting on the theoretical work of several writers, including Michael Omi and Howard Winant's racial formation process, as a way to analyze and assess the current pro-immigrant rights actions. As Omi and Winant (1986) state, the conceptualization of race, as it has been generally agreed by social scientists, is a contested arena. The concept of race is dynamic. Its meaning is constantly changing. Race cannot be described objectively, nor can it be treated simply as an illusion (Omi & Winant, 1994).

IMMIGRATION AND CIVIL RIGHTS

Immigration policies have been founded on a racially determined conception of who should be included and who should be excluded from legal participation in U.S. society and therefore who has rights and who doesn't—in essence, who is White and who isn't White. As a consequence, U.S. immigration policy's effect has been to diminish full participation by immigrants through a system of institutionalized oppression that reproduces inequalities in civil society and in educational institutions. Social construction theory serves as the framework for exploring the historically racial nature of immigration policies based on White privilege, and for examining the immigrant rights movement's opposition to racial and legal barriers that increase the challenges immigrants face in their life in the United States.

The civil rights movement has had an important effect on my awareness of race and racism in the United States. The institutions organized during the civil rights years demonstrated the power of reframing and reconstructing the debate on racial and social equity. Most important, the civil rights movement provided an example of what an empowered citizen could do, individually and collectively, in order to change the unequal treatment and discrimination perpetuated by racism and White entitlement. Organized groups like the Southern Christian Leadership Conference (SCLC) and the Student Nonviolent Coordinating Committee (SNCC) made considerable efforts by creating citizenship schools resulting in millions of new voters and increased electoral power (Payne, 1995). These grassroots organizations have been vehicles for social action that have influenced my understanding of what is possible when communities of color get organized and use their social and cultural capital to gain ground in their fight for justice. As institutions of learning and social change, citizenship schools served native-born citizens in their quest to become more active in their communities by their vote, and shifted the imbalance of power in the broader political landscape toward racial, social, and economic equity.

The language of inclusion and exclusion perpetuates definitions and concepts that increase or decrease the rights of immigrants in civil society and in educational institutions. There is a clash between who people think we are and who we truly are. For example, people have asked me if I am from China and if I speak Chinese, but I am from Peru, speak Spanish, and my ancestry is Chinese. The perception of others can put me within the space of acceptance or, depending how I answer, can send me orbiting to the outer edges of marginality and away from privileged space. I believe that community-based organizations are effective in pulling us back into our cultural centers. Through a collective process of dialogue and participation, we begin to construct a positive self-identity that facilitates an engagement in civil society.

SOCIAL CONSTRUCTION OF RACE

A critical reflection in these areas can increase an understanding of the nature of power and of the positionality of immigrants and the institutional systems that oppress them. Historically, adult education began as a call to citizen participation in order to fulfill this country's democratic ideals of full participation and shared leadership and decision making. In order to have a diverse democracy, the concept of race must be expanded and viewed as being in a constant process of formation, as a dynamic racial epistemology reflective of the experiential complexity of living in a changing world with transnational identities. According to Omi and Winant, the concept of race must be understood "as an unstable and 'decentered' complex of social meanings constantly being transformed by political struggle" (1994, p. 55).

Race has played a central and historical role in this country's immigration policies, and subsequently, the institutionalization of those policies has perpetuated a separation of new immigrants from mainstream society because of their status and, at times, racial affiliation. New immigrants are subjected to separation from their families, to barriers to educational opportunities, to a lack of well-paying jobs, and to abuse by law enforcement in cases of racial profiling (Mass, 2009). These activities are seen as normal actions against undocumented immigrants. According to Delgado and Stefancic (2007), racism is imbedded in daily life as the common experience of many people of color, and White privilege serves a purpose, the self-interest of White elites. Groups can become racialized depending on the economic needs of the labor market. Some groups may be favored over others at different times, with images that brutalize or soften their racial stereotypes. This development is called *differential racialization* (Delgado & Stefancic, 2007). The dominant race ideology arises from the friction and clash of a myriad of micro and macro social projects over decades that result in the racialization of different groups at different times for different social, legal, and economic purposes.

On Becoming a Citizen: A Study on Racial Identity Formation Among New U.S. Citizens

Just as the word *hope* is an active verb, so is the word *include*. We, as much as others, partake in the act of including. We are included as much as we include ourselves. As individuals, we have little or no power in seeking social inclusion. So how do we build institutions or social movements that advocate for citizen inclusion? Can a citizenship class serve as a starting point in developing a path to becoming a citizen and therefore enriching one's sense of identity?

In a study I initiated to examine whether a citizenship course aimed at engaging immigrant students in critical thinking and reflection about U.S. history succeeded in its aim and also to look at what impact race has on learning, I found that the course provided the motivation to learn about U.S. civics and about American history, including the struggles of African Americans, the right to vote and be counted, labor history, and civil rights. Students began to value the importance of passing the citizenship test as a way of providing their families with economic security. As a result of this study, I discovered that in addressing immigrant learners' needs, it is important that we determine the role of place, the use of the citizenship school or program, the purpose and function of the site as a place of resistance, and the need to construct a preferred future through understanding and propagation of dialogue (Kong, 2008).

Place and Legal Status Race formation does not necessarily come about without the friction generated by the opposition of adversary communities with different cultural points of view. New citizens maintain their sense of social and cultural identity by sustaining community relationships through organizations such as churches, community cultural events, and family gatherings like baptisms, marriages, or funerals that bring people together to share common experiences. New citizens perpetuate multiple identities by integrating relevant aspects of their life experience with a newly found sense of belonging and identification.

Legal status and the interpretation of legal language relating to immigration directly affect the civil and human rights of a person and whether he or she is authorized or unauthorized to reside in the United States. The importance of a comprehensive immigration reform has been on the news, with politicians arguing for and against proposals ranging from such extreme measures as criminalizing immigrants for what in the past was a civil offense to providing a path to citizenship for millions of undocumented immigrants and their families. The citizenship schools become relevant in their role as a site of resistance and as a space that could be opened to immigrants' own subversive kind of cultural performance (Butler, 1990).

Citizenship Schools   Citizenship schools, citizenship courses, and adult education programs grounded in critical pedagogy can be influential in developing critically reflective learners by providing a space for dialogue and meaning making among participants as an antihegemonic expression of resistance. In the early 1950s, the Highlander Center's education director, Septima Clark, together with Esau Jenkins and Bernice Johnson, instigated the creation and expansion of citizenship schools in order to teach African Americans how to read and write so they could pass a state literacy exam (intended to exclude them) and be able to vote (Horton, 1990). Citizenship schools are active historical sites that contribute to the engagement of their students in social action. As Jacobs (2003) notes, Highlander cofounder Myles Horton envisioned hundreds of involved citizens who, through the work of teachers, would be able to read and write and would become active community participants because teachers "began by assuming that they could be citizens" (p. 145). Both students and teachers are partners in socially constructing what is to come by learning from each other through sharing stories and negotiating curricular content (Arnold, Burke, James, Martin, & Thomas, 1991). The curriculum can play a major role in the construction of this complex, dynamic reality.

Pinar (1993) explains the importance of curriculum as a negotiated racial text that exposes, in the act of teaching, an instructor's own understanding of race and identity. He says, "to understand curriculum as a racial text suggests understanding ourselves as racial texts. By exploring the denied past, we might push back the blacked-out, repressed areas and in so doing understand our nonsynchronous identity as Americans" (p. 63). An understanding of the curriculum as a racialized text is significant in the exploration of citizenship courses and their effect on learners' ability to become new citizens. According to Pinar (1993), identity responds to constantly changing influences arising internally and evolves through the intersection with historical events and through gender and racial formation. He states that race is "a complex, dynamic and changing construct" (p. 61).

For the immigrant learner, becoming a citizen is about managing the contradictions of the here and now, about propagating roots that will not be pulled out, and about anticipating and acting on a preferred and negotiated future (Cooperrider et al., 2003).

Sites of Resistance: Citizenship Schools and Becoming a Citizen

Citizenship schools can act as a critical vehicle against socioeconomic oppression and marginalization of both irregular and regular migrants. Social actions and learning about the nature of citizenship can provide an environment for dialogue, analysis, and action. The concept of participatory citizenship and citizenship schools as sites that counter hegemony and socioeconomic oppression and marginalization is an important element in shaping adult education practices with immigrants who are becoming naturalized citizens. The informal settings of citizenship schools create a space for dialogue and reflection about political and social systems in the United States and their relationship with the adult student's life and challenges.

Propagating Social Change

There is a need to shift to a new paradigm, to an antireductionist and antiessentialist view of immigrants that removes them from boxes with labels like "illegal" or "alien" that do not fit the current patterns of twenty-first-century global migration and border realities. The dynamic nature of postcolonial migration, the historical influences on the concept of race, and the dynamic and changeable nature of racial identity that counters the hegemony of a racialized society impel us to find new ways of seeing and defining oneself.

Freire commented in his last writings (compiled in *Pedagogy of Indignation*, 2004) that a sense of just ire is a source of motivation to act. He said, "I have the right to be angry and to express that anger, to hold it as my motivation to fight, just as I have the right to love and to express my love for the world, to hold it as my motivation to fight, because while a historical being, I live history as a time of possibility, not of predetermination" (p. 59). Immigrants have the right to determine how they engage in civic and economic life, with supporting social and educational institutions that motivate them to act as agents of democratic social change.

EDUCATING TO PRODUCE SOLUTIONS, NOT PROBLEMS

The complexity of racial identity is influenced by a multiplicity of phenomena distributed historically over time and place (Omi & Winant, 1994). The individual is constantly influenced by collective action and the community is influenced by the individual awareness of self and place in the struggle for political validation. A study I conducted with older immigrant learners provided me with a window on their life experiences as they navigated the path toward citizenship, and became increasingly knowledgeable and reflective about their rights, their sense of place, and the importance of citizenship schools in directing them to what they can become in civic life (Kong, 2008).

The field of adult education must make space to confront the myth of racial differences and the discrimination and privilege that arise from those beliefs. As adult educators, we must continue the dialogue on race and education in a world where globalization and neoliberal ideologies threaten to rob immigrants and other actors on the socioeconomic stage of the tools with which they can build a strong meaning into their racial, economic, and political identity. As educators, community organizers, and immigrant rights advocates, we need to know more about what works in organizations and what energizes people to take action, so that we can begin to construct a historical reality that produces more creative solutions than problems (Kong, 2005).

REFERENCES

Arnold, R., Burke, B., James, C., Martin, D., & Thomas, B. (1991). *Educating for a change.* Toronto: Doris Marshall Institute for Education and Action.

Butler, J. (1990). *Gender trouble: Feminism and the subversion of identity.* New York: Routledge.

Cooperrider, D. L., Whitney, D., & Stavros, J. M. (2003). *Appreciative inquiry handbook.* Bedford Heights, OH: Lakeshore Communications.

Delgado, R., & Stefancic, J. (2007). *Critical race theory: An introduction.* New York: New York University Press.

Freire, P. (2004). *Pedagogy of indignation.* Boulder, CO: Paradigm.

Fukumoto, M. (1994, January). Influencia Asiática en las Américas: Chinos y Japoneses en la América del Sur. *Anthropología, 11,* 311–323.

Gergen, K. J. (1999). *An invitation to social construction.* Thousand Oaks, CA: Sage.

Horton, M. (1990). *The long haul.* New York: Doubleday.

Jacobs, D. (Ed.). (2003). *The Myles Horton reader.* Knoxville: University of Tennessee Press.

Kong, L. (2005). Immigrant civic participation and leadership development in citizenship schools: A research study using appreciative inquiry. *Adult Education Research Conference Proceedings, 2005.* Athens, GA: University of Georgia.

Kong, L. (2008). I am more from here than from there: The role of citizenship schools in the construction of racial identity among older adult immigrants. *Adult Education Research Conference Proceedings, 2008.* St. Louis, MO: University of Missouri.

Mass, J. H. (2009, April 3). *De-ICEing the sheriff: The ACLU sues the Sonoma County sheriff & U.S. immigration.* Keynote address at the ACLU-NC Sonoma County Chapter 2009 awards ceremony. Santa Rosa, CA.

Omi, M., & Winant, H. (1986). *Racial formation in the United States: From the 1960s to the 1980s.* New York: Routledge.

Omi, M., & Winant, H. (1994). *Racial formation in the United States: From the 1960s to the 1980s* (2nd ed.). New York: Routledge.

Payne, C. M. (1995). *I've got the light of freedom: The organizing tradition and the Mississippi freedom struggle.* Berkeley: University of California Press.

Pinar, W. F. (1993). Notes on understanding curriculum as racial text. In C. McCarthy & W. Crichlow (Eds.), *Race identity and representation in education* (pp. 60–70). New York: Routledge.

Rodríguez Pastor, H. (1996). Del Kon Hei Fat Choy al chifa peruano. In O. W. Rosario (Ed.), *Cultura, identidad y cocina en el Perú.* Lima: Universidad San Martín de Porres.

Stewart, W. (1970). *Chinese bondage in Peru: A history of the Chinese coolie in Peru, 1849–1874.* Westport, CT: Greenwood Press.

15

A River Runs Through It

Building Bridges Across Racial Divisions in Urban Graduate Education

CATHERINE H. MONAGHAN
CATHERINE A. HANSMAN

We begin by asking the question (using the critical white studies framework, Dyer, 1997), "How do we as White women knowingly and unknowingly engage with the universal norms of Whiteness as we teach?" Of course we intellectualize and read about White privilege, but when we are in the classroom we must admit that White privilege and how we benefit from it is not always primary in our thinking as we consciously analyze the class material or structure. We try to use the critical white studies lens when we are interacting with students; however, we think that our focus is more about race and less about White privilege. It is clear that our privilege as White women affects how we view the world and thus the way we approach teaching. Therefore we strive to keep our privilege foremost in our minds during interactions with students, even when our students—particularly the White students—may not see this as a priority. It is a struggle for us to keep this lens in place.

We recognize that we live in a society divided by race, class, gender, and sexuality. In our city the racial divisions reflect the demographics of location and space—the eastern suburbs are a mix of Whites and African Americans, while the western and southern suburbs are primarily White. The river that runs through the city neatly divides it into these sections. Within the city bounded by the river and Lake Erie, the population is largely African American, with a growing number of Asians, Middle Easterners, and Hispanics. This city has the dubious distinction of consistently ranking as the poorest city in America (DeNavas-Walt, Proctor, & Lee, 2006).

These facts situate us and our stories of teaching at an urban university in a Midwestern city desperately trying to reinvent itself from its manufacturing roots. We are middle-aged, middle-class White women, with doctoral degrees, teaching in adult education master's and doctoral degree programs. The students in our programs reflect the diversity of our city. In addition, many of our students are the first in their families to attempt graduate study. Education is promoted as the key to economic recovery, yet the city and the university where we teach struggle to provide access to educational and economic opportunities for the diverse population.

Our programs and courses address issues of race, class, sexuality, and gender through curriculum, class discussions, and course activities. Students respond with varying degrees of engagement, particularly in mixed race classrooms where race, privilege, and power become main topics of discourse. As White women, we recognize that the intersection of power and privilege resulting from our race may make it difficult for students, both White and Black, to fully engage in these discussions or to see our concerns as legitimate. Conversely, as Johnson-Bailey and Cervero (1998) have discussed, because of our Whiteness our classroom dialogue and discourse concerning these topics may be viewed by the students along a spectrum from trivial to some to laudable to others. We challenge ourselves to practice what we preach in exposing how power and privilege shape our own practices of adult education, exploring how we center discourse regarding race and create change within our classrooms. In order to promote a more equitable world and critical consciousness about the world, we believe that dialogues of race and racism are essential to helping ourselves and our students promote transformation.

FRAMING OUR WORK: CRITICAL THEORIES

To frame our discussions, we examined several theories that could ground our work with students regarding race. One of the first important frameworks we considered is *critical white studies* (CWS), rooted in critical race theory. The foundation of critical race theory is "the uncompromising insistence that 'race' should occupy the central position in any legal, educational or social policy analysis" (Darder & Torres, 2004, p. 98). CWS comes from this tradition in an attempt to "examine the rhetorical struggle over the cultural production of Whiteness with the aim, in Richard Dyer's words, 'to dislodge it from its centrality and authority'" (Lipari, 2004, p. 83). Within this context the aim is to dethrone the unacknowledged lens of White privilege that pervades the academy, our classrooms, and other aspects of adult education from literacy to training and development. CWS is focused on "interrupting White privilege" (Cassidy & Mikulich, 2007), as Whites acknowledge their "white supremacist consciousness" (European-American Collaborative Challenging Whiteness, 2002) and its impact on society.

Without an acknowledgment of the White supremacist consciousness that drives our society, ideas and policies meant to bring about an equitable society are twisted in ways that maintain White privilege as the cornerstone of society while promoting the illusion of greater inclusiveness. For instance, in the beginning of the movement to make discrimination illegal, "color blind meant lifting barriers to full citizenship, but the term now means blind to the effects of prejudice on people because of their color" (Gallagher, 1997, p. 9).

CLASSROOMS REFLECTING SOCIETY

Too many times in our classrooms, the African American students act as storytellers to White students who can choose to engage or to sit on the sidelines of class discussions. In this context, White students may interpret stories of racism as hostility by African Americans, confirming White students' stereotypes of Blacks. Although we as educators see White students' interpretations of the stories as projected hostility, such an interpretation can stop the classroom dialogue, allowing White students to be observers, without engaging or investing in the discourse, and further, it thrusts the African American students into the role of unwilling teacher. Over the years we have begun to take note not only of student exchanges but also of our roles during those exchanges. We have become more aware of our roles and of the way that sometimes, rather than being a facilitator, we take on the role of observer. As instructors, we need to move beyond encouragement and require the engagement of the White students by asking them to recount their own stories and experiences about their awareness of their Whiteness. If nothing else, it might open a discussion about why, as White persons, we do not have any stories because we do not think of our Whiteness as a racial characteristic. Approaching discussions in this way will, we hope, bring to the forefront the real work that needs to happen in the classroom: White racial identity development. White racial identity development (Helms, 1990; Tatum, 1992, 1994) is something that is very rarely discussed or talked about anywhere in our White society; instead, multiculturalism is the focus. As professors of adult education, however, we need to include White racial identity development along with other discussions of race, class, gender, and sexuality in the classroom.

WHO SPEAKS? WHO HEARS? TRANSFORMING HEGEMONIC NOTIONS

Through our discussions of race, class, and gender in our classrooms, we attempt to promote transformational learning among students. *Transformational learning theory* purports that through experiences and discussions, people may come to realize the limitations of their ideas and worldviews (Mezirow, 1991). Although dialogue and discussion may help individuals to change their way of seeing things and making meaning in the world, Mezirow postulates that a disorienting dilemma is the first step in bringing about transformation. Cranton (2002) discusses the importance of critical reflection in change, describing it as a way to work through beliefs and values in light of new experiences.

Given this, we have made a conscious and deliberate decision to seek out ways in which students in our classes can work through their differences and find common threads of understanding (Sheared, 1999). We strive to provide the opportunity for discourse and reflection in our classrooms that can lead to change and transformation. Nevertheless, change does not always occur, and at times, class discussions reinforce the very hegemonic ideas about race and class we are trying to counter. For instance, we discuss developmental and learning theories that honor tradition and norms of women and races other than the White race. But the theories that students seem to remember by the end of their master's study are "traditional" White views of development and learning—from Maslow, Piaget, Knowles, and so forth. So although we promote transformation, in reality our actions may not support transformation. Therefore we fail when we do not spend equal amounts of time talking about the contributions of the many African American founding fathers and mothers, such as Allan Locke (1936) and Septima Clark (1990). There are a number of reasons why we fail to focus more time on the scholarship of peoples of colors: (1) we do not have a solid grounding of our own in this area of scholarship, and (2) we tell ourselves that we are preparing our students for real-world experiences and knowledge. Then we look at other programs and even conference presentations and see that most scholarship is grounded in the White perspective. In focusing on the White founders, we reinforce our students' understanding that the field of adult education is one of Whiteness.

THE RIVER THAT DIVIDES US

The perception of many of our students is that the river that runs through the city divides the inhabitants based on race, class, gender, power, and privilege, with more White students living west of the river and many Black students living east of the river. Some of our students have never crossed the river, either literally or figuratively, in either direction, resulting in wide separations of geography and experience among our students. For example, this divide manifests itself when learners engage in group projects, a staple of adult education. Our White students' and Black students' perceptions of each other affect the way they are able to work together, and can prevent them from understanding and working collaboratively. The racial stereotypes that negatively affect students are operative even though there are many times when African American students have greater education, higher skill levels, and more important positions in their work environments than the White students do. The assumption of the White students that they have more knowledge or better project management skills sometimes results in African American learners moving to the side while less competent White students take over the group projects.

A perfect illustration of this problem of stereotyping is seen in the story of a White woman advisee who came to see one of us about a group project. Her group was made up of two White women and two African American women. The White student implied that she and the other White woman in her group were doing all the work, referring to the other group members as "those people," as in, "I know those people need an education too, but why do I have to work with them?" She assumed that the African American women had few skills to bring to the project, never thinking that perhaps the African American women in the group had decided that the White women were not interested in learning about their skills, so they had moved aside and let the White women manage the project.

What was telling about this situation was that the White woman assumed that we, as White women, would agree with her assessment of the Black students in her group. When we challenged her remarks, she quickly dropped her complaints and left. However, we doubt that our arguments changed her perceptions and assumptions. This incident illuminates the question we continually struggle with: How can we, as critical White adult educators, heed the impact of White supremacy in our lives and the lives of our students, and engage in the work of dismantling it through our programs and courses?

BRIDGING THE DIVIDE: SHIFTING THE TIDE

As White educators, we stand on both sides of the river. On one side is the classroom and the realization that if we are not working to dismantle White privilege there we are perpetuating a racist system that oppresses others on a daily basis. "Fundamental issues of how knowing, thinking, believing, and living are organized—questions of epistemology, hermeneutics, and praxis—are implicated in the maintenance of White supremacy" (Harvey, Case, & Gorsline, 2004, p. 12). On the other side of the river is our need to engage in our own personal journey of grounding our work consistently and consciously in the reality of White privilege and in the struggle to dismantle it. It is only through an analysis of how White supremacy functions that we can generate specific strategies for change (Harvey et al., 2004). The work on this side of the river must be done first if we are to have any impact in the classroom.

For years we have struggled with questions about the effectiveness of our efforts in the classroom to foster transformation in students' thoughts and actions around the issues of race, power, and privilege. We wonder: How far and hard do we push? How often do we engage our students in discussions and activities that focus on power and privilege? What do we do with the resistance that we will encounter? (Chan & Treacy, 1996). Monaghan and Cervero (2006) found that even in classes where the objective was to critique the system of capitalism that "the course simultaneously reinforces different, even opposing orientations at the same time" (p. 379). It appears that in some ways we may be reinforcing ingrained ways of engaging with the dominant system.

The example of White students experiencing stories told by African American students as being delivered with hostility points to the difficulties in engaging White students in deep discussions about racism. We believe that such reactions among White students are common in these circumstances, reflecting White Americans' desire to maintain "the *White* illusion of *White invisibility* that derives from White fear of being seen by people of color" (Lipari, 2004, p. 98). It is unsettling for Whites to hear stories that confirm that African Americans or other people of color are well aware of the racist attitudes and actions of others. White Americans want to maintain the stance that racism is an isolated instance in our society, only perpetrated by those who are hateful toward others, so that they do not have to wrestle with the fact that they can never escape their privilege. In fact, no matter how engaged we are in the critique of the system, as Whites we cannot escape benefiting from the very hegemonic system that we critique.

Through our discussions and reflections in writing this chapter, we have thought of some possible classroom and program ideas that might help us build bridges across the river that tends to divide Whites and other racialized individuals in our classes. We believe these activities can be used to help students initiate steps toward dialogue and discussion about race, racist thinking, and racism. We believe they will help instructors to engage students in reflection and discourse regarding race, class, gender, power, and privilege.

Instead of assigning students papers that discuss only traditional theories, such as self-directed learning, create assignments for course papers that ask students to compare and contrast White theories as traditional mainstream theories with the feminist Afrocentric perspectives found in, for example, Rosemary Closson, Mitsunori Mitsuwa, Mary Alfred, and others writing in this handbook, and also in the work of Patricia Hill Collins (see, for example, Collins, 2000), bell hooks, Juanita Johnson-Bailey, Vanessa Sheared, Peggy Sissel (see, for example, Sheared & Sissel, 2001), and Molefi Kete Asante. Books and journals that include the voices and philosophical perspectives of Blacks, Asians, Latinos and Latinas, and other racialized groups can assist all students to gain a better understanding and grounding in other ways of knowing. More diverse authors and critical topics can be added to texts that are authored solely from the viewpoint of White Americans.

Classroom group work can be structured to enhance students' opportunities to learn about and articulate their racial identities using common frameworks such as CWS. One useful structure is *collaborative inquiry,* described by Kasl and Yorks (2002) as a systematic way to learn from experience. "Participants organize themselves into small groups to address compelling questions that bring the group together...collaborative inquirers engage in cycles of reflection and action, evoke multiple ways of knowing, and practice validity procedures" (p. 3). *Whole-person learning* (Yorks & Kasl, 2002) expands on these ideas by "casting experience as a verb instead of a noun—that is, conceptualizing experience phenomenologically instead of pragmatically" (p. 186). In essence the phenomenon is *learning-within-relationship,* "a process in which persons strive to become engaged with both their own whole-person knowing and the whole-person knowing of their fellow learners" (p. 184). Another group approach is *multiple-group inquiry into whiteness* (European-American Collaborative Challenging Whiteness, 2002). Participants in this approach form groups that are centered on the race of the members of each group; each group's members can then explore critical race theory, CWS, or other theoretical constructs to further their knowing about their own and others' racial identities. In our classes we both have experimented with forming students into *communities of practice* (CofP) (Monaghan, 2007). Communities of practice are groups of people who share common purposes and a desire to learn from each other, constructing their own knowledge about whatever it is they are studying (Hansman, 2001, 2007). Although this may seem similar to other group approaches, the point of participating in CofP is to construct knowledge actively with other community members through dialogue, discourse, and experiences. In CofP, students may use CWS to reflect about their group process and how their own race contributes to perceptions and expectations. The hope is that this will engage them in meaningful dialogue surrounding issues of race, class, gender, and sexuality. CofP, collaborative inquiry, and multiple-group inquiry can help students to look carefully at these issues, not just in the abstract but also in concrete ways that allow for organic and holistic ways of knowing that are inclusive of many others besides those who benefit most from the hegemonic dominant system.

SUSTAINING THE MOMENTUM

Our issues of positionality as White women bring unique challenges to the learners and ourselves as we try to bridge the river of racial division in urban graduate education. In this chapter we examined racial biases that affect our classroom practices related to the issues of race, equity, and social justice. We discussed theories that influence our reflections and hopes for the work that can be done in a graduate classroom to bring about a more equitable society, and we discussed some practical approaches for critical adult educators to use in their classrooms.

As White female educators we believe that in order to sustain the momentum we have started, we must continue to engage in critical dialogue with each other and also work with others who are engaged in the struggle to end oppression. We therefore will continue to explore our own White racial identities and the ways that power and privilege play out in our classrooms and interactions with students, colleagues, and administrators. Hayes and Colin III (1994) have said, "Racism and sexism are societal problems that affect all human interactions and social institutions" (p. 14). From our vantage point of seeing both sides of the river that divides individuals, we know that we need to work on our own sense of White racial identity and how it informs the ways that we interact in the world. Included in our work should be examinations of how we personally perpetuate the system and how we can be instruments to change the system, to question continually the meaning and standards of good adult education.

Finally, when we first started writing this chapter three years ago, an African American man and a White woman, along with many White men, were candidates for the office of president of the United States.

As we conclude our writing here, we are both filled with new hope for America, as Barack Obama, an African American, is now president. For the first time, we think it may be possible that our country can build a bridge over the river of racial inequality—that we can live in a nation where people will not "be judged by the color of their skin but by the content of their character" (King, 1963). We will continue our personal work on dismantling White privilege, encouraging students to examine critically how their perceptions of race and class shape them, and engaging students in the work that allows the audacity of hope that we all can bridge the river that divides us.

REFERENCES

Cassidy, L. M., & Mikulich, A. (Eds.). (2007). *Interrupting White privilege: Catholic theologians break the silence.* Maryknoll, NY: Orbis Books.

Chan, C. S., & Treacy, M. J. (1996). Resistance in multicultural courses. *American Behavioral Scientist, 40*(2), 212–221.

Clark, S. P. (1990). *Ready from within: Septima Clark and the civil rights movement* (C. S. Brown, Ed.). Trenton, NJ: Africa World Press.

Collins, P. H. (2000). *Black feminist thought: Knowledge, consciousness, and the politics of empowerment* (2nd ed.). New York: Routledge.

Cranton, P. (2002). Teaching for transformation. In J. Ross-Gordon (Ed.), *Contemporary viewpoints on teaching adults effectively* (New Directions for Adult and Continuing Education, No. 93, pp. 63–71). San Francisco: Jossey-Bass.

Darder, A., & Torres, R. D. (2004). *After race: Racism after multiculturalism.* New York: New York University Press.

DeNavas-Walt, C., Proctor, B., & Lee, C. (2006). *Income, poverty, and health insurance coverage in the United States: 2005* (U.S. Census Bureau Current Population Reports, P60–231). Retrieved March 10, 2007, from http://www.census.gov/prod/2006pubs/p60–231.pdf.

Dyer, R. (1997). *White.* New York: Routledge.

European-American Collaborative Challenging Whiteness. (2002). A multiple-group inquiry into Whiteness. In L. Yorks & E. Kasl (Eds.), *Learning from the inquiries: Lessons for using collaborative inquiry as an adult learning strategy* (New Directions for Adult and Continuing Education, No. 94, pp. 73–81). San Francisco: Jossey-Bass.

Gallagher, C. A. (1997). White racial formation: Into the twenty-first century. In R. Delgado & J. Stefancic (Eds.), *Critical White studies: Looking behind the mirror* (pp. 6–11). Philadelphia: Temple University Press.

Hansman, C. A. (2001). Context-based adult learning. In S. Merriam (Ed.), *The new update on adult learning theory* (New Directions for Adult and Continuing Education, No. 89, pp. 43–51). San Francisco: Jossey-Bass.

Hansman, C. A. (2007). Adult learning in communities of practice: Situating theory in practice. In C. Kimble & P. Hildreth (Eds.), *Communities of practice: Creating learning environments for educators* (pp. 293–309). Greenwich, CT: Information Age.

Harvey, J., Case, K. A., & Gorsline, R. H. (Eds.). (2004). *Disrupting White supremacy from within: White people on what we need to do.* Cleveland, OH: Pilgrim Press.

Hayes, E. R., & Colin, S.A.J., III. (1994). Racism and sexism in the United States: Fundamental issues. In E. R. Hayes & S.A.J. Colin III (Eds.), *Confronting racism and sexism* (New Directions for Adult and Continuing Education, No. 61, pp. 5–16). San Francisco: Jossey-Bass.

Helms, J. E. (Ed.). (1990). *Black and White racial identity: Theory, research, and practice.* New York: Greenwood Press.

Johnson-Bailey, J., & Cervero, R. M. (1998). Power dynamics in teaching and learning practices: An examination of two adult education classrooms. *International Journal of Lifelong Education, 17*(6), 389–399.

Kasl, E., & Yorks, L. (2002). Collaborative inquiry for adult learning. In L. Yorks & E. Kasl (Eds.), *Learning from the inquiries: Lessons for using collaborative inquiry as an adult learning strategy* (New Directions for Adult and Continuing Education, No. 94, pp. 3–11). San Francisco: Jossey-Bass.

King, M. L., Jr. (1963). "I have a dream" speech. Retrieved November 7, 2008, from http://www.usconstitution.net/dream.html.

Lipari, L. (2004). "Fearful of the written word": White fear, Black writing, and Lorraine Hansberry's *A Raisin in the Sun* screenplay. *Quarterly Journal of Speech, 90*(1), 81–102.

Locke, A. (1936). Adult education for Negroes. In D. Rowden (Ed.), *Handbook of adult education in the United States, 1936* (pp. 126–131). New York: George Grady Press.

Mezirow, J. (1991). *Transformative dimensions of adult learning.* San Francisco: Jossey-Bass.

Monaghan, C. H. (2007). Communities of practice: Modeling lifelong learning. *Journal of Continuing Higher Education, 55*(2), 10–16.

Monaghan, C. H., & Cervero, R. M. (2006). Impact of critical management studies courses on learners' attitudes and beliefs. *Human Resource Development International, 9*(3), 379–396.

Sheared, V. (1999). Giving voice: Inclusion of African American students' polyrhythmic realities in adult basic education. In T. C. Guy (Ed.), *Providing culturally relevant adult education: A challenge for the twenty-first century* (New Directions for Adult and Continuing Education, No. 82, pp. 33–48). San Francisco: Jossey-Bass.

Sheared, V., & Sissel, P. A. (Eds.). (2001). *Making space: Merging theory and practice in adult education.* Westport, CT: Bergin & Garvey.

Tatum, B. D. (1992). Talking about race, learning about racism: The application of racial identity development theory in the classroom. *Harvard Educational Review, 62*(1), 1–24.

Tatum, B. D. (1994). Teaching White students about racism: The search for White allies and the restoration of hope. *Teachers College Record, 95,* 462–476.

Yorks, L., & Kasl, E. (2002). Toward a theory and practice for whole-person learning: Reconceptualizing experience and the role of affect. *Adult Education Quarterly, 52*(3), 176–192.

Looking Inward
A Journey Through Dialogue and Reflections on Race

How does one's personal history or a group's historical legacy shape personal or group views on race? Each of the authors in Part Three, "Theoretical Responses to Race and Racism," grappled with the question, and each chapter offered a different perspective. Overall the chapters in this section offer an insight into the workings of assumptions about racial groups, especially one's own racial group, and the ways these assumptions can limit one's worldview and become a barrier to developing a proactive agenda to eliminate racism. Providing insights from their own practices and revealing their own perspectives, these writers tell what they have learned about race and, more important, how they work to end racism. Despite having theory as an impetus to direct their writings, they attempted to defy the theoretically based edict that race is permanent.

As the section editor and chapter authors talked on the telephone in the process of finalizing their individual chapters, they struggled to find familiar ground and common beliefs on which to base their discussions of race and racism. The driving force behind these conversations and

Part Three as a whole was the section editor, Elizabeth Peterson. Near the end of the process, Elizabeth died. But her presence is ever visible in the words of the chapter authors: Rosemary Closson, Mitsunori Misawa, Mary Alfred, Taj Johns, Luis Kong, Catherine Monaghan, and Catherine Hansman. Here is an excerpt from a transcript of one of their conversations that will allow you to sense Elizabeth's influence. She questioned and asked each of the authors to deal with the permanency of race and racism. Elizabeth began by asking:

> What are the effects of race and racism in a society where privilege is pretty evident?...As we move forward, I supposed that the argument is [whether racism is]...permanent, and if it is not permanent or if we feel like we can make some changes as we move forward, how can we make those changes?...The fact is that there has been endemic racism but that perhaps it's not permanent but there is hope for healing.

So the questions and answers that these authors grappled with over and over dealt with whether they believed healing was indeed possible and what the role is each of us can play in uncovering and discovering the avenues to that place of healing that leads to greater understanding among the races. Elizabeth went on to say:

> I have talked to a number of people about the impact of slavery...
> I remember having a conversation with one woman and she [was] like..."nothing positive came from it."...And I said, I think that we have to begin to think about that differently because I think there were some victories for us as a people just—even based upon survival.... I think that it is a lesson [not just] for African Americans but it is a lesson for all people. To see what can be done in the face of tremendous hardship and resilience that all people can draw lessons from.

While the authors in this section discussed race as it centers around Blacks and Whites in the United States, they also paid attention to race and racism as it exists among and within other ethnic and cultural groups. Elizabeth noted this in her comments concerning conversations she had had with individuals from other racial and ethnic groups:

I have had some discussions with people who are from, you know, Europe and Asia and...there is just this sense around the world, I guess, that African-Americans have not risen up beyond their circumstances...and I say, What's the difference? Well, Africa was colonized by all these nations but they [the Africans] were still at home and they still resisted and so...at this point in time they've got their land. They have their home and we [African Americans] don't have that. And we have not risen up...claimed...our existence in that same way.... One of the things that I took away from Obama's [race] speech the other day was that...some of the changes have already occurred. But [Obama said] that there is still a ways to go. And the other thing about...[racism is that it's a disease] and like any illness you have to work your way back from the root cause. I think that the root cause is something that is very elusive.

The authors in Part Three remind us how difficult conversations on race can be when you begin to have them with members of varying races. Not only do you have to deal with what is in the moment but you also have to consider the history, the storytelling, and the life stories, as well as your own views about the subject, all of which either helps with or prevents moving the conversation to a place of healing and understanding. So what we can note from the stories and experiences shared in this section is that as we all talk about race and racism, we must continue to grapple with the multifaceted nature of discussing and analyzing race and racism, just as described by Elizabeth. Elizabeth and the section authors provide us with an inside view of the complexity of making theory live and work in practice. Foremost in their offering is the importance of connecting theory to one's experiences. According to them, a means for doing this is examining our own place and positionality by analyzing our personal narratives and then working to be part of the solution.

After Elizabeth's death, the remaining editors of this book took over the process of completing Part Three. As we (Vanessa, Juanita, Scipio, and Stephen—three black women and one white male) debriefed ourselves about what we had read and then listened to the chapter authors talk about their experiences, we found ourselves reflecting not only on their words but also on their feelings and their experiences. We begin to wonder and ask ourselves what we had learned about race and racism and its ultimate impact on these authors as well as on ourselves. What we had done with these authors, we ask you now to do with us—read and listen to our words and thoughts. Ask yourself, what can I learn by listening to someone talk about race and racism?

We began our conversation after having read the chapters in this section and having listened to a series of conversations that the authors had had about their chapters. It took place around a table in a well-established hotel in Chicago. Juanita began the part of our dialogue we focus on here by saying, "But I keep hearing that the battle is won. There is a Black man in the White House and we now live in postracial and postethnic America." Stephen then picked up that point and summarized some key ideas of Part Three:

> I think most...would say that this is a transformational moment and marks a massive movement forward in this country.... And in fact a more plausible interpretation is that this situation will be co-opted to underscore how enduring our structures will be. While we see...his face...that sort of public face has not really changed anything. It's made racism even easier because now it is going to be even more covert and subtle and anyone can just say of course things have changed because now we have the nation's first African American president.
>
> I'm also thinking about it, for me, in terms of how some of the authors approach this dilemma of the double consciousness. Because to some extent I see the authors in this...section...have either resolved the dilemma or are in the process of doing it. My sense,

in putting it back to a historical time…what you're talking about is the power to define…. My experiences and my understanding initially of racism are grounded in the Euro-American, African American and African Diaspora context. That's how I understand racism. But not as being a perpetuator. Because there's a power differential. And there's social cultural racism and there's intellectual racism.

Although race and racism were at the heart of the conversation, we began to see that the authors in this section were challenging us to look within ourselves to find out how we had begun to look at ourselves as being different and similar, all at the same time. As each of us reflected on the words on the pages, we found that the way each author responded to the issue of race and racism was the same but also different and rather interesting, for each of these authors seemed to say that racism is in all of us. So it was really interesting to take what the authors had said in their telephone conversations and compare it to what they had written. They appeared to be formulating and framing a counternarrative to critical race theory. They also appeared to be focusing in on internalized racism and the ensuing acculturation, assimilation, and internalized oppression that come with living out the counternarrative. We also noted with great interest that during the conversations the authors had on the phone with Elizabeth, there was agreement that racism is endemic, but there was also a lot of commentary about how it wasn't necessarily permanent, or that the authors hoped it was not permanent, which leads one to begin to theorize about what it mans if racism is not a permanent state. This seems contradictory to the narrative that critical race theorists express: that is, that racism is a permanent state and needs to be addressed wherever it surfaces. The authors in this section present a new counternarrative to the existing narrative that racism is permanent. The struggle for understanding how one's race is influenced by racism looms large in the chapters in Part Three.

Although we noted their clear ongoing struggle to deal with the ways in which race and racism had negatively affected their lives, we found hope in what these authors had spoken and written. As we reflected on their written and spoken words, we began to notice the importance to them of seeking and discovering hope, which they had expressed in both mediums, and we noted the importance to them of finding hope in their lived experiences. It is not just in what they wrote and said about their own individual lives; it is also in what they suggested they saw within each other. That is, we must search within. We also began to note the connection between looking inward and seeking and working for justice, not just for oneself but also for others. Each author shared the belief that CRT is a perspective that spreads the blame—that equalizes the playing field for others. And if you equalize it, then it's easier to bring people together. In other words, people begin approaching the eradication of racism as a shared responsibility, that begins to give one a sense of comfort.

We believe that this, ultimately, is how you bring people together. By taking them away from the classroom table in the academy and bringing them home to their kitchen tables. It is through people's shared understanding, through the mixing and blending of ideas that occurs best at places of free expression like the kitchen table, that individuals will uncover and discover greater knowledge of and respect for each other. When we, you and I, share a kitchen table dialogue, it's not a conversation just about you and it's not just about me either—it's about *us*. So you not only help yourself and I not only help myself but we help each other. The kitchen table dialogue allows us to engage in a conversation with a perspective that is beyond theory and practice. It is a conversation that touches our souls and the lived contexts of our everyday lives.

As the members of the editorial collective read through each of the chapters in this section, it became clear that as the ideals and concepts of critical race theory are introduced into the conversation, in addition to gaining greater understanding, one begins to recognize that change must occur in the way all of us see and talk to one another. Moreover, one sees more clearly than ever the need to obtain social justice for those who are disenfranchised and made invisible because of the color of their skin—their race. More often than not the majority of people talk about social justice, but what do they actually do? As Scipio aptly states, "It's like being downstream and rescuing people from the river .... At some point someone has to go to the source of the river and rescue people before they fall into the waters."

And so as we sat around our kitchen table in our editorial roles, we found no resolution but were somewhat taken aback by the words of these six authors who were grappling with theory as a means of finding answers to their fervent questions about race and racism. What we had expected from them were lofty treatises and complicated discourse. What we found instead were the sounds of hope and the longings of a weary few for a better day.

PART FOUR

Reframing the Field Through the Lens of Race

The five chapters in Part Four, "Reframing the Field Through the Lens of Race," examine the paradigmatic perspectives people use in relation to race and racism, discussing how focusing on centering these sociocultural factors can change or reframe the ways in which we teach, learn, and work in adult education. The contributing authors provide insightful analysis and in many instances culturally grounded analytical and interpretive frameworks that can be employed in research, scholarship, and practice. These chapters open new areas of discussion and expand the dialogue about the role of race and the impact of racism on adult education practice and knowledge production. The information provided in this section, if reflected and acted upon, will result in significant progress toward the conceptual reconfiguration of the content of adult education and will encourage a much needed paradigm shift in the purposes and goals of our practice.

When the chapter authors began their work, there was no discussion regarding the existence of racism. As one author stated, "You can't encounter what doesn't exist, and I am sick and tired of discussing that." And so were the others. So the discussion started with each sharing her experiences, which seemed a natural beginning. It is interesting to see the kind of affective comfort zone that emerges when individuals are sharing space with others who *know* what they are talking about. Although the majority of the authors' lived experiences were within the usual context of Black-White encounters with racism, the inclusion of the Asian perspective in this group not only expanded the discussion but reinforced what many knew, that the "other" in U.S. society includes more groups than the members of the African Diaspora.

As the authors discussed their personal encounters with sociocultural and intellectual racism, it became apparent that each one, by rejecting the ideas of racial inferiority, had resolved what DuBois (1903/1995) referred to as the "dilemma of the double consciousness." In essence, as their personal narratives indicated, each author had engaged in acts of conceptual disobedience that led to the reconstruction of meaning constructs and in some cases the introduction of new ones. And then the question was asked, "So what? So what if we understood the racial socialization process that deems one group superior and others inferior and the implications? So what if we knew that those who have conceptual and definitional power use that power to shape behavior?"

As they spoke of what they do in their practice, it became clear that each author, in different ways, had committed herself to incorporating acts of *conceptual disobedience* into her practice. Although the approaches varied, it was clear in these authors' racialization of the discourse that there was no conceptual comfort zone for White racism.

In Chapter Sixteen, "Mammies, Maids, and Mamas: The Unspoken Language of Perceptual and Verbal Racism," Doris Flowers focuses on the racist use of language and its role in shaping attitudes and influencing behavior. She introduces critical discourse analysis (CDA) as an analytical tool for understanding the dominant role of language in the formation of racist images and behaviors. Additionally, she presents an instructional strategy, real conversation in real time (RCRT), that facilitates the learner's understanding of the conceptual correlations between language and racist perceptions and behaviors.

Barbara Ford in Chapter Seventeen, "The Race Card," employs elements of the African-centered paradigm as an analytical and interpretive frame in constructing the context of discourse that looks at the impact of racial socialization on identity development and learning. She presents culturally grounded concepts to frame discussions about the racial socialization process and how it influences identity development and the learning process.

In Chapter Eighteen, "Expanding the Racialized Discourse: An Asian American Perspective," Ming-yeh Lee expands the discussion beyond the traditional Black-White dichotomy by offering an Asian-centered interpretation of the concepts of heterogeneity and polyrhythmic realities. She centers her discussion on the impact of racist connotative and denotative descriptors on adult education curricula and research.

LaJerne Terry Cornish's "Challenges and Approaches to Racializing Discourse in a Privileged, White Dominant Society," Chapter Nineteen, offers a way to racialize the discourse on White identity development from the perspective of the "us" (Euro-Americans). She advocates the use of White identity development models to assist students to identify and understand the culturally grounded beliefs and assumptions that undergird racist behavior, whether it be intentional or unintentional.

"Using an African-Centered Paradigm for Understanding Race and Racism in Adult Education," by Derise Tolliver, Chapter Twenty, provides an introduction to the Africentric philosophical concepts of twinness and complementarity, not only as a way of knowing but as analytical tools and interpretative tools.

REFERENCE

DuBois, W.E.B. (1995). *The souls of Black folk.* New York: New American Library. (Original work published 1903)

16

Mammies, Maids, and Mamas

The Unspoken Language of Perceptual and Verbal Racism

DORIS A. FLOWERS

Over the course of the last eighteen years, I have thought many times about the varied experiences I've encountered on my way toward becoming a full professor in the university, a position in which I now find myself working. I went from the point at which I was offered the position to the point at which I had to rethink, reflect, and reassess whether or not I would stay in the field of communication studies to the point of making a decision about moving into the field of adult education. For you see, my journey into adult education did not begin by choice but by necessity. A necessity forced upon me, as a result of students and faculty colleagues to whom I had entrusted my career but who then seemed to turn their backs on me. Initially, I found myself asking questions like, "Why is this happening?" and, "What have I done to cause my colleagues to take their support away from me?" As I reflect back over the last eighteen years, upon experiences and incidents that have occurred in my life, these two factors stand out—language and race.

As a Black American woman member of the academy, I know that my academic experiences of teaching, research, student advisement, and collegial interaction, and even those experiences that appear more social, have all been shaped by skin color and language. For many Black Americans born in the United States before the 1960s, it is probably no surprise that race, as defined by skin color, is a factor in how they think, act, and are treated in American society. And given the historical and social context, along with the legislative acts that have addressed issues of race in America, it is clear that for many their social or economic strata were affected or determined by the color of their skin. And even though changes have occurred because of laws passed or policies enacted, like voting and housing rights acts or affirmative action, these changes have not eliminated the ultimate and very distinct act of racism. It is my belief that the lived experiences of Black Americans are multilayered, which means they include issues of race, gender, language, age, history, politics, economics, and class, to name a few. Although I believe all of these factors have an impact on how Black Americans have come to see themselves, over the last eighteen years I have come to believe that the intersection of race and language is a factor that we do not spend enough time discussing. And more important and on a more efficacious level, how do racism and the language that is used to encourage it or diffuse it affect teaching and learning and ultimately actions between and among racial groups?

Society has had an interesting way of structuring the language that references and describes "others." We, as social beings, encounter one another with words, therefore language is a completely social construction that requires there be a relationship. This communication relationship is already designed as a hierarchical language encounter, given that one person controls the knowledge through language. Racist language as I will refer to it throughout this chapter is often grounded in the social construction of race, ethnicity, gender, and other marginalizing characteristics related to the more dominant power group's assumptions that exclude "others" from either resources or opportunity. These prejudicial attitudes about "others" are usually formed out of a belief system that is communicated about other individuals and groups. So, in order to know racist language, one must use racist language that communicates prejudices. Van Dijk (1987) states that apart from—often minimal or even absent—observation and interaction, White people learn about minorities mainly through talk and text. The intent of this chapter is to examine how language is used to communicate prejudice, bigotry, and discrimination. In doing so, I offer some contextual application of racist language, out of my personal experience. Finally, I offer a model of how we might be able to use language to engage one another in conversations that promote awareness, understanding, and truth about others.

So this chapter attempts to provide us with an opportunity to focus on these factors. And so I am left to critically reflect and ask myself, "And I'm still a nig____ woman?" I will reflect on this ever present question using *imagery* and *perception* throughout this chapter.

RACISM AND LIVED EXPERIENCES

After receiving my doctoral degree I accepted a postdoctoral position at a Big Ten university. I was excited and anxious as I began my career in academia as a researcher, scholar, and professor. I worked with another research assistant who was a White male. Our research focused on children and adults who had language-processing difficulties. After I conducted a test on a White child, his mother insisted on speaking to my colleague. I heard her ask him, "How did he do with that nig____ woman?" Those words reverberated in my soul as if I were in an echo chamber. While I cognitively understood the historical reasons for her behavior, reasons that made African Americans invisible, even those in positions of authority, I was not affectively prepared for the question. After twenty-five years of education that included earning a PhD degree from the University of Virginia, I was still a nig____ woman, being viewed through a racist lens as subservient and uneducated, with the perceived identity of a mammy, maid, or mama. I was reminded of what Malcolm X said when asked, "do you know what white racists call black Ph.D.'s?" His answer was, "You call him a nig____" (Malcolm X & Haley, 1973, p. 284).

RACISM CONVEYED THROUGH LANGUAGE: WHO AM I?

This chapter's title, "Mammies, Maids, and Mamas," was chosen with the intent to (1) provoke the imagery associated with these words; (2) convey the social meaning of discriminatory practice through language, and (3) uncover the complexities of racism. The expression of power in this instance is in the syntactical and contextual metaphor. However, we understand too that power and position have a significant role in our understanding and interpretation of racism.

Even though less overt, dismissive statements are used quite casually within our profession in our conversations and scholarship. The seemingly innocent act of communicating through scholarship and curricula is saturated with language that often marginalizes peoples of color. It is the language of deception and tends to exclude many people of color from the complete dialogue, from conversation, and ultimately, from full participation in activities. Collins (1998) and hooks (1993) suggest that racism is acted on using language that is less overtly racist and more subtle. Collins (1998) refers to this as "racially coded language," which does not explicitly refer to race but race is embedded within its context. Matsudo, Lawrence, Delgado, and Crenshaw (1993) describe race-based language as a form of hate speech that is used to demean and degrade and that evokes or conveys a message of inferiority and of persecutory and degrading acts toward marginalized or oppressed individuals or groups. It leads them to ask, "Who am I?" and, "Who am I in relation to those in power?"

MAKING THE CONNECTION: RACISM AFFECTS RELATIONSHIPS

It is through language that we make human connections. It is after all the defining characteristic of human beings, distinguishing them from all other mammals. Language is a repository of a culture's worldview, an instrument of social interaction, an indicator of social identity, and the primary vehicle of learning and maturation for education. Recognizing the importance of language to humans is critical to understanding the inequities that exist among groups of people. Language, both spoken and written, can be racially coded to implicate certain groups, and language is most certainly political. It is politicized as an instrument for not only describing events but also shaping their meaning and thus shaping the political roles officials and the general public play (Edelman, 1977). Language is used covertly to structure social problems that are then categorized into various political departments that scatter and diffuse the issues even more. This often makes the issues, whatever they are, appear unrelated to the real issue of *race*.

Racism is not just an active gesture; much more importantly it is words, language, and perceptions that have been institutionalized and operationalized daily. Clearly, language is the ultimate channel of communication used to define our thoughts and ideas. It is important that we, as adult educators, examine the use of language as a racial instrument that validates the assumptions embedded in the ideology of White supremacy, and as an instructional tool that can facilitate a critical dialogue regarding race and racism.

ASSAULTING WITH WORDS

Words, letters, sounds, and symbols are spoken and used like weapons to hurt and dehumanize people every day. Words are hurled like stones or knives at a target—"bitch," "ho," "nig___," "jigga-boo," "coon," "spook"—to either kill or, at a minimum, bruise the soul. How many times have you been referred to (called a name) or described using words that are meant to insult and assault you? Not just offensive language but language that is attached to prejudicial belief toward you based on your race, ethnicity, gender, religion, or sexual orientation? Language meant to discriminate against or harm a person is hateful and racist and is referred to today as *hate speech*. It is language used too often and with an increasing level of comfort in our society.

Recently, we witnessed the broadcast degradation of Black women by a public figure when Don Imus, who at the time was a radio and TV talk show host, uttered those words referencing the Rutgers University female basketball team as "nappy-headed hos." It literally was the shock (jock) heard around the world. Although this is not the only example of a public display of verbal assaults, it is the one that most Americans heard loud and clear. Not since the civil rights movement has this country witnessed such a resurgence of the acceptance of hate speech, racist language, and verbal attacks. Leets (2001) suggests that derogatory speech content, ethnophaulisms, and unpleasant paralinguistic communication can all be experienced as verbal aggression, which hurts feelings, causes mental anguish, and damages the personal and social identity of the target of such utterances. Hate speech is intentional language used to cause damage to the receiver.

USING CRITICAL DISCOURSE ANALYSIS

Earlier I offered my personal experience as an example of the racist nature of language and the power that words have for the speaker and for the receiver of those words. Within language, racism is hidden within the context and content of the dialogue or conversation. According to critical discourse analysts, language is not powerful on its own. Language gains power by the use powerful people make of it. This explains why critical discourse analysis (CDA) often chooses the perspective of those who suffer, and critically analyzes the language use of those in power who are responsible for the existence of inequalities and who also have the means and opportunity to improve conditions. CDA emphasizes the need for interdisciplinary work in order to gain proper understanding of how language functions in constituting and transmitting knowledge, in organizing social institutions, or in exercising power. And ultimately, language gains its power from the person using it. So when words are racist, homophobic, sexist, or biased in any other form, language hurts.

RECOGNIZING RACISM EMBEDDED IN CONTEXT

Although the incident I shared was a conscious and overt use of language, most racist language is integrated and injected into our lexicon more covertly. Since that time I have had the opportunity to explore language from many perspectives. As a speech and language pathologist, I was taught to view language usage or nonusage through a lens of deficiency. From this perspective, language is assessed to determine whether it is impaired or deviated from what is considered normal, and normal language is what is produced when one is able to articulate and produce language structures that are within a standardized system that is commonly known as *Standard English.* While this perspective is warranted and not uncommon for the profession or professional, it has been met with concern over the years when words such as *deviant* and *deficient* are applied to the speech characteristics of African Americans.

Racializing language in this instance relegates the speech and speaking of all African Americans to a category labeled as inferior or substandard and different from the mainstream language. This idea of deviancy within the spoken vernacular (Ebonics or Black dialect, for example) of African Americans is not a new phenomenon. In fact, language spoken by African Americans has historically been viewed as defective and flawed, resulting in its being scrutinized, criticized, and condemned by most speakers of Standard English, who are often White Americans.

HEARING THE SILENT LANGUAGE OF RACISM: SILENCING

When we talk about *silencing,* we typically think of the individual or person whose voice or language is left out or excluded from the conversation or intellectual discourse. However, silence can occur as a passive way of avoidance and can become racist when we don't confront the usage of language that evokes racist behaviors or thinking (in other words, our silence can say, if it's not coming from us, then it's not our issue). The silent language of racism can also be seen through the exclusion of voices and perspectives, the mystification and coding of language, and the use of semantics that erase race and gender from the discourse. Racist language tends to masquerade in the rhetoric of *color blindness*. While this is relevant, there are also other occurrences of taking away people's voices and silencing them. People impose semantic silence so as not to deal with the substance of what is being described and discussed, so others can never get to the true meaning.

ENGAGING IN REAL CONVERSATION IN REAL TIME

I introduced the concept of *real conversation in real time* (RCRT) in Flowers, Sheared, Martin, and Lee (2005) and Flowers, Wiessner, Lee, and Sheared (2007). RCRT is an instructional strategy that I developed as a way to help me address the issues of race and racism in the adult education and the equity and social justice courses that I teach. It has become a tool that I use with my students to engage in conversations that are difficult and painful for many, as they often have to confront issues about their own beliefs and actions as they pertain to race and racism. Although the use of dialogue is not new, what I needed was a way to address these issues with immediacy and authenticity while removing the constraints on language so as to extend the conversation.

Real conversation in real time is about having an authentic voice and sustaining conversations on difficult issues such as race and racism. The ultimate goal of this process is for students to become aware of the critical issues that create barriers to understanding the conceptual correlation between language and racism. The strategies for engaging students are fairly simple however highly effective when given the right circumstances. Listed in the following sections are a series of steps that I believe we can use to encourage real conversation in real time.

Creating a Learning Community

When we are creating a learning community, hooks (2003) states that we need to forge a community that values wholeness over division, and that the democratic educator must work to create closeness by facilitating the establishment of relationships that are built on trust and honesty. Participants are required to honor the lived experiences of others and as much as possible to be open and honest with what they say. This means that we are all willing to engage in dialogue or at least willing to listen to others.

A learning community allows students to critically reflect on their lives and also on their positionality and how it relates to other experiences. While we all understand the passion that these topics carry, everyone is held accountable for his or her language and any verbal or nonverbal expressions. This learning community is developed over time, which allows for critical self-reflection.

Facilitating and Relationship Building

The class begins with the students developing guidelines by which they will operate; this provides the first opportunity for them to engage in conversation or dialogue. Additionally, they are assigned a topic in which they will facilitate the discussion. It is interesting to note that the students of color typically respond to the topics on race and racism with the passion and sincerity that is reflective of their lived experiences. The Euro-American students are eager to engage until the conversation moves into the area of racial oppression and how it benefits Whites. Up to that point they can theorize but are reluctant to make the personal connection or to engage in moral imagination. Pugh, Ovando, and Schonemann (2000) describe *moral imagination* as the ability to reason from multiple perspectives and experience empathy. A lack of moral imagination prevents people from connecting with the experiences of others, thus preventing the conversation from moving forward.

Sustaining Dialogue on Difficult Topics

As the students progress in the class, they are given numerous opportunities to engage with their peers and me in critical dialogue on race and racism. I make myself a part of the process of racializing the discourse, following Freire's (2002) suggestion that the instructor must de-center himself or herself. The students are initially surprised and skeptical about my new role. But what happens in the classroom are conversations that acknowledge and explain the lived experiences of others.

There may be some initial reluctance because some are unfamiliar with the process, but they do make the effort to enter the conversation at some point. RCRT is about effective communication that includes recognizing and respecting silence. More times than not, this *silent space* is a place of critical cognitive and affective reflection.

USING LANGUAGE THAT GIVES VOICE

There is no doubt that race and racism are among the most difficult topics on which to engage mixed-race groups in dialogue. In adult and higher education, those who believe that we should engage in conversation about these topics would without hesitation say that race and racism are not off limits. However, the truth is really that in order to truly enter the conversation on race and racism, individuals must reveal themselves in a way that means relinquishing all rights and privileges that Whiteness or positionality (as a professor, for example) bestows. This sense of entitlement is what prevents the discussion to move past the abstract. And while theory has its place in the literature as it relates to race and racism, it often uses language which (1) continues to exclude those who have been oppressed, (2) obfuscates and denies the racialized lived experiences of people of color, and (3) disconnects race and racism from human relations and instead simplifies its impact on people and reinforces negative and false images of African American people. Theorists such as Matsudo et al. (1993) suggest that the experiential knowledge of peoples of color can lead to a better understanding of the impact of race on marginalized groups and the overt and covert benefits that members of the dominant society derive from this oppression.

And so as an African American woman professor in higher education, if I am to make a difference in the perception of Black women as mammies, maids, and mamas, then I must challenge the status and use of racist language with other language that provokes imagery, conveys the social meaning of discriminatory practice, and uncovers the complexities of racism. Because language is socially constructed and requires a relationship, it is already designed to set up a hierarchical framework that intersects with race, ethnicity, gender, and other factors that identify otherness or marginalization. Racist language often masquerades as acceptable speech and is used quite inconspicuously in textbooks, policy, and everyday conversations. That means real conversation in real time is critical to our profession if we desire truth through our exploration of knowledge and if we desire to understand others while accepting the differences among us all. There is tremendous power in the relationship that develops through authentic conversations. RCRT is an attempt to bring the critical issues to the forefront so that there is no longer a hidden agenda or curriculum or knowledge. It becomes a necessary method for inquiry purposes that adult and higher education professors can and should include in their curricula and apply to their practice in order to engage their students and their colleagues in authentic dialogues and discussions about both perceived and verbalized acts of racism, race, and linguicism. The goal is to move us from and through our own perceived notions of race and others to an awareness that brings clarity and understanding by developing a relationship to promote dialogue and discussions that use language to empower.

REFERENCES

Collins, P. H. (1998). *Fighting words: Black women and the search for justice.* Minneapolis: University of Minnesota Press.

Edelman, M. (1977). *Political language: Words that succeed and policies that fail.* New York: Academic Press.

Flowers, D., Sheared, V., Martin, L., & Lee, M. (2005, June). Women of color on teaching race. *Adult Education Research Conference Proceedings, 2005.* Athens: University of Georgia.

Flowers, D., Wiessner, C., Lee, M., & Sheared, V. (2007, June). All-American apple pie or chocolate sundae: Introspections from the margins of race and gender. Paper presented at the 48th annual Adult Education Research Conference and the 26th Canadian Association for the Study of Adult Education conference, Mount Saint Vincent University, Halifax.

Freire, P. (2002). *Pedagogy of the oppressed.* New York: Continuum.

hooks, b. (1993). *Teaching to transgress: Education as the practice of freedom.* New York: Routledge.

hooks, b. (2003). *Teaching community: A pedagogy of hope.* New York: Routledge.

Leets, L. (2001). Explaining perceptions of racist speech. *Communication Research Journal, 28,* 676–706.

Malcolm X & Haley, A. (1973). *The autobiography of Malcolm X.* New York: Ballantine.

Matsudo, M., Lawrence, C., Delgado, R., & Crenshaw, K. (1993). *Words that wound: Critical race theory, assaultive speech, and the First Amendment.* Boulder, CO: Westview Press.

Pugh, S., Ovando, C. J., & Schonemann, N. (2000). Political life of language metaphors in writing about diversity in education. In C. J. Ovando & P. McLaren (Eds.), *Politics of multiculturalism and bilingual education: Students and teachers caught in the cross fire* (pp. 3–21). Boston: McGraw-Hill.

Van Dijk, T. A. (1987). *Communicating racism: Ethnic prejudice in thought and talk.* Thousand Oaks, CA: Sage.

17

The Race Card

BARBARA FORD

As an African American woman scholar, I determined upon entering the field of teacher education and Black studies, or Africana studies as it is now referred to, that I would dedicate my research and teaching practices to the development of young Black children. So, for the past ten years I have taught courses both in Africana studies and elementary education. As I have reflected on the issues and needs of the students who enter my classes, I have discovered that no matter what ethnic, racial, language, gender or sexual orientation, religious, age, or other background they bring to the classroom environment, the factor or topic that causes them the most trouble is race. Whenever that term *race* comes up, I note that students are either very open or resistant to examining how it affects the teaching and learning environment or the developmental stages of the Black child. Nowhere do these types of conflicting thoughts become more present than in the classes that I teach in Africana studies on Black children. So my task here is to talk about my experiences in this class, as I hope this will provide adult and higher education instructors with some strategies to help us all increase our understanding about, first, the importance of talking about race and racism and, second, the ways in which the race card affects how we think, act, and behave whether in higher or adult education.

THE CONTEXT

The classes I taught in Africana studies were generally made up of undergraduate and graduate majors, many of whom came with their own particular, often Eurocentric, view of Black people. Often about one-third of the students were Black females. All of these students' polyrhythmic realities were shaped by their encounters with racism (Sheared, 1999). Like my students, as an African-centered educator in higher education, I too am informed by my polyrhythmic realities, being also a Black female, mother, and grandmother. The recognition of this, along with an understanding about the ways in which these intersecting points of reality affect how we operate and speak in the teaching and learning context, required me to negotiate through what Boykin and Toms (1986) refer to as the *triple quandary,* or three realms of experience. The three realms involve (1) the *mainstream realm,* or dominant cultural racial socialization; (2) the *minority* realm, in which you learn to cope with racial and economic victimization because of racial group status; and (3) the *Black cultural realm* and an ultimate grounding in Africentrism. Negotiating these realms is the process of racial socialization that most successful, healthy African American adults must master in order to navigate a racist society.

Therein lies the tension and the point at which I enter into the discourse about how to reframe the teaching and learning environment through the lens of race. The generative paradigm that I developed is designed to challenge and expose the *new racism* described by Cross (2005), whereby White privilege is maintained through invisible, insidious operations of power that foster Whiteness and racism. This power is no longer enacted primarily through physical violence but is achieved mostly through more symbolic means.

AN AFRICAN-CENTERED PARADIGM

So, as I reflected on what I wanted the students in the Black children course to understand, recognizing who they were and what type of learning and personal experiences they were likely to have prior to entering this class, I had to reframe what and how I asked them to engage in class. Given that I have used the African-centered perspective to frame my scholarship and research, I found that this particular course afforded me an opportunity to introduce the Africentric paradigm as an analytical and interpretative frame for both content and instructional strategies. More important, I found that I was able to teach the course from an African-centered perspective. For purposes of this discussion I offer the following definitions used by Nobles and Asante. Nobles (1995) states that the term *African-centered*

> categorizes a quality of thought and practice which is rooted in the cultural image and interest of African people and which represents and reflects the life experiences, history and traditions of African people as the center of analyses. It is therein the intellectual and philosophical foundation which African people should create their own scientific criterion for authenticating human reality.

Asante (2005) uses the term *Afrocentricity* and defines it as

> a paradigm based on the idea that African people should re-assert a sense of agency in order to achieve sanity . . . . Afrocentricity becomes a revolutionary idea because it studies ideas, concepts, events, personalities, and political and economic processes from a standpoint of black people as subjects and not as objects, basing all knowledge on the authentic interrogation of *location* . . . there is something more than knowing in the Afrocentric sense; there is also *doing*.

Nobles and Asante have both offered definitions that many African-centered scholars have used to explain the perspective or theory. While Nobles (1995) refers to this perspective as *African centered* and Asante refers to it as *Afrocentricity,* scholars of this perspective use either or both terms, and have chosen not to debate whether one is more appropriate than the other. To do so makes a false start to any discussion on race, shifting the discourse to the nonessential and making invisible those the theory or paradigm intends to redress. The use of the *race card* demonstrates how White and Black students attempt to engage or redirect any conversation or dialogue about race; and the use of the African-centered paradigm offers us a way to counter the impact of the race card or racism in adult and higher education teaching and learning contexts. In the following discussion I offer an example of how we might move the dialogue on race and racism forward using an African-centered perspective.

THE RACE CARD

One of the first things I ask students on the first day of class is, "Why are you taking this course?" Often students say such things as, "I'm taking it to satisfy my general education requirements"; others say such things as, "I plan on teaching and working with young Black children." Rarely do you hear or think that the first thing someone is going to say is what one Latino student said to me: "I hope you are not going to play the race card?" Although I was shocked that this was said, I understood that this question reflected a Eurocentric interpretation of the term. According to Dei and Karumanchery (2004), the *race card* is a metaphorical reference to card games in which there is a trump card, reflecting how race and racism are too often viewed and used. Blacks view the race card as providing them with an advantage, and Whites view it as allowing them to challenge, devalue, and minimize valid claims of racism posed by Blacks. Elise (2004) provides an Africentric interpretation and argues that the game metaphor renders White privilege as a set of rights that is attached to Whiteness and maintained through the deployment of White racism under a set of rules that shifts under the whims of Whites in power. Thus it is not Black people who play the race card to their advantage; it is Whites who hold the race card that trumps all cards dealt to Blacks, by conferring privileged access to power, freedom, and rights on themselves.

THE JOURNEY

So, how can dialogue about race and racism occur if the race card is used? Using the remark from the Latino student as an example, I ask the students to engage and to go on a journey of uncovering and discovering new ways of speaking and talking about race. We begin by examining where we are now and where we would like to be or could be if we agreed to engage in an honest conversation with one another. Not only do we examine who we are with regard to our racial identity, but we also think about what we each gain or lose with regard to perceived or real power in the classroom. While clearly this is a beginning, Mojab (2005) notes that critiquing power relations is not enough, and suggests that alternative analytical frames be introduced to expose students to perspectives, ideologies, and new meaning contexts. Cross (2005) concludes that this will enable students to challenge the new racism, which had previously enabled White privilege to be maintained through invisible, insidious operations of power that both protect and perpetuate the ideology of White supremacy. The next three steps, preassessment, examining and reframing language and culture, and the turning point to racial socialization, help students move from thinking and dialogue to action.

Preassessment

In order to find out what background knowledge and experiences students bring to the course, students complete a preassessment. The survey includes one statement and six questions which they respond to.

Students are asked first to respond to a statement quoted from Fuller (1974): "If you don't understand White supremacy (racism)—what it is, and how it works—everything else that you understand will only confuse you." This statement helps the instructor prepare and direct students in a conversation about racism and the ideology of White supremacy and racism. This generally helps the instructor understand the students' perspectives.

After defining whom the class is about, not just the descendants of enslaved Africans who live in the United States but Africans in the Diaspora, I acknowledge that people of color will find themselves reflected in the knowledge and scholarship that is presented in the class. I also require students to capitalize the "B" in Black, because they are not referring to a color but to a people who have sociocultural and intellectual histories.

Examination and Reframing of Language and Culture

The journey (course) begins with a critical examination of the prevailing paradigm that defines White middle-class males as the norm. The journey then proceeds to examine research and policy, which are part of this pathological paradigm. Using Black scholars almost exclusively is purposeful, as we define this pathological paradigm and develop an understanding about alternative paradigms and ways of knowing (what could be or is). This includes an examination of an ancient African paradigm, which emphasizes the socialization and development (Hilliard, 2002) of individuals in the African Diaspora. After examining the historical factors, we introduce the social, economic, and political structures and institutions that are produced by the existing paradigm, making sure that we examine contemporary institutions and practices that continue to regenerate the pathological paradigm. Students are generally quite engaged and involved during this phase of the course. Adult learners are able to connect to their lived experiences, as many of these institutions were built using a familiar pathological paradigm.

The importance of Black, or African, culture is introduced and then this culture takes on meaning for the students during the discussion on Ebonics. Nobles (1999) defines *culture* as

a vast structure of behaviors, attitudes, values, habits, beliefs, customs, rituals, language, customs and ceremonies peculiar to a particular group of people which gives them a general design for living and patterns for interpreting reality.... A people's indigenous culture anchors them to reality and must be the starting point for all learning.

Ebonics also brings up a lively discussion and debate. Dispelling myths and misunderstandings regarding the language of Africans in the Diaspora is truly an interesting challenge. According to Smith (1998, p. 54):

Ebonics refers to the language of West African, Caribbean, and U.S. (en)slave(d) descendants of Niger-Congo African origin. It is the verbal and paralinguistic features of Black people . . . it represents an underlying psychological thought process.

As we examine, reflect on, and reframe our understanding about the ways in which language and culture shape our ideas and actions, I reintroduce the concept of the triple quandary.

These concepts resonate with Black and other adult learners of color. I then use my own personal experiences to illustrate how this works.

The Turning Point to Racial Socialization

This is really the turning point in our journey. Race now begins to have a different meaning for all participants. The use of multimedia helps bridge the gaps between students. For example, I recommend that you use videos like *Tupac Resurrection* to expose students to the complexity of being an extremely bright and talented young Black male and the impact of social, economic, and political institutions on him, his family, and his community. You and the group can analyze Tupac's life and development, as well as discuss what the findings of this analysis mean for students interested in teaching and learning. I also use several other videos that are very effective and instructive during the journey. For example, *Raising Tennis Aces* offers an extremely important story, as the students see not only the development of Venus and Serena Williams but also the extraordinary parenting of Richard and Oracene Williams.

The last leg of the journey takes students into a discussion about the significance of racial socialization and connects directly with Boykin and Toms's (1986) concept of learning to navigate and negotiate the triple quandary. This affects all persons of color, especially Black people. The success of the discussion, and perhaps the course, for the most part depends on it. Messages such as "you must not only do well, but you must be twice as good" are an important part of our racial socialization, as they prepare us to be successful in a world that is both hostile and racist. This is the point at which I suggest you use the *Raising Tennis Aces* video.

Since racial socialization is all about race and racial socialization, this video can help you counter the race card that results from the ideology and practices of White supremacy. This White race card is being used daily against Africans in the Diaspora.

Hilliard (2002) posits that our survival depends on proper intergenerational transmission of our culture and discusses re-Africanization in socialization as a way to counter cultural genocide. McAdoo (2001) and also McWright (2001) describe how intergenerational racial socialization is a practice evident in Black children's development; however, McAdoo (2001), more importantly, concludes that racial socialization should be a village responsibility. According to Stewart (1996), if you do not recognize the role of race in development then you may be committing another form of abuse.

THE JOURNEY IS PERSONAL

This is where the journey becomes personal for the students and instructor. Students begin to recognize that institutional pathologies are based on the ideology of White supremacy and the resulting racist policies that are practiced and enforced within schools and society. In other words, they begin to acknowledge the fact that the *race card* is exactly as Elise (2004) has described: the trump card of power and privilege that Whites use to trump all other cards dealt to Blacks and others. As they transform, they begin to talk about helping others transform their ideas, thinking, and action.

The journey that students take, and the Africentric paradigm that undergirds it, seems to result in the following outcomes: students begin to question what had previously been taught, informally and formally, about Black people; many begin to challenge the status quo. They begin to question and apply this new knowledge to their personal and professional lives. Almost all of us who have taken this journey have begun a process of transformation and understand that socialization and education are about transformation.

And what about the student who hoped that this course was not going to be about the race card? In responding to a question on the final exam, he wrote:

> [T]here are parents who racially socialize their children and those who do not engage in the [discussion of the] existence of race . . . the ones [adolescents] who have dialogue absent of race are the ones that are struggling . . . . I myself have to take this knowledge and apply it. This means helping Black children to understand their history, their African language system—Ebonics. It is important to hold teachers and school districts accountable for their inability to conform to Black cultural experience.

In this statement the student implicitly acknowledges that race is a critical variable, that his original conceptualization of the meaning and holder of the race card was framed in the Eurocentric paradigm, and that in reality it is Whites who hold the trump card.

REFERENCES

Asante, M. K. (2005). Afrocentricity. Retrieved December 8, 2009, from http://www.asante.net/articles.html.

Boykin, W., & Toms, F. (1986). Black child socialization: A conceptual framework. In H. P. McAdoo & J. L. McAdoo (Eds.), *Black child development: Social, educational, and parental environments* (pp. 33–52). Thousand Oaks, CA: Sage.

Cross, B. (2005). New racism, reformed teacher education, and the same ole' oppression. *Educational Studies, 38*, 263–264.

Dei, G., & Karumanchery, N. (2004). *Playing the race card: Exposing white power and privilege.* New York: Peter Lang.

Elise, S. (2004). How Whites play the rAce card: Drylongso stories reveal "the game." *Sociological Perspectives, 47*, 409–438.

Fuller, N. (1974). *The united-independent compensatory code/system/ concept: A textbook/workbook for thought, speech, and/or action, for victims of racism (White supremacy).* Author.

Hilliard, A. G. (2002). *African power: Affirming African indigenous socialization in the face of the culture wars.* Atlanta: Makare.

McAdoo, H. P. (2001). The village talks: Racial socialization of our children. In H. P. McAdoo (Ed.), *Black children: Social, educational, and parental environments* (2nd ed., pp. 47–56). Thousand Oaks, CA: Sage.

McWright, L. (2001). African American grandmothers' and grandfathers' influence in the value socialization of grandchildren. In H. P. McAdoo (Ed.), *Black children: Social, educational, and parental environments* (2nd ed., pp. 27–46). Thousand Oaks, CA: Sage.

Mojab, S. (2005). Class and race. In T. Nesbit (Ed.), *Class concerns: Adult education and social class* (New Directions for Adult and Continuing Education, No. 106, pp. 73–82). San Francisco: Jossey-Bass.

Nobles, W. (1995, Spring). African centered paradigm. *The Drum, 1.* Retrieved December 8, 2009, from http://www.ritesofpassage .org/ds95–1.htm.

Nobles, W. (1999, July 10–14). The Nsaka Sumsun: Touching the spirit. Presentation at the Center for Applied Cultural Studies and Educational Achievement (CACSEA Summer Institute), Richmond, CA.

Sheared, V. (1999). Giving voice: Inclusion of African American students' polyrhythmic realities in adult basic education. In T. Guy (Ed.), *Providing culturally relevant adult education: A challenge for the twenty first century* (New Directions for Adult and Continuing Education, No. 82, pp. 33–48). San Francisco: Jossey-Bass.

Smith, E. (1998). What is Black English? What is Ebonics? In T. Perry (Ed.), *The Real Ebonics Debate* (pp. 49–58). Boston: Beacon Press.

Stewart, N. (1996). Melanin, the melanin hypothesis, and the development and assessment of African infants. In D. Azibu (Ed.), *African psychology in historical perspective* (pp. 99–138). Trenton, NJ: African World Press.

18

Expanding the Racialized Discourse

An Asian American Perspective

MING-YEH LEE

Eight years ago, while flying to Northern Illinois University to receive the Adult Education Research Conference Graduate Student Research Award, excited and nervous about the acceptance speech, I began jotting down some ideas. My thoughts were suddenly interrupted by a middle-aged White man, who asked, "Are you practicing your English?" I responded that I was writing a speech for an award that I was receiving. He smiled, but did not respond.

To my mind, his question reflected certain Eurocentric assumptions regarding my English proficiency based upon who he saw, an Asian in America. By simply looking at me, he had *labeled* me as the "other," a non-English-speaking foreigner or, at best, an immigrant. Takaki (1993) found that this is a common encounter for Asian Americans, many of whom were born in this country and many with families that have lived here for generations.

As a first-generation Asian American woman, I have experienced the impact of race and racism since immigrating to the United Sates. Socio-cultural and intellectual racism is experienced by all peoples of color, but its impact and influences vary and depend on one's racial or ethnic group membership. For me, it has been a painful and ongoing learning process. Having to sort through and manage daily interactions framed by racist assumptions while realizing the unwillingness of practitioners in my field to engage in a discussion regarding racism's presence or perpetuation is common.

In the early 1990s, a number of African American adult education researchers significantly expanded our knowledge base on the impact of racism on African Americans and challenged the prevailing paradigm regarding the accuracy of our theories and the appropriateness of our practice (Colin III, 1994; Johnson-Bailey & Cervero, 1996; Sheared, 1994). Yet there has been little or no discussion by scholars of Asian descent regarding an analytical framework that would facilitate our understanding regarding the impact of racism on Asian Americans' experiences and on their practice as adult educators.

In order to develop a more comprehensive analytical framework to further address the racial dynamics in our society, it is imperative that adult educators expand the racialized discourse by initiating discussion on the ways racism operates in shaping the lives of Asian Americans and influencing adult education practices. Therefore this chapter is specifically devoted to this analytical framework, using the concept of heterogeneity and the polyrhythmic realities (Sheared, 1994) expressed in intragroup descriptors that reflect the diverse linguistic, religious, and cultural diversities of Asian Americans as units of analysis. The paradigm shift suggested here will assist adult educators in reframing and racializing the discourse in the field of adult education for members of the Asian Diaspora.

It is my hope that the following discussion will facilitate a critical analysis of the impact of racism on the personal and professional lives of Asian Americans, thereby reshaping the content and goals of adult education practices and research foci. So that adult educators can accurately understand the diverse cultures of Asian Americans and the Asian Diaspora, I believe that it is important for us to talk about the ways in which history, language, legislative policies, and homogeneity have shaped our lived experiences.

ASIAN AMERICANS AS A HETEROGENEOUS GROUP

There are currently ten million individuals of Asian ancestry (roughly 4.21 percent of the total population) in the United States, representing fifteen countries. The largest ethnic groups are Chinese, Filipino, East Indian, Vietnamese, and Korean (U.S. Census Bureau, 2002). Although the dominant society has constructed an ethnocentric conceptualization of a homogeneous "Asian American population," this view ignores distinctive ethnic identities and disregards the historical, cultural, linguistic, and religious differences within the Asian Diaspora. Furthermore, Asia's history of wars and political conflicts means that much of any posited "universal Asian American experience" is nonexistent. Given all this, I believe that the concept of *heterogeneity* offers a more accurate description of the differences and diversity found within this population.

I also believe that it is precisely this heterogeneity that explains why there have not been any integrated analyses or interpretations that adequately frame the ways in which Asian experiences and intellectual thought have had an impact on the American landscape. Given the culturally encompassing and diverse nature of the Asian population, there is a real danger in using homogeneous assumptions to frame research or practices about Asians as a group. As increasing numbers of Asian immigrants continue to arrive in the United States, adult educators need to be keenly aware of their intragroup cultural differences and the educational implications of these differences (Lee & Sheared, 2002).

Socioeconomic differences make up another set of intragroup realities that have a bearing on the ways in which immigration status and educational attainment affect Asians. Asian Americans are found in all economic strata from richest to poorest. As a group they range from refugees with very few resources to wealthy entrepreneurs. In short, Asians of the Diaspora are parallel to other racial groups in the United States in terms of class divisions and their multiple and varied realities and set of experiences (Amott & Matthaei, 1996; Martin & Midgley, 1994; Ong, 2004).

ANTI-ASIAN DISCRIMINATION AND THE CONTEMPORARY STEREOTYPES

Like other people of color, Asian Americans have suffered from past policies and ordinances that were legislated as either a way to control or as a means to perpetuate prevailing stereotypes. Violence against Asians began when Chinese and then Japanese men were brought to the United States as cheap labor in mid-1800s. As anti-Asian sentiments prevailed, legislation was passed in the late nineteenth and early twentieth centuries to impose unequal tax laws, to establish unreasonable quarantine procedures, and even to exclude Asian laborers or their families from immigrating to, entering, or becoming naturalized citizens in the United States. Fong (2002) notes that many of these policies were not abolished until 1965.

The period following the World War II bombing of Pearl Harbor offers one of the most overt examples of racism in the United States. All Japanese Americans in the United States were evacuated from their homes and relocated in concentration camps. This command was based on fabricated, anti-Japanese hysteria about Japanese Americans possibly aiding the Japanese military or returning to Japan so that they could attack America. In addition, the competitors of Japanese Americans took control of Japanese Americans' land and assets after the rightful owners had been forced to relocate (Amott & Matthaei, 1996). Although a small numbers of German and Italian aliens were relocated, this effort did not compare to the mass internment of Japanese Americans on the West Coast (Fong, 2002).

In addition to the denigration of Asians during World War II, many Asians were labeled as "aliens." The alien label cast Asian Americans as outsiders whose loyalty to America was subjected to suspicion and criticism. The Japanese people's experience in concentration camps during World War II highlights the assumptions Whites held about other ethnicities or groups that were not White. Rather than referring to Asians as "Asians in America" or "Asian Americans," terms like "alien" were used and often promoted stereotypical and racist thinking and actions toward Asians, both those who came to America as immigrants and those who were born in America. As Wu (2002) explains: "Asian Americans cannot seem to convince non-Asian Americans . . . when we ask not to be blamed for what Asians have done . . . . Conflict with Asia makes Asian Americans vulnerable, because there has been a history of anti-Asian moods leading to anti-Asian American actions" (p. 11).

Clearly, Asian Americans are negatively affected by domestic and legislative policies as well as by international crises and conflicts. If the past is an indicator of the present and future, it is highly unlikely that Asians will be viewed as solely Asian Americans. As long as folks who sit with you on planes only see what you look like first, Asians will continue to be viewed as aliens first and Asian Americans second. Moreover, the widespread use of stereotypes that depict Asian Americans as the *model minority* continues to isolate Asians from other peoples of color. Furthermore, this concept continues to frame the perceptions of many Euro-American adult educators, who refer to Asian Americans as *pseudo-Whites* and see them as people who also enjoy many privileges Whites have held since the founding of the United States. This has resulted in Asian American experiences being excluded or invalidated when issues of race are discussed.

THE MODEL MINORITY

The myth of Asian Americans as a model minority prevails and has led educators in higher and adult education to stereotype Asians and to develop classes that fail to fully recognize the contributions of Asians in America. Educators as well as others always think of Asians as being high achievers in education (particularly in math and science). This has led to those who desperately need instructional assistance being ignored because they are categorized as the model minority and assumed to be successful, when in fact they are struggling to learn (Walker-Moffat, 1995). Furthermore, placing an emphasis on the model minority, at the expense of other people of color, has led to the unequal distribution of educational and economic resources in schools that serve the poor and other people of color. When the existence of a model minority is assumed, the public may be misled into believing that the educational playing field is level and that individuals in any racial group can and should be able to make it by pulling themselves up by their bootstraps.

Thus, the thinking goes, no additional efforts or resources are needed to enhance the practice of education (Fong, 2002). This myth of Asian Americans as the model minority not only obfuscates the real experiences of Asian Americans but serves to negate and isolate those experiences. In addition to making them a model minority, this myth makes them invisible. If our experiences are homogeneous, then the fact that we are heterogeneous, representing various groups and experiences from different countries, can be ignored. This way of thinking damages not only people of the Asian Diaspora but other people of color as well.

ADULT EDUCATION PRACTICE: HEALING

To respond adequately to the effect of race and racism on Asian Americans in the teaching and learning context, those of us who are adult educators must begin to address these issues in our teaching practices and research agendas. We need to question in order to understand why we as adult education practitioners need to develop racially inclusive curricula. We also need to think about ways to include issues of equity and social justice in the curriculum, as well as to find ways to include the lived experiences of all learners. We need to devise instructional strategies that engage students in antiracist acts as they participate in our classes.

I believe that this is an imperative, given that research has shown that racial group membership is one of the salient sociocultural impact factors that affect identity development and educational involvement (Johnson-Bailey, 1998, 2001; Sheared & Sissel, 2002). Therefore, it is extremely important for adult educators to create a space in which they can engage students in a real dialogue on race and racism in order to effectively deal with the real oppressions in their lives.

As an academician, an adult education practitioner, and a concerned member of the Asian American community, I believe our roles and responsibilities as educators are grounded in our positions at the university and also in the community outside the institution of higher education. We must embrace and challenge issues that confront our communities. Swaminathan (2004) strongly suggests that as scholars of color, we should serve as healers, community builders, and consciousness raisers within and on behalf of our communities. Our enhanced knowledge about the shared history of resistance practice among people of color will help us identify a common vision, enhance community networks, and explore possibilities to build coalitions across the multiple racial communities.

ADULT EDUCATION PRACTICE: REFLECTION OF THE OTHER

Given all that I have discussed so far, I believe we as adult educators should reflect on the following questions and respond via our pedagogy, curriculum development, and research agendas. How and in what ways are the Asian American experiences reflected in educational literature in general and adult education literature specifically? Are these experiences reflected in adult education, history, philosophy, and adult development and learning curricula? Are Asian Americans included in the sociocultural context of adult education? In what ways do race and racism affect our lives on the individual, institutional, and societal levels? In what ways do race and racism affect our schooling experiences? And how can we include race and racism in our pedagogy so that students begin to have a real dialogue about these real issues in their lives?

Even though I don't think we can answer all these questions here, I do believe that as we develop our classes so that our students come to recognize and understand the role of race in teaching and learning, we must review these questions and find time to address at least four or five of them before we begin our classes. I strongly suggest that strategies using consciousness raising and transformative-learning processes such as critical incident analysis, reflective journaling, critical debate, and support groups be included (Cranton, 1994). If we do this, I believe it will enhance the discourse on race and racism in our classes.

REFRAMING THE FIELD THROUGH RESEARCH

As researchers in adult education, we need to be cognizant of how our racial identities frame and inform our research agendas. Emerging Asian and Asian American researchers have begun to examine how racial identity and racism affect the learning experiences of the Asian American adult population (Lee, 2004). We still have a long way to go, but this is our beginning.

The invisibility of Asian Americans is apparent in the foundational literature of our field, as oftentimes Asian Americans' experiences are either missing or treated within a "people of color" group. The historical, linguistic, and political contexts of Asian Americans are rarely considered, while the stereotypes regarding Asian American learner characteristics, such as being a model minority, good at math and science, and silent learners, seem to prevail among adult education practitioners.

Asian American academicians in particular and other academicians in general have a primary responsibility to "make the invisible visible" by actively participating in the process of knowledge production and distribution in relation to the Asian American population. Employing an Asian-centered analytical and interpretative framework is the first step. It is also important that we conduct empirical studies involving Asian Americans as primary research participants in order to expand the breadth of knowledge about the lived experiences of people of color. These research efforts will expand our field's knowledge base and frame our practice, so that we serve Asian American learner populations better.

THE VISIBLE ASIAN AMERICAN

The purpose of this chapter was to discuss the significance of expanding racialized discourse of adult education by developing and incorporating an Asian-centered analytical framework. Members of the Asian Diaspora are not homogeneous but they are heterogeneous. A study that gives us an overview of the prevailing racial stereotypes regarding Asian Americans and the impact of racism on the lives and learning experience of Asian Americans must be conducted if we are going to develop classes and programs to adequately address these students' needs. Adult educators must begin to examine the history, language, experiences, and demographics of the Asian Diaspora in order to gain a better understanding about this population. Until we do this, we will continue to perpetuate stereotypes and racist ideologies about Asian Americans as the model minority, and we will fail to see them as diverse members of the Asian Diaspora.

REFERENCES

Amott, T., & Matthaei, J. (1996). *Race, gender and work: A multicultural economic history of women in the United States.* Boston: South End Press.

Colin, S.A.J., III. (1994). Adult and continuing education graduate programs: Prescription for the future. In E. Hayes & S.A.J. Colin III (Eds.), *Confronting racism and sexism* (New Directions for Adult and Continuing Education, No. 61, pp. 53–62). San Francisco: Jossey-Bass.

Cranton, P. (1994). *Understanding and promoting transformative learning: A guide for educators of adults.* San Francisco: Jossey-Bass.

Fong, T. (2002). *The contemporary Asian American experience: Beyond the model minority.* Upper Saddle River, NJ: Pearson Education.

Johnson-Bailey, J. (1998). Black reentry women in the academy: Making a way out of no way. *Initiatives, 58*(4), 37–48.

Johnson-Bailey, J. (2001). *Sistahs in college: Making a way out of no way.* Malabar, FL: Krieger.

Johnson-Bailey, J., & Cervero, R. M. (1996). An analysis of the educational narratives of reentry Black women. *Adult Education Quarterly, 46*(4), 142–158.

Lee, M. (2004). Negotiating my space in academe. In M. V. Alfred & R. Swaminathan (Eds.), *Immigrant women of the academy: Negotiating boundaries, crossing borders in higher education* (pp. 105–118). New York: Nova Science.

Lee, M., & Sheared, V. (2002). Socialization and immigrant students' learning in adult education programs. In M. V. Alfred (Ed.), *Learning and sociocultural contexts: Implications for adults, community, and workplace education* (New Directions for Adult and Continuing Education, No. 96, pp. 27–36). San Francisco: Jossey-Bass.

Martin, P., & Midgley, E. (1994). Immigration to the United States: Journey to an uncertain destination. *Population Bulletin, 49*(2), 2–46.

Ong, A. (2004). Higher learning: Educational availability and flexible citizenship. In J. Banks (Ed.), *Global space in diversity and citizenship education: Global perspectives* (pp. 49–70). San Francisco: Jossey-Bass.

Sheared, V. (1994). Giving voice: An inclusive model of instruction—A womanist perspective. In E. Hayes & S.A.J. Colin III (Eds.), *Confronting racism and sexism in the United States: Fundamental issues* (New Directions for Adult and Continuing Education, No. 61, pp. 27–37). San Francisco: Jossey-Bass.

Sheared, V., & Sissel, P. (Eds.). (2002). *Making space: Merging theory and practice in adult education.* Westport, CT: Bergin & Garvey.

Swaminathan, R. (2004). Relational worlds: South Asian immigrant women talk about home/work. In M. V. Alfred & R. Swaminathan

(Eds.), *Immigrant women of the academy: Negotiating boundaries, crossing borders in higher education* (pp. 89–104). New York: Nova Science.

Takaki, R. A. (1993). *Different mirror: A history of multicultural America.* Boston: Little, Brown.

U.S. Census Bureau. (2002). *The Asian population, 2000.* Retrieved March 8, 2009, from http://www.census.gov/prod/2002pubs/c2kbr01–16.pdf.

Walker-Moffat, W. (1995). *The other side of the Asian American success story.* San Francisco: Jossey-Bass.

Wu, F. (2002). *Yellow: Race in America beyond Black and White.* New York: Basic Books.

19

Challenges and Approaches to Racializing Discourse in a Privileged, White Dominant Society

LAJERNE TERRY CORNISH

I had my first known encounter with racism as a student at Goucher College. I was taking precalculus and performing quite horribly, so I made an appointment to meet with the math professor to discuss my lack of progress and to seek additional assistance with the course. During our meeting she acknowledged that I was not doing well with the class, but then she suggested that my poor performance was expected because "Black people can't do math." I did not know what to do affectively or cognitively with such a racist comment. When I was an undergraduate student, there was not one professor or professional member of color in my school and no one there who looked like me who could help me move beyond the emotional impact of this statement. I remember suffering silently and then moving on. Now, three decades later, I find myself teaching and talking about race at the same institution. I wonder if this is coincidence or providence. I choose providence.

Currently, I am an assistant professor of education at Goucher College, a predominantly White, small, liberal arts college in Baltimore. Since Goucher's founding in 1885 the racial and ethnic composition of the student body and faculty has remained largely unchanged and is one of the institution's continuing challenges. Because of the current racial and ethnic composition of the student body, I am often the only person of color in my classroom. My students are quite comfortable talking about their views on race and racism and the sources of each. Although I am the only African American in the classroom, my position as the instructor has made me *racially invisible* to them. Clearly, talking about race and racism in a privileged White environment creates many challenges for me. Students are often lulled into a false sense of cognitive security as a result of the absence of racial and ethnic diversity in the classroom, so I find that the racial and ethnic composition of the institution has afforded me the opportunity to push students in their thinking about race and racism.

For the past seven years I have taught ED 103, Adolescent Development, which is my favorite course. I use elements of Helms's (1990) and Marcia's (1980) racial identity development models, fiction, film, and personal experience to help students identify their racial development process, the validity of the assumptions that frame it, and the appropriateness of subsequent behaviors. Both development models help students achieve an implicit and explicit understanding of racial identity formation and personality development. Without theoretical constructs to inform conversation, discussions about race can be difficult, contentious, and meaningless. So I believe these models provide frameworks in which meaningful discussions about race and racism can begin in the classroom. The theories postulated in the following discussion allow young adult learners to analyze their assumptions regarding the "other" and themselves relative to their attitudes and behaviors toward people of varying racial, gender, linguistic, religious, class, and cultural backgrounds.

WHITE RACIAL DEVELOPMENT MODELS

Helms (1990) developed a six-stage theory of racial identity formation that enables students to recognize their privilege and choose to relinquish it. Helms further states that a psychological defense supports each stage, and the model helps Whites understand race-related experiences. There is an inherent resistance mechanism reflected in each stage that requires a conversation about race and racism, and this affords Euro-Americans an opportunity to understand where they are with regard to their own White racial identity formation and how their actions influence their interactions with people of color. The six stages are contact, disintegration, reintegration, pseudo independence, immersion/emersion, and autonomy.

The *contact* stage is the first phase in the model. This is the stage in which White individuals espouse values of superiority that are embedded in their internalized beliefs regarding people of color. Often students have trouble at this stage in believing that racism exists. And because they lack social interaction with the "other" or because they do not know anyone who has experienced racism firsthand, they struggle to understand how they could exhibit superiority over a person of color. If they lack intergroup social mobility, White individuals in the contact stage could remain in that stage for life. If they don't get stuck, they move on to stage 2—where disintegration occurs.

During the *disintegration* stage the individual begins to realize and acknowledge the existence of racism and the resulting sociocultural implications of racism. This is the time in which White individuals realize that people may indeed be treated differently because of their race. Armed with this knowledge, White individuals may also begin to recognize the privilege that comes with Whiteness and may also begin to exhibit their own feelings of discomfort. They realize the privileges that come with their racial group membership. A caveat here is worth mentioning, and that is, even though White people may realize the privileges they have that are associated with group membership, the ideology of White supremacy may cause them to think that such privileges are a right that they have been granted or have earned.

During stage 3, *reintegration* occurs. As the White person begins to reflect on his or her disintegration a sense of discomfort may occur. If it does, then the person will experience disequilibrium for a period of time. In order to restore their equilibrium, individuals in this stage often reject what they learned about the experiences of people of color in the disintegration stage and develop an idealized view of their own culture. According to Diller and Moule (2005), White people emphasize "the superiority of White culture and the natural deficits in Cultures of Color" in an effort to manage their discomfort (p. 58).

During stage 4, the person moves into a form of *pseudo independence.* This is characterized by a desire to learn more about people of color, or the "other." Individuals acquire an intellectualized understanding of racial differences and the resultant racist attitudes and behaviors that they may exhibit toward the other. At this point, they begin to support social justice activities on an intellectual level, but this commitment is neither personal nor internalized. It is not uncommon for people in the pseudo independent stage to proclaim, "I have a Black friend," in an effort to show how culturally progressive they perceive themselves to be.

During stage 5, an *immersion/emersion occurs,* as individuals immerse themselves in their cultural heritage and history. In this stage, White people may seek to redefine Whiteness and attempt to understand racism. More important, they may try to ascertain the ways in which they benefit or have benefited from the oppression of others, particularly people of color. So while disintegration brings a realization of the privilege associated with Whiteness, immersion/emersion brings an understanding of the degrees to which privilege is a direct result of racial oppression stemming from the ideology of White supremacy. It is in this stage that White people realize that their privilege is a result of group membership and not something earned through their efforts or hard work.

In the last developmental stage, *autonomy*, White people accept their Whiteness and actively seek to partner with people who are the "other," in an effort to effect societal change. This stage finds White people becoming more comfortable in their own skins, acknowledging the privilege that comes with their racial group membership, and possessing the ability to "approach those who are culturally different without prejudice" (Diller & Moule, 2005, p. 59).

In addition to Helms's work on identity development, Marcia (1980) has developed a theory of identity statuses, or categories, that explain how an individual can resolve his or her way of acting once he or she understands his or her racial identity. The four identity statuses—identity diffusion, identity foreclosure, moratorium, and identity achievement—are defined by the presence or absence of crisis and commitment. According to Marcia, crisis and commitment are necessary if one is going to realize or achieve identity. In this model, the *crisis* leads to an exploration of alternatives and *commitment* involves the degree to which an individual's ways of being reflect his or her own values, beliefs, or philosophy. Originally applied to vocational, religious, and political domains, Marcia's identity status categories have implications for racial identity formation as well.

With regard to *identity diffusion,* identity formation for Whites often begins with a lack of awareness about differences. Because diffused individuals have experienced *neither crisis nor commitment* as characterized by the diffused status, identity-diffused individuals are often children who have yet to intentionally denote differences in the people around them and have yet to be socialized to see differences in others. The identity-diffused state normally ends with the onset of adolescence. It rarely continues into adulthood.

In *identity foreclosure,* White people *commit* to particular beliefs about their own culture and that of others *without experiencing any crisis.* They claim a racial identity without exploring options or alternatives because they have not been subject to any situation that calls their particular value system into question. While in foreclosure, Whites have limited contact with groups outside their own culture. Foreclosed individuals from the majority may downplay differences, often saying, "I don't see color." Whites in the foreclosed status are not only unaware of the scope of the social and political implications of oppression but also may deny the existence of oppression.

> While they have been breathing the "smog" and have internalized many of the prevailing societal stereotypes of people of color, they typically are unaware of this socialization process. They often perceive themselves as color-blind, completely free of prejudice, unaware of their own assumptions about other racial groups [Tatum, 1999, p. 95].

While White students are in foreclosure, they will more than likely reflect the values and beliefs of their families. They have learned to think as their families do, talk as they do, and behave as they do. Unless members of the majority experience a crisis that causes them to reevaluate their ideology and explore other ways of being, foreclosure may be a lifetime status for some Whites. Remaining in foreclosure, a phenomenon Marcia (1980) calls *structured foreclosure,* can be dangerous (Muuss, 1996, p. 64). Foreclosure can become a permanent part of an individual's personality if he or she commits to an ideology, position, or value system without ever considering or being challenged to consider alternatives. Hence, structured foreclosure can prevent individuals from having an achieved identity, because they never experience the crisis that comes as a result of experiencing moratorium.

Moratorium is characterized by *crisis without commitment.* For White people, their understanding of their majority membership status comes into question during the moratorium stage. This often begins in college, during interactions with people of color in classes or sports activities. During this time of engagement, Whites begin to recognize and acknowledge the existence of discrimination and prejudice. Acknowledgment of individual and institutionalized forms of oppression may be accompanied by feelings of helplessness, guilt, and perhaps frustration. Because of the discomfort these feelings create, moratorium may cause some Whites to retreat further into their own culture or actively explore friendships with persons from other cultures. Discomfort may cause some Whites to refrain from mixing with other cultures and to accentuate the positives of the majority culture. In moratorium, members of the majority may even become critical of minority groups, blaming them for the majority members' personal condition, or members of the majority may distance themselves from cultural issues entirely by focusing on issues such as world hunger. For White students, moratorium represents a time of intense feelings, a time of exploration, and a time of crisis in the absence of commitment—all of which are necessary to identity development. Muuss (1996) describes it this way:

> Experiencing moratorium issues often creates subjective discomfort. Moratorium subjects are inclined to express their disenchantment by challenging what they see and hear. Their desire is to change government, politics, the church, education, in short, the system. While they are frequently very good diagnosticians and effective critics who can point to limitations, inconsistencies, and imperfections of the "system," moratorium subjects are not equally effective in producing viable, realistic alternatives, because to do so requires life experiences, identity, willingness to compromise, and a more permanent commitment [p. 67].

Identity achievement involves *crisis and commitment.* To be fully achieved, one must commit to a value system, ideology, or way of being as a direct result of exploring the alternatives available during crisis. For White students, identity achievement is characterized by an ability to recognize and accept the privilege associated with being a member of the majority in a society that has been or is ruled by a majority, especially economically. Movement from an intellectual understanding of differences to a genuine acceptance of differences demonstrates that identity has been achieved. Comfortable with their identity and Whiteness, White individuals begin to build bridges across racial and class lines. They begin to do this in an effort to eradicate oppression of any kind. For members of the majority, identity achievement is moratorium's reward and society's gain. Identity achievement requires work, and those who do the work help those who are merely observers to recognize just how much is possible when crisis results in commitment.

The goal of White racial identity formation is to enable White people to develop a positive White identity based in reality, not on an assumed or socialized belief of superiority. Helm's racial identity development and Marcia's identity status categories enable White students to recognize their White identity and enable them to understand Whiteness in relationship to race and racism. With this new understanding, White students begin to value and respect other ways of knowing, beliefs, and behaviors; and they find new ways of acting and behaving toward those whose language, race, religion, or gender or sexual orientation is different from their own.

WHERE DO I GO FROM HERE?

As a teacher of teachers, I believe it is important that my students know and understand how their views on race and racism shape and frame their attitudes, and ultimately influence their interactions with people of color. So I spend a significant amount of time discussing and providing them with tools to help them understand identity development through the lens of Whiteness. To facilitate this reflective process, I ask my students to write short reaction papers based on theories of White racial identity development. I frame these learning activities around Helms's (1990) White identity development model. I have the students go on a journey of self-exploration in an effort to realize an achieved identity.

I think it is important for White students to recognize their own stages of identity development and to understand how identity development can inform behavior. To that end I use fiction and film to facilitate my students' ability to apply the theories learned in class to characters in books or movies, thereby increasing not only their understanding of racial identity formation but also their own awareness of the effect of identity formation on individual and group behavior.

Fiction such as *Black Ice* (Cary, 1991), a coming-of-age story about an African American female who attends a predominantly White boarding school in the northeastern United States, clearly shows Whites as they go through various stages of identity development and shows how they might react and or change given their new understanding. From contact through autonomy, teenage and adult characters in the book show how each stage informs behavior.

Films such as *The Breakfast Club* (1985), *Finding Forrester* (2000), and *Freedom Writers* (2007) allow students to see racial identity formation play out on the big screen as well. As with fiction, film allows students to use their knowledge of identity formation for character analysis. Reflection papers, in which students have to choose the character from the text or film they most resemble, help students deepen their understanding of themselves and others as they continue their engagement with the other. Videos such as *Skin Deep* (1995) and *What's Race Got to Do with It?* (2006) give students the opportunity to witness how other young adult learners deal with issues of race while obviously displaying their own stage of racial identity development, and the theoretical frameworks by Helms (1990) and Marcia (1980) help students analyze what they see on the screen.

For me, the primary purpose of discussing race in any classroom should be to help students understand themselves, understand others, and understand their interactions with others. With a clear understanding of the formation of identity in general and White racial identity in particular, White students will be equipped to understand themselves, to understand others, to change if necessary, and to effect change when possible.

REFERENCES

Cary, L. (1991). *Black ice.* New York: Vintage Press.

Diller, J. V., & Moule, J. (2005). *Cultural competence: A primer for educators.* Belmont, CA: Thomson Wadsworth.

Helms, J. E. (Ed.). (1990). *Black and White racial identity: Theory, research, and practice.* Westport, CT: Greenwood Press.

Marcia, J. E. (1980). Identity in adolescence. In J. Adelson (Ed.), *Handbook of adolescent psychology* (pp. 159–187). Hoboken, NJ: Wiley.

Muuss, R. E. (1996). *Theories of adolescence* (6th ed.). Boston: McGraw-Hill.

Tatum, B. D. (1999). *Why are all the Black kids sitting together in the cafeteria?* New York: Basic Books.

20

Using an African-Centered Paradigm for Understanding Race and Racism in Adult Education

DERISE E. TOLLIVER

When asked to write about my experiences regarding my encounters with race and racism in adult education, I first wondered if there would be enough space to recount how my White colleagues often privilege objectification over lived experiences and the poignancy of faculty and staff of color's reports of racist practices and White supremacist attitudes in the workplace. I was overwhelmed by the many examples that came to mind.

Should I talk about the time when a senior administrator scheduled a White colleague, with new interest in Africa, to speak to the new provost to represent our unit's Africa initiatives? In doing so, she "overlooked" the following facts: (1) that I and another African American faculty member have long-standing and deeply rooted teaching, scholarship, and service interests in African and African American issues; (2) that we, the Black faculty, had previously provided consultation on curriculum and professional development to a South African university; (3) that we had close to ten years of experience with directing study-abroad programs to West Africa; (4) that we had participated in several faculty development trips to southern Africa; and (5) that we were both members of a cross-unit, cross-discipline, university-level committee titled Africa Initiative. Additionally, what about the suggestion from a colleague that I teach "real" psychology, rather than the course I currently teach, Psychology from an African-Centered Perspective?

What emerges when you put these and other encounters with racism together is what Christian (2006) describes as "a consistency of experience, or phenomena" (p. 709). These experiences reflect a pervasive and ongoing backdrop to my work that constitutes something more than what Peters and Massey (1983) refer to as the "occasional misfortune" (p. 193). It is akin to the *mundane extreme environment* identified in the 1970s by psychiatrist Chester Pierce, "an environment where racism and subtle oppression are ubiquitous, constant, continuing and mundane" (Carroll, 1998). Carroll finds that this environment leads to mundane extreme environmental stress (MEES):

> Mundane, because this stress is so common a part of the day-to-day experience of all Blacks that it is almost taken for granted; extreme, because it has a harsh impact on the psyche and world view of Blacks;... environmental, because it is environmentally induced and fostered; stress, because the ultimate impact on African Americans is indeed stressful, detracting and energy-consuming [p. 271].

AFRICAN-CENTERED PARADIGM

If, as Akintunde (1999) purports, White supremacy is "the progenitor and true underlying problem of racism and racist ideology" (p. 2), then a Eurocentric framework cannot be expected to adequately address racial inequities nor to dismantle racism, nor can other structures of oppression and injustice, as this paradigm has been and is responsible for and organized to perpetuate the negation of the identity and essence of people of African descent (Alkebulan, 2007; Kambon, 1998).

The African-centered paradigm is more accurate and appropriate for understanding the lived experiences, concerns, and needs of people of African descent. The philosophical and conceptual elements of this paradigm affirm peoples of African descent and support the goals of optimal functioning and actualization. These elements can also be employed as an analytical and interpretative framework to guide the development of liberatory educational strategies (Colin III & Guy, 1998; Schiele, 1994). As a critical and practical framework, the African-centered paradigm has an important place in adult education discourse as it provides a structure for meaning making and interpretation of reality from an African worldview (Brookfield, 2003; Kambon 1998; Sheared, 1999).

The paradigm also provides guidance for effective, responsible, and authentic engagement in life that will contribute to positive development of the African community as well as the larger world. As Tolliver (2002) states: "It implores one to act upon the world to transform it, in support of social justice, social change, and social transformation" (p. 7).

THE PRINCIPLES OF TWINNESS AND COMPLEMENTARITY

As Akbar (1975) concludes, the principles of *twinness* and *complementarity* are critical to the African ethos and the African-centered paradigm. Although all elements of the paradigm are important and interrelated, these two principles are of significance because of their particular usefulness as frames for understanding and responding to issues of race and racism in adult education.

Gyeke (1988) describes the principles of twinness and complementarity in his discussion of traditional African philosophy, particularly communalism and individualistic values. He notes that these two seeming opposites are neither "exclusive nor antithetical" (p. 58). In fact, the talents and uniqueness of the individual are not rejected in the traditional African culture that embraces communalism. Rather, both concepts must coexist, as their interaction is critical for the optimal development of individual members of the group as well as for optimal development of the group itself. The needs of the group and of the individual are to be balanced, attesting again to complementarity and twinness. Complementarity exists within the individual and also in the individual's relationship with others and with various elements of the universe. The manifestation of twinness throughout various African cultures represents *ubuntu,* diversity in unity (Venter, 2004).

Ani (1994) invokes the twinness principle to explain the genesis and perpetuation of racism. She states that the dualistic mind-set—the cultural and intellectual legacy of the Platonic view and Aristotelian ethics existing in the Eurocentric paradigm—has contributed to the antagonistic stance that is manifested in racism and similarly oppressive systems, such as patriarchy (Wise, 2006). Dualism, dichotomous thinking, and splitting can lead to irreconcilable judgment and valuation. Specific to the issue of racism, *non-Whiteness* becomes a category that is dichotomous and diametrically opposed to *Whiteness* (Akintunde, 1999). Non-Whiteness and Whiteness become binary opposites that cannot comfortably coexist owing to the nature of the Eurocentric worldview (Ani, 1994). The opposite of Whiteness is perceived to be threatening, defined as inferior and deficient, thus justifying the need to have it controlled by Whiteness. Ani's (1994) consideration of the concept of twinness uses one of the major cultural precepts of an Afri-centric paradigm as a framework for analyzing and understanding the systemic ills of racism, oppression, and Eurocentric hegemony, and can be a useful way of combating internalized oppression and developing personal and collective approaches to address the negative impact of racism and oppression.

Not only does this articulation of this principle highlight the interconnectedness of seeming opposites with each other, it also embodies the possibility of conceptualizing the opposite as a *helper,* one that, simultaneously, can be a problem and can provide the motivation for right action and positive transformation (Stepteau-Watson & Tolliver, in press). Through cognitive restructuring about the nature of the purpose of the "opposite," one can have more agency in the face of racism, acting in resistance to oppression and domination (Thomas & Hollenshead, 2001). Saying that racism, White privilege, oppression, and other similar issues can be reframed as helpers is not to say that they are good or desirable. To reach that conclusion, in fact, is reverting back to the dualistic thinking that characterizes the Eurocentric paradigm. Such reversion is not surprising, given that most of us in academia are trained in programs, regardless of the discipline area, that are grounded in Western European hegemony.

The demand to think and operate within the African-centered paradigm, therefore, requires conscious effort to shift one's perspective from the conventional Eurocentric framework. Continuing with the example, the reality of racism and institutionalized oppression is accepted, not rendered invisible, under the cloak of a color-blind norm (Thompson, 2001). Racism is not to be nurtured as helper, but as Somé (1999) says about conflict, "it is to be listened to," so that our actions emerge as a restoration of harmony and balance, in support of self-determination, renewal, and transformation (p. 110). The concept of twinness can help us, in the face of racism, to extract ourselves from being oppressed and injustice-driven, so that we can proactively pursue social justice. Kambon (1998) concluded that the response to this reality, considered within the African-centered paradigm, comes from a place of self-affirmation, not weakness or vulnerability.

FROM THEORY TO PRACTICE

As an adult educator, I ground my practice within an African-centered paradigm because it reflects my commitment to challenging and confronting racist ideas and practices in multiple areas through my being and actions. However, given that I have been educated and work within institutions that are based upon Eurocentric values and assumptions, I must also constantly engage in self-assessment to ensure that my actions are not distorted by the invisible norms of Whiteness. I begin by self-examining, by acknowledging, and confronting the negative effects of Eurocentrism in my own life and work, and then I use this process to provide a model for learners and colleagues, so that they too can confront their own problematic behaviors and attitudes.

My classroom becomes a space where learners are exposed to learning materials that support the legitimacy of the African-centered paradigm as a conceptual framework in order to foster critical consciousness in school and other areas of their lives. For example, in one class, students are assigned *The Mis-education of the Negro,* by Carter G. Woodson (1933), and music and lyrics by Nina Simone. As they read and listen to these works that speak to the human condition from an African-centered interpretative frame, they learn about the history and cultures of people of African descent and broaden their understanding of the meaning of scholarship and what constitutes literary classics. Similarly, music, movement, and poetry, as well as other representations of knowing and being in the world, are provided and legitimized as tools for facilitating learning, with critical analysis of their potential for supporting emancipation or perpetuating oppression of different peoples. These choices of curricular content and learning methodologies challenge the conventional privileged approaches to knowledge dissemination. The application of the principle of twinness provides a framework for examining the purpose and outcome of these educational decisions.

The African-centered paradigm emphasizes collective and social relationships as well as spiritual connectivity. This is consistent with major precepts of the African-centered paradigm. So in my courses I endeavor to construct an atmosphere that embraces holistic learning, to be experienced cognitively, affectively, kinesthetically, and spiritually. I also support learning that occurs both through the individual's effort and within the context of the group. This is, again, another example of the twinness and complementarity principles in action.

In mentoring students, in particular those who are experiencing extreme uncertainty, self-doubt, and a sense of failure, I use the twinness principle to help them connect to the companion affect and to positions of competence, confidence, and success. I encourage them to identify elders and ancestors whom they perceive to have been successful, and I then encourage them to connect with the oneness shared with those role models. Working with this African-centered principle often allows students to see a different, more positive possibility for themselves, through the connection with a successful other. I help them affirm aspects of themselves that have often been devalued or dismissed when assessed by a cultural paradigm that is asynchronous with their lived experiences and realities.

Given the centrality of spirituality in the African-centered paradigm, I also honor nonmaterial, nonrational ways of knowing, understanding, and being the world with my students. This is the complement to the material and rational. One of the favorite activities in all of my courses is beginning with the ritual of centering, which allows time and space for focused breathing and guided meditation in order to prepare for the upcoming activities in the classroom. Students report this to be inspirational, and they often find themselves connecting or reconnecting to some aspect of their spirituality to assist in their classroom work.

It has also been important for me and other colleagues of African descent to remind students which alternatives to Eurocentric ways of knowing and being in the world are valid and legitimate. Here again, operating from an African-centered lens can facilitate action that addresses the invisibility of the Eurocentric norm. A recent example of this occurred at a meeting where concern was expressed about the viability of a collaboration that did not have a specific individual designated as director. I challenged the insistence upon a solution based on the individualistic focus and advocated for consideration of a more collective approach to leadership. This was, in fact, more compatible and consistent with the values and culture of the people with whom we would be partnering.

The African-centered paradigm also provides guidance for the content and methodologies of my creative and scholarship activities, many of which involve issues of race and culture. As Mkabela (2005) notes: "The collective as well as the holistic orientation suggest that research should disclose and apply codes, paradigms, symbols, and circles of discussion that strengthen the centrality of indigenous African ideals and values as a legitimate frame of reference for collecting and interpreting data"(p. 186). In keeping with this view, I have asked people to respond with symbols rather than words in answers to survey questions used in my research; I have also presented symbols and nonverbal prompts to stimulate responses. I have presented data with poetry and in visual, nonliterary forms. I have also used community-based collection processes, within a cultural location, to enhance the data that were received.

EMBRACING THE AFRICAN-CENTERED PARADIGM

Clearly, the effort to incorporate issues of race and culture into pedagogy in the field of adult education is not new. Many have championed consideration of the African-centered paradigm in adult education practice (see, for example, Colin III, 2002; Sheared, 1999; Johnson-Bailey, 2001; Alfred, 2001). It is on their strong and often weary shoulders that I stand as I write my words now.

Adult education is racialized, grounded in the principles that emerge from Western European intellectual traditions and conceptualizations (Brookfield, 2003). As such, its expectations for theory and practice and for knowledge production and knowledge dissemination are often at odds with the expectations of those whose lived experiences emerge from a different cultural and conceptual base. The appeal to use an African-centered paradigm for critical analysis of issues of race and racism (while not limiting its use to these areas) necessarily presents a challenge for adult education as a field that like most, is grounded in the tenets of a Eurocentric theoretical framework. The African-centered paradigm neither denigrates nor precludes adopting Western theorizing where it is appropriate and not an imposition (Mkabela, 2005). This paradigm does, however, expose falsehoods and problems with the Eurocentric framework. In that respect, its principles are relevant to oppressed and dominant groups alike (Asante, 1994).

Although many adult educators may not choose to embrace the African-centered paradigm as a personal guide for living, we can all recognize that it is a legitimate conceptual framework with which to not only examine and understand the lived experiences of people of African descent but also to better understand and generate empowered responses to issues related to race and racism. We can learn much from its precepts and principles, with the awareness that others also live by these precepts and principles and use them as personal resources.

Embracing the African-centered paradigm as valid and legitimate epistemology will lead to deep discussion about concepts that often make people very uncomfortable: race, oppression, White supremacy, Eurocentric hegemony, and liberation of oppressed people. The centers of knowledge will necessarily shift to include multiple worldviews that represent cultural synchronicity, consistent with the lived experiences and values of people of African descent. Can adult education embrace the metaphoric, symbolic reality of this paradigm? Can scholarship that references spirit and spiritual technologies or dissemination be accepted in top-level journals? Can proverbs be considered alongside empirical data as legitimate evidence, or will measurement and objectification continue to be privileged?

If adult education is truly committed to undoing systems of oppression and marginalization within its own ranks, it must take the risk of telling the truth about cultural imposition and racist assumptions and ideologies that have operated in various practices, often invisible to many, rather than embracing a sweet falsehood of itself as a race-neutral, color-blind profession. The African-centered paradigm provides an avenue for the profession to move to a more pluralistic reality. It will be in its twinness, through the death of the old hegemony and the birth of new considerations, that the field of adult education will become more welcoming, vibrant, and alive.

REFERENCES

Akbar, N. (1975). Rhythmic patterns in African personality. *Journal of Psychiatry, 130*, 223–241.

Akintunde, O. (1999). White racism, White supremacy, White privilege and the social construction of race: Moving from modernist to postmodernist multiculturalism. *Multicultural Education, 7*, 2–8.

Alfred, M. V. (2001). Expanding theories of career development: Adding the voices of African American women in the White academy. *Adult Education Quarterly, 51*, 108–124.

Alkebulan, A. A. (2007). Defending the paradigm. *Journal of Black Studies, 37*, 410–427.

Ani, M. (1994). *Yurugu: An African-centered critique of European cultural thought and behavior.* Trenton, NJ: Africa World Press.

Asante, M. K. (1994). *The Afrocentric idea.* Philadelphia: Temple University Press.

Brookfield, S. (2003). Racializing criticality in adult education. *Adult Education Quarterly, 53*, 154–169.

Carroll, G. (1998). Mundane extreme environmental stress and African American families: A case for recognizing different realities. *Journal of Comparative Family Studies, 29*(2), 271–284.

Christian, M. (2006). Black studies in the 21st century: Longevity has its place. *Journal of Black Studies, 36*, 698–719.

Colin, S.A.J., III. (2002). Marcus Garvey: Africentric adult education for selfethnic reliance. In E. Peterson (Ed.), *Freedom road: Adult education for African Americans* (pp. 41–65). Malabar, FL: Krieger.

Colin, S.A.J., III, & Guy, T. (1998). An Africentric interpretive model of curriculum orientations for course development in graduate programs in adult education. *PAACE Journal of Lifelong Learning, 7*, 43–55.

Gyeke, K. (1988). *The unexamined life: Philosophy and the African experience.* Legon, Ghana: Sankofa.

Johnson-Bailey, J. (2001). *Sistahs in college: Making a way out of no way.* Malabar, FL: Krieger.

Kambon, K. K. (1998). *African/Black psychology in the American context: An African-centered approach.* Tallahassee, FL: Nubian Nation.

Mkabela, Q. (2005). Using the Afrocentric method in researching indigenous African culture. *The Qualitative Report, 10*(1), 178–189.

Peters, M. F., & Massey, G. (1983). Mundane extreme environmental stress in family stress theories: The case of Black families in White America. In J. M. Patterson, H. I. McCubbin, & M. B. Sussman (Eds.), *Social stress and the family: Advances and developments in family stress theory and research* (pp. 193–218). Binghamton, NY: Haworth Press.

Schiele, J. H. (1994). Afrocentricity: Implications for higher education. *Journal of Black Studies, 25,* 150–169.

Sheared, V. (1999). Giving voice: Inclusion of African American students' polyrhythmic realities in adult basic education. In T. Guy (Ed.), *Providing culturally relevant adult education: A challenge for the twenty first century* (New Directions for Adult and Continuing Education, No. 82, pp. 33–48). San Francisco: Jossey-Bass.

Somé, S. (1999). *The spirit of intimacy.* New York: Morrow.

Stepteau-Watson, D., & Tolliver, D. E. (in press). Substance abuse in African American adolescents. In H. Grey (Ed.), *Psychological treatment of ethnic minority populations.* New York: Oxford University Press.

Thompson, A. (2001). *Summary of Whiteness theory.* Retrieved May 12, 2007, from http://www.pauahtun.org/Whiteness-Summary-1.html.

Thomas, G. D., & Hollenshead, C. (2001). Resisting from the margins: The coping strategies of Black women and other women of color faculty members at a research university. *Journal of Negro Education, 70,* 166–176.

Tolliver, D. E. (2002). *My journey into the sacred art of teaching.* Unpublished manuscript.

Venter, E. (2004). The notion of *ubuntu* and communalism in African educational discourse. *Studies in Philosophy and Education, 23*(2–3), 149–160.

Wise, T. (2006, May). Paleness as pathology: The future of racism and anti-racism in America. *LiP.* Retrieved December 9, 2009, from http://www.lipmagazine.org/~timwise/palepathology.html.

Woodson, C. G. (1933). *The mis-education of the Negro.* Washington, DC: Associated.

Inpowering the Self
A Journey Toward Ending Racism

What we have seen in these chapters in Part Four, "Reframing the Field Through the Lens of Race," is an ideological development schema regarding *White racism*. In these chapters the authors use their various perspectives to advocate their individual understandings of the impact and influences of these intersections of White racism with their own educational practices. These authors, who are all educators, discuss how they have addressed the impact of White racism on their practices through the interjection of new perspectives, curriculum content, and instructional strategies.

In some ways these discussions had a sense of a gathering of sister scholars who had traveled through a cognitive and affective *mind field* to sit around a kitchen table together and to discuss their approaches and strategies for dealing with the intrusive disruption of *White racist ideology*. At times the discussions also took on the tone of a meeting of members of a resistance movement engaged in battling the intellectual apartheid of the academy.

Each of these authors demonstrated a commitment in her practice to introducing analytical and interpretive frames that she and her students could use not only to facilitate an understanding about the impact that toxic racism has on us all but also to develop a knowledge scheme that, by framing the discussion within the context of White racist ideology, would identify the true owners and perpetrators of White racism. As educators, these authors examined the marginalization they experienced in their own classrooms, which often left them with a sense of being "in the world, but not of it." As educators who refuse to lead unexamined academic practices, each author shared in the awareness that if assumptions regarding racial superiority and inferiority go unchallenged they will become realities for educators and for their students.

As these authors and educators shared the challenges and victories of their authentic lived experiences in the battle against White racist ideology, the conversation went beyond chitchat among like-minded scholars and rose to the level of a sage discourse that produced a battle plan. Their spoken words in their discourse and their written words on the pages serve to liberate and *inpower* (not *empower*) us. We all, section editors and authors, made the decision to use the descriptor *inpowering* once we realized that it best described the early stages of the respective journey each of us takes as we transition from our public selves, which are constructed upon racist assumptions and framed within stereotypes of inferiority, to our true racial selves. You inpower yourself when you first assume the power to define who you are. This action in turn determines what you should commit to. The authors in Part Four suggested that this realization could occur in various ways. However, they all agreed that indeed, the first necessary action involves the reclamation and reaffirmation of our racial humanity.

Yes, we and all who have been the objects of racism have at some point in our lives had those moments of shedding bitter tears, but for those of us in the struggle, these tears wash away the veil that prevents us from seeing our true selves; as DuBois described, no more double consciousness, no more dilemmas. In various ways, our shared experience of being conceptually colonized and our choice to engage in our own decolonization process, a kind of deprogramming process, begins to unite us. But first, we separately make the choice to be actors in our own lives, to rescue ourselves. The writers of these chapters determined that one has to decide to move beyond the process of merely naming one's self and actually become that self: to think it, be it, and act it. In other words, to no longer be the *noun,* or the object that is acted on, but to choose instead to be the *verb,* the actor, the source of the action. It is a decision one has to make; we all have to choose the validity of our sociocultural histories and our lived experiences that reflect our true selves and reject the perverted racist creation of that "public person."

Through their spoken and written words, the authors in these chapters lead all of us into a discussion about how we as teachers, community activists, and leaders can provide this same kind of liberatory transformative process for both our students and our colleagues. The approaches provided in these chapters highlight a common goal of instituting a pedagogy that is reflective of a sociocultural understanding of both the oppressed and the oppressor. It becomes clear as one reads through these chapters, that in racializing the discourse we begin to recognize that *methodological mediation* is not a viable option if we expect to understand the import and impact of race and racism on the socialized self.

It became even more apparent to us as editors progressing through this project that along with obtaining a greater sense of understanding comes a sense of responsibility that all of us must engage in certain actions. This engagement is not predicated upon, or done *because of,* some level of collegial or institutional support (for we have all learned that mission statements more times than not are words from the shallow well of good intentions), but rather it is taken up *in spite of* the fact that this support has been missing at crucial stages.

For the editors of this section, the emotional uplift that resulted from interacting around our metaphorical kitchen table with these authors and sisters of color who had become comfortable in their own skins was balm to heal the wounds we had each endured. Somehow, the stories brought the group together as we recognized that even though we had traveled different roads to this convergence, each of us had survived a similar journey. Somehow we found ourselves at the same place, in our now perfectly fitting skins, seeing ourselves through the empathetic understanding eyes of racial pride and not seeing ourselves through the eyes of White racism. As you examine the words on these pages, we hope that you too find yourself quieting your thirst for external validation and drinking from the deep wells of cultural centers.

As the authors of the chapters in Part Four engaged in a critique on race and racism and the possibilities of the future, they challenged us to explore within our own lives and to ask ourselves

- Who has the power to define me save myself?
- How does language racialize my existence?
- How can I make a difference in my place of practice? How can I build fighting racism in as a course objective?

Answering these tough questions begins with acknowledging that racism does exist and that fighting racism is a moral issue. It is important in this resistance movement to understand that power is used to determine the norms and to influence what is examined and what goes unexamined, to determine acceptable and unacceptable behavior. As educators who are committed to engaging in the struggle to fight racism in our classrooms and programs, it is necessary that we commit to detoxifying our practices.

These authors demonstrate that in order to change how we see others, we must show an acceptance and a commitment to work and we must walk through the pain that will result from exploring and raising our own consciousness. We must accept and embrace the unpleasant parts of the journey. For how else will we be able to assist our students and colleagues in going through this journey if we have not done so ourselves? Does this personal and professional paradigm shift require a level of risk? Yes! But clearly the commitment of each of us, in the words of an anonymous soul mate, is to "Be that kind of woman that when your feet hit the floor each morning the devil says, 'Oh crap, she's up.'"

PART FIVE

Individual and Collective Responses to Race and Racism

This, the final leg of our journey, begins with the four editors of this book, Vanessa, Juanita, Scipio, and Stephen, collectively reflecting on what we have learned about race and racism from the experiences shared by the authors in this book. We'll start by letting you in on a conversation that we had on race and racism as we sat around the *kitchen table*, a heartwarming and safe setting where difficult conversations on any subject can occur. It is a location where you find families partaking of food and information about what has transpired during the day. In this symbolic space people share expectations, hopes, joys, tribulations, and pains. So while we use the term *kitchen table*, we recognize that your table might be one in your classroom, your home, or your office, or it might be any space in which people gather in a group to work through problems, resolve issues, gain understanding, or find ways to just get through. So, as we come to this final conversation around the proverbial kitchen table, we do so first as a collective, moving next to individual reflections, and then to presenting strategies from our professional and personal practices.

OUR COLLECTIVE RESPONSE: CHANGE ISN'T EASY, BUT IT'S NEEDED

Here we address what we have learned about the intersection of race, racism, power, privilege, and gender as a result of working on this book project. From our changing practices we address issues that we have encountered and offer some insights for the field of adult education. When we began this endeavor, each of us had a hope that at the end of the road all four of us would know the differences and similarities between *racism* and *privilege*: Are these concepts one and the same, or are they two distinct correlates bound by people's perceptions of who they are as individuals and who they are in the context of a collective bound by race, gender, culture, and beliefs? We engaged in a series of dialogues with each other and asked others to engage with us in similar conversations. We also listened to our contributors' stories, trying to ultimately ascertain the definition of racism. According to Colin III and Preciphs (1991), racism "permeates the roots of American society and is reflected in all its societal institutions, and that racism was created by White Americans and is perpetuated by them." The Anti-Defamation League (2001) describes racism as the "belief that a particular race is superior or inferior to another, that a person's social and moral traits are predetermined by his or her inborn biological characteristics. Racial separatism is the belief, most of the time based on racism, that different races should remain segregated and apart from one another."

Each of the four of us agrees that racism exists when a person or group exerts power and control over another individual or group as a result of his or her racial identity—an identity that is defined by the melanin in one's skin. Each of the authors in this book isolated some form of racism or aspects thereof through which they exerted power over others (see Part Two on White privilege) or others exerted power over them (see Parts One and Four)—a power or force that negated its objects or obfuscated their existence in a given social, political, or historical context.

When we began this project, George W. Bush was in the beginning of his second term as president; and the United States was at war in Iraq and Afghanistan, on Orange Alert against terrorists, according to the Homeland Security rating system, and full of people concerned about threats to their way of life and the ideals of their nation. Since then the political landscape has changed tremendously: (1) the nation's first African American president, Barack Hussein Obama, has been elected; (2) the first Latina justice, Sonia Sotomayor, has been appointed to the U.S. Supreme Court; (3) a Latino, Leon Panetta, now heads the Central Intelligence Agency (CIA); (4) a Latina, Hilda Solis, is secretary of labor; (5) Hillary Clinton, a Euro-American woman who ran a strong campaign for the Democratic presidential nomination, has become secretary of state; and (6) Eric Holder is the first African American U.S. attorney general. Several more cabinet-level appointments also signal remarkable differences: Kenneth Salazar, a Latino, is secretary of the interior; Steven Chu, an Asian American, is secretary of energy; and Eric K. Shinseki, an Asian American, is secretary of veterans affairs. All of these strides forward signal a change in U.S. politics, and yet and still the topic of racism is alive and well.

This time of transformations has been referred to as the period of post-racial and post-ethnic America, as if to suggest that race and racism are concerns of the past and subjects that we no longer need to talk about or seek to change. There are those in America who would like to just forget that slavery occurred and who see the U.S. internment of the Japanese in camps during World War II as just a bad mistake. Further, many Americans believe that the Black power, civil rights, women's rights, Chicano rights, United Farm Workers, and American Indian movements have all served their purpose and that those who once suffered have been compensated. So there is no longer a need for us to dwell on or talk about race, racism, marginalization, or any other thing that speak to the negation of people's rights, because after all, in America if you work hard, you too can have the American Dream.

We, the editors of this book, do not debate that working hard is a good common goal, but we do want to remind our readers that having a leg up and an opportunity to work hard is not something that all people are afforded. In part, we believe that racism has played and continues to play a significant role in whether a person or a people can believe in life chances and finding opportunities. While we believe that racism is real, we also acknowledge that how we talk about it in social circles has oftentimes led us into circuitous and sometimes light-hearted chatter. This is usually because of our discomfort in discussing this topic. Talking about such things is difficult at best, especially given how such talk deeply worries those who exert the power and control in this society and threatens the disenfranchised with the possibility of harm. As we engaged in conversations with each other about this topic, we often, since we were working on a book on the subject, addressed race and racism as a practical business matter. This let us off the hook for dealing with the topic among ourselves as if we were devoid of any fault. Another technique we used was to occupy or move into an intellectual comfort zone, discussing philosophical and theoretical ideals or the lack thereof.

ENTERING THE DIALOGUE: AM I SAFE?

When we began the process of creating this book, we talked about who would be responsible for what, negotiated who would take the lead, and found ourselves mired in a set of issues and factors separate and apart from our own assumptions about race and racism. To some extent there was a sense of relief at the end of these conversations; yet a sense of frustration persisted too, for we found it all too easy to end the conversations without ever talking about how we, the editors, could talk about race. Generally, we found that conversations on race and racism often started off with people jousting back and forth about technical matters; this seemed to be a testing of the waters to determine how safe it was to enter the discussion. In reflection we noted that this occurred repeatedly. With this revelation a fog lifted and a clouded perspective became clear, and we moved into very deep conversations about how race and racism affected our work within and across racial lines. For example, the following exchange between Vanessa and Stephen occurred after several minutes of these two going back and forth in discussing the questions we had asked the chapter authors. Vanessa, talking about the elections, asked Stephen:

> Do you think Barack Obama being elected has changed things?... because that is what I hear now. Now that Barack Obama has made it over to the other side, to the highest office, that Whites think that this is really evidence that things are changing. And could you see that... just looking at your community and where you are?

Stephen responded:

> Yes, I think most of my White friends would say this is a transformational moment and marks a massive movement forward in this country. I don't think they would say it is the end of racism but they would say that it is an incredibly hopeful sign and they would attribute to it something very significant. It is never going to be the same. We have a qualitative movement forward here. So I do think that most Whites would regard it that way. I was teaching a class a couple of weeks ago where we talked about this. I was talking not about a critical race theory but critical theory perspective on it that said the forces of power are far too enduring for this to be the transformation that you think it is. And in fact a more plausible interpretation is that this situation will be co-opted to underscore how enduring our structures will be—while we see Barack Obama in office and we see his face and we see Michelle's face that that sort of public face has not really changed anything. It has made racism even easier because it is now going to be even more covert and subtle and anyone can just say "of course things have changed because now we have

the nation's first African American president." And that is something that I think a lot of the White students were resistant to hear.

Vanessa asked Stephen to explain this further, and he continued:

Yeah, they just thought I was being overly negative and cynical and a lot of my students say that "you always see race here and always talk about race in situations that it doesn't exist." . . . I think that Whites are at different points in their individual trajectories of being able to confront their own racism. When there's already a stated commitment to doing that then you can have [a more open conversation about racism] . . . . But in the majority-White classes I often teach I think there's a real reluctance, because of a sense that racism is now over, to focus on race. Students ask, "Why are we still talking about it now we have an African American president; can't we move on to something else?" And I have to say I feel this in me too—I think, "Do I really have the energy and commitment to raise race again when I know students are going to resist talking about it, or when they're going to mark me down on my end-of-course evaluations because I keep bringing it up?"

As you will note, even though we had the best of intentions, we found as a collective that we often were trapped in a cycle of conversations that remained aloof and detached. Even when inroads were made and we began to share more about things that mattered to us, as Stephen did in talking about his classroom experience, we still struggled to say how racism felt when we encountered in our own lives—in that moment. So at best we tried and at worst we failed to define for ourselves and each other what we thought racism meant to each of us in our personal lives. We often had more success when we kept the topic and examples related to our professional lives in the abstract. Although racism touched us in our professional roles, it was clear we had the intellectual prowess to talk about it from a theoretical and philosophical standpoint. We worked through the business and the intellectualization of racism, but we never really had that conversation that was earth-shattering. While we had made an inroad, we recognized that we had not moved to the point where we all felt truly safe; yet clearly we had moved beyond just talking about the mechanics of developing, writing, and editing the book.

INTENTIONALITY, RACE, AND RACISM: THE BEST-LAID PLANS

So, what did we learn about ourselves or our intentions concerning the development and completion of this book on race and racism in adult and higher education? Upon completion of this project we had learned that a beginning dialogue on race requires that an individual be open to not having all the answers. All too often people stop trying because they think that unless they know the outcome or have a specific outcome in mind they should not attempt or begin something. We often felt that because we didn't have the answers, we couldn't find the right entry point to discuss race and racism, that we had no right to push the conversation forward. As we sat around the kitchen table we established in Chicago, we started and stopped many times. Were our intentions to engage in a dialogue on race enough? Should we be doing more? This exchange between Vanessa and Scipio, spurred by our reading a draft of one of the chapters in the book, offers a glimpse into why intentions matter. Scipio commented:

> I think we have to go by our experiences. I mean there's no doubt that there have been times in my life when I have identified something and the response has been, "Well, you're just too sensitive." And my response has been, "Well, you may not be sensitive enough." I think that is a cop-out. Now, conversely, everything that happens is not racist. I think now I have my own internal gauge so that if I say this is racist it is. That I have processed it. I know what it looks like. I know what it feels like. So I don't look for external evaluations.

Vanessa responded with further reflections:

> I think that's an important feature because I think that people do tend to use race and racism on almost anything. It has now

been co-opted by conservative Whites, if you will, so that it now allows them to call the disenfranchised and marginalized racist when they don't agree with or [when they] challenge majority group members.... [Conservative Whites] are now saying that [disagreement] was once evident as racism. That's not racism.... And in fact it isn't a racist comment. Or is it? And that's why I think we do have to be careful and think very hard about what we're calling racism. And what is racism? Having a clear definition for it is important. And so when we look at the chapter, the reason why we're looking at it and going . . . oh, this is kind of scary on the one hand . . . on the other hand, isn't it good that we have a space for this conversation to take place. And that's a part of it. If we don't have that conversation happening we don't know we need to have a response to it. This now allows us a way to talk about race and to frame it or discuss racism as being permanent. There are those that believe that, yes, racism is color-blind. But the reality is that this is what we believe racism is. If we define it, it has to have these elements to it.

Intentions, definitions, and actions, as well as a willingness to engage in dialogue about race and racism, matter. We discovered as we moved forward that while these things matter, it is far easier to describe what and how than it is to do. When individuals come together in groups to discuss race and racism, initially there may be a great deal of jousting back and forth between group members, to the extent of rendering attempts to engage in dialogue null and void. This does not lead to movement forward, and group members may become trapped in this cycle unless one person takes the risk of asking a question that pushes the members beyond talking abstractly and into talking more concretely about how race and racism influence their lives. They then begin to share examples from their lived experiences and that leads them to meaning making as they answer the question, Just how do race and racism affect how one lives and works in the world? *Pushing forward* is what we call the action that occurs when you think you've reached the end but then you find yourself asking the one question that causes you to pause, reflect, and react either in word or deed.

PUSHING FORWARD

What we learned at the end of our journey, during the two days we spent together in Chicago and the three years we spent drafting and crafting this book via conference calls and e-mails, is that most people, including ourselves, have a long way to go before they find a comfort zone in which to discuss the topic of racism and its profound effect upon who they are, how they view others, and in what ways they interact with those of different races. We recognized that of all the mediums we had used to communicate with one another, face-to-face dialogue offered us the most valuable and unique set of opportunities to push each other. (Not to take away from the other mediums used—we also recognized that if we had not laid the groundwork for the face-to-face meeting, we would not have been able to go as far as we did in Chicago or with this book project.) Although we didn't come away from this project with over-the-top aha moments, we did come away with a deeper understanding of why it is so difficult for many people, even good friends like us, to discuss racism. At the same time, we still think there are things educators and others can do to encourage this type of conversation. In the last portion of Chapter Twenty-One, our epilogue, we offer some of these activities and processes that you can use to tackle this very difficult topic.

THE ENGAGEMENT: PUSHING THE DIALOGUE FORWARD

As we suggested at the beginning of this project, we did not want to engage just in a dialogue about the issues of race and racism in our lives and practices; we wanted to, in the end, provoke thought and provide some possible ways in which we all might generate solutions to uncover, discover, and resolve the issues of race and racism in our lives and in our practices. So our hope is that the stories, voices, shared experiences, and strategies presented by the authors and storytellers in this volume will evoke thought and will remind you that you are OK and that there is nothing wrong with you for thinking that perhaps what you thought or experienced and felt in a certain moment was not an illusion but was indeed an act of racism toward you or an act of racism committed by you.

Racism pervades everyone's life, for it has been institutionalized in our curricula, schools, corporations, businesses, and politics. Each chapter author in this book has shared ways in which racism occurred in his or her life or was perpetuated by something he or she did. These authors shared how they overcame or are overcoming these acts, individually recognizing that telling their stories, although not easy, was necessary in order to begin the internal healing process and to begin the act of healing with the "other." As one does so, the other becomes a part of the self, and the self is renewed and begins to generate a new reality. The reality of one person does not negate the experiences or racial differences of another but allows space to respect or accept the experiences and feelings that are grounded in another's cultural, historical, and political antecedents. Once this occurs, healing can begin to take place, thereby allowing a common thread of experience to be discovered and recovered among and between racial groups that were once divided by racist ideologies. As we ourselves, along with each chapter author, have struggled to share, we understand that while this has been important it is only a beginning step.

In Chapter Twenty-One we offer you additional strategies that we have learned through the acts of courage disclosed through the lived experiences of our authors, and also methods and tactics imparted from our own praxis. We do not make these suggestions or share our approaches with the intent of saying that we have definitive answers. We, like many of you, are works in progress and practice. And so we offer these recommendations to you for advancing your own praxis.

REFERENCES

Anti-Defamation League. (2001). *Racism.* Retrieved December 10, 2009, from http://www.adl.org/hate-patrol/racism.asp.

Colin, S.A.J., III, & Preciphs, T. (1991). Perceptual patterns and the learning environment: Confronting White racism. In R. Hiemstra (Ed.), *Creating environments for effective adult learning* (New Directions for Adult and Continuing Education, No. 50, pp. 61–70). San Francisco: Jossey-Bass.

21

Epilogue
Implications for Curriculum, Programming, and Research

SCIPIO A. J. COLIN III
VANESSA SHEARED
JUANITA JOHNSON-BAILEY
STEPHEN D. BROOKFIELD

The intent throughout this book has been to demonstrate that if people share their experiences, listen to their own stories and those of others, and reflect on the meanings that underlie their thoughts and feelings, then as teachers, scholars, students, parents, administrators, and citizens of the world, they can create new opportunities to work and communicate with one another. There are no simple answers or solutions, as we have demonstrated throughout this book. However, if one is willing to engage, push forward and tap into the self, and open up to new ways of being and operating, then the difficult conversations on race and racism are possible, meaningful, and life changing. We offer four paradigms in this epilogue, but recognize that there are many others from which you could choose. The stories shared by the authors in this book, along with the suggestions that follow reveal steps that can be taken to move the discourse on race and racism from the kitchen table into institutions, schools, board rooms, churches, and other organizations in an effort to eliminate the ways in which racism has adversely affected these settings.

SCIPIO: AFRICENTRISM IN PRACTICE

Africentrism is also referred to in the literature as *Afrocentrism, African-centered,* and *pan-Africanism.* These descriptors all reflect the same salient purposes, concepts, ideas, philosophies, and theories. The differences lie in the form of descriptors and do not denote what some refer to as *Black studies* or *Black philosophy,* terms that reflect various modes of philosophical inquiry and other culturally grounded intellectual paradigms. This is an important point to be made, as there is a prevailing assumption that one who advocates or articulates the learning and precepts of philosophers of the African Diaspora speaks in an authoritative voice regarding Africentrism as both a paradigm and a discipline. This issue can be reframed as a guiding question in a discussion of racializing the discourse: "At what point do we know more about ourselves than others?" (Carruthers, 1999; Colin III, 2002b). I define *Africentrism* (Hayes & Colin III, 1994) as a

> sociocultural and philosophical perspective that reflects the intellectual traditions of both a culture and a continent. It is grounded in these seven basic values (the Swahili term is provided first, followed by its English translation): Umoja (unity), Kujichagulia (self-determination), Ujima (collective work and responsibility), Ujamaa (cooperative economics), Nia (purpose), Kuumba (creativity), and Imani (faith) . . . . The term Africentrism was originally used by Colin III (1988, p. 3).

This paradigm is an analytical and interpretive frame that is employed by a specific group of scholars, Africentric and Africanist, who have chosen to ground themselves in the African-centered knowledge base by engaging in the analysis of the impact of sociocultural and intellectual racism on Africans and members of the African Diaspora, using ideas, concepts, philosophical frames, and theoretical constructs that are culturally grounded, or African centered (Asante, 1990; Colin III, 1999/2007, 2002a). Asante (1988) describes this mode of inquiry as *Africology* and explains that it

> denotes the Afrocentric study of African concepts, issues, and behaviors. In recent years Winston Van Horne of the University of Wisconsin at Milwaukee has promoted Africology as a more fluent term to describe the discipline.... As used by Van Horne, Africology is the transgenerational and transcontinental Afrocentric study of African phenomena. There are three fundamental existential postures that one can take with respect to the human condition: "feeling, knowing and acting, which are sometimes known as the affective, cognitive, and conative positions. Africology recognizes these three stances as being interrelated, not separate" [pp. 19–20].

I suggest that the introduction of this paradigm should follow the same conceptual sequence as any other. There must be a determination of (1) what it is that one must know regarding the Africentric paradigm (what the salient elements are of this intellectual tradition); (2) what is it that one must understand regarding the philosophical groundings (the values, beliefs, and so forth); and (3) what one should be able to do (the implications for practice). I offer the following suggestions.

Curriculum and Resources

The sources used in the course must be drawn exclusively from the Africentric bodies of literature. The salient commitments and goals of Africentric and Africanist scholars are to pull from the African-centered knowledge base and scholarship to identify, analyze, and articulate. This will aid in determining the most appropriate actions to take and goals to set, with the aim of addressing the impact that sociocultural and intellectual racism has on the lives of Africans and African peoples. This is in line with the purpose and goal of Africentrism, that is, to combat intellectual racism and challenge the assumption that Africans and members of the African Diaspora have but one role in the area of knowledge production. The assumption has been that they are only consumers and not producers. Additionally, the aim is to challenge the assumption of White racist ideology that members of the African Diaspora are intellectually inferior. And moreover, given that knowledge is culturally grounded, the aim is to present accurate sociocultural and intellectual histories of African Americans in the United States, as well as throughout the African Diaspora (Colin III, 1994).

I believe that when we know and understand the conceptual groundings from whence a particular tree of knowledge emerged, we begin to understand why the fruits (ideas, concepts, theories, philosophies, and so forth) of that tree should be placed (centered) in a specific intellectual basket (tradition).

Role and Responsibilities of Africentric and Africanist Scholars

It is imperative that adult learners understand that the Africentric intellectual paradigm is an analytical and interpretative frame that is used by a specific group of scholars (Africentric and Africanist) who have chosen to ground themselves in an intellectual tradition both cognitively and affectively. All share the same goal of the liberation of Africans and African peoples of the Diaspora. As such, each has shared values, beliefs, and a commitment to centering himself or herself intellectually, socioculturally, and sociohistorically within an African-centered context or construct. This involves the presentation and continuous development of both accurate and appropriate sociocultural and sociohistorical contextual meaning constructs in which the values, beliefs, ideas, and knowledge are culturally grounded. These elements are reflected in Colin III's (1999/2007) credo for Africentric scholars:

An Africentric Scholars Credo

I believe in the placement of Africa and the African Worldview in the center of any sociocultural and sociohistorical analysis of African Peoples (Africans and members of the African Diaspora).

I believe that racism is the primary impact factor relative to African Peoples.

I believe that Africans and members of the African Diaspora need to reclaim and regain a sense of selfethnic and cultural identity through the serious study of an accurate African Peoples History.

I am committed to the eradication of the impact and influence of sociocultural, sociohistorical and intellectual racism on the spheres of life of African Peoples, through research and culturally grounded knowledge.

I am committed to the use of African Centered concepts, philosophies and theories as units of analysis and interpretation.

I am committed to the incorporation of these elements in the development of a Selfethnic Liberatory Pedagogy.

I will not present these intellectual products (ideas, concepts, theories and philosophies) as having universal relevance or applications to those other than African Peoples. Note: While I acknowledge the possibility of relevant application regarding other peoples of color, I respect their right to "Bell Their Cat."

These scholars have a responsibility to engage in the analytical process to identify and resolve the impact of sociocultural and intellectual racism on Africans and members of the African Diaspora by using culturally grounded concepts, philosophical frames, and theoretical constructs as the units of analysis (Colin III, 1999/2007).

Development of an Africentric Philosophy

Educators should include an introduction to Africentric philosophy in philosophy of education courses. I believe students should understand that this culturally grounded centering involves elements of both accurate and appropriate sociohistorical and sociocultural contextual meaning constructs whose values, beliefs, and knowledge are indigenous to precolonial Africa. Students should also understand that this is a philosophical mode of inquiry and a required cultural perspective that is embedded in African-centered ideas, concepts, definitions, and theoretical frames that are required if an appropriate analysis and interpretation of this group's lived experiences is the focus and the rehumanization of Africans and their descents is the goal. There is no more powerful tool that can stop the African dehumanization process (Gyekye, 1987; Karenga, 1980; Oruka, 1991; Outlaw, 1996; Serequeberhan, 1991). This paradigm serves, as Hord and Lee (1995) state, as a tool to "evaluate and counter the dehumanization to which people and ideas of African descent have been subjected through the history of colonialism and European racism" (p. 5).

Africentric philosophy as a mode of inquiry challenges the racist assumptions that are a product of the scientific racism that says Africans and African peoples are incapable of "rational thought" and that is produced by mainstream institutions such as Harvard, Yale, and the University of Chicago. These same assumptions of intellectual inferiority are, to a great extent, reflected overtly and covertly in our field. In response, the use of culturally grounded meaning constructs as a philosophical mode of inquiry begins with addressing a basic philosophical question: "What is one's human nature?" As so aptly stated by Jones (1977/1978):

> What is at stake here is the power and authority to define. Is the white philosopher to be the sole definer of reality? Is his perspective alone to be afforded philosophical merit? With this understanding of what is at stake, it is unobscure that blacks dehumanize themselves if they don't insist upon the right to make history the point of departure for their philosophizing. Blacks announce their own inferiority if they do not force the established philosophies to revalidate themselves and reconstruct their normative apparatus in light of the black perspective [p. 157].

Implications for Practice

Given that all knowledge is culturally grounded, the African-centered paradigm, by its nature and design, is a challenge to the racist assumptions that Africans and peoples of African descent neither had nor have a culture that has intellectual products of any value worthy of space on the intellectual landscape. It is through the presentation and use of this knowledge base that Africentrism claims its rightful place as both an intellectual paradigm and a discipline. I believe that, "if reason rules and logic prevails," Africentric concepts and goals should frame adult education programs for members of this group, specifically Africentric culturally grounded community programs (Colin III, 1999/2007). I have stated that these programs

> Provide both formal and informal educational activities (which include the introduction of new knowledge/information and/or deprogramming regarding knowledge and/or understandings held as a result of a miseducative process) that are reflective of the sociocultural realities and lived experiences that are indigenous to African Peoples as a result of the impacts of sociocultural and intellectual racism. The specific programmatic goals reflect the African Centered Principles of the Nguzo Saba [Umoja (unity), Kujichaguila (self-determination), Ujima (collective work and responsibility), Ujamaa (cooperative economics), Nia (purpose), Kuumba (creativity), and Imani (faith)]; the reconfiguration and enhancement of the selfethnic image; the development of selfethnic reliance and the liberation of Africans and members of the African Diaspora [p. 8].

As stated earlier this African-centered paradigm, or worldview, is culturally grounded (Colin III, 1992) in that the African worldview needs to be the conceptual center of any sociocultural and sociohistorical analysis of African peoples. As such, this paradigm reflects a particular value system, out of which emerge philosophical frameworks, conceptual constructs, and theoretical formulations that can be used by educators of adults in the development of relevant educational programs and activities.

Although the impact of racism should not be news to anyone, it is often mistaken, or usurped, by Whites as being something that can be done to them. The very act of racism or of being a racist assumes that you have power over someone as determined by your race and your position of power used as a result of that. In 1994, Elizabeth Hayes and I coedited the monograph *Confronting Racism and Sexism,* which included my article titled, "Adult and Continuing Education Graduate Programs: Prescription for the Future" (Colin III, 1994), where I stated that

> [b]efore we can confront the issue of societal racism, members of the professoriate must first confront the racism that is reflected in their perceptions of and attitudes toward people of color.... Our curricula must incorporate knowledge that comes from outside the Eurocentric, dominant cultural and ideological framework.... Acceptance of the Eurocentric worldview excludes the sociocultural and intellectual histories and life experiences of African Ameripeans [and Africans and members of the African Diaspora].... Given the racial and cultural diversity of American society, adult and continuing education graduate programs can no longer rely on the Eurocentric approach [p. 59].

And now in 2010 we are still addressing the impact of racism on us as adult educators and on our field and suggesting ways to racialize the discourse. In some ways, for me, this feels like an academic version of a Verizon telephone commercial in that I must ask, "Do you hear me now?"

VANESSA: WOMANIST IN PRACTICE—GIVING VOICE

I do want to make sure that every person hears and is given an opportunity to be heard. I introduced the concept of "giving voice" using a womanist framework to the field of adult education as a process that educators seeking to change the discourse in their classrooms could use as a way to aid them in moving toward a more democratically and just learning environment. For years the overall frustration for some has been that the concept did not come with a list of tools that one should use in order to ensure that an instructor or facilitator was indeed giving voice. Over the course of the last fifteen years, I have tried to describe some things one could do, as well as a set of principles that an instructor or facilitator might use. I have included some of those here for you to consider as you begin to engage in this work around uncovering, discovering, and resolving issues of race and racism in your curriculum or practices.

Before moving into this, I think that it is also important for me to share with you the overall intent of giving voice. Giving voice is not a new ideal or concept for those seeking to make their spaces more inclusive with regard to race, gender, class, language, religion, and so on (Sheared, 1994). For those who've been engaged in this work, the "aim is based on the proposition that all knowledge is grounded in a social, political, economic and historical context." And giving voice

> requires us to acknowledge different realities and understand that there are different ways of interpreting reality. "Voice is related to the means whereby teachers and students attempt to make themselves present in history and to define themselves as active authors of their own worlds" (Weiler, 1988, p. xiii).... Voice is the active engagement of students and teachers in dialogue with one another. Both are heard and "define themselves as active authors of their worlds...it is the unique instance of self-expression through which students affirm their own class, cultural, racial, and gender identities" (Giroux and McLaren, 1986, p. 235) [Sheared, 1994].

Giving voice is situated within the womanist (Walker, 1983) epistemological framework because of its focus on addressing and reflecting upon the interconnecting and intersecting realities of race, gender, class, language, religion, age, and sexual orientation, and the ways these factors have been affected throughout history, varying body politics, and socioeconomic and sociocultural trends within our society (Sheared, 1994). The womanist epistemological perspective is situated within the Africentric theoretical framework, and adds the dimension of gender specifically to its analytical framework. It recognizes the fact that the African tradition, ethos, and way of knowing is significant, and that the contributions of Black women of the African Diaspora to that tradition are an essential component to this way of knowing and being.

The assumption is that in order for us to engage in any conversation about race and racism we must value and respect the lived experiences (Sheared, 1999) of those in the room. You cannot do that if any one person's lived experiences has been negated or devalued within our research, literature, or cultural texts as defined by history, politics, or socioeconomic or sociocultural standing. So an acknowledgment of one's African-ness and relationship to slavery in the United States is essential to engaging in a discourse about race and racism. Listed below are some of the steps you can use to give voice.

Start with General Knowledge and Common Language

In order to gain an understanding about one's lived experiences, one must be willing to introduce varying perspectives, histories, and cultural aspects into the curriculum, so that there is general and common language and information. This does not mean that all have to agree, but if you don't start with a common language or set of information, you end up going off on tangents that lead to distractions. Using a common language doesn't mean that you all have to agree on where the information will take you, but it does mean that you are willing to agree to engage in a discussion about that which is on the agenda.

Create a Set of Ground Rules

Before moving forward within any discussion, establish a set of common ground rules about the time, time-outs, goals, and expectations of the facilitator and the participants, and also discuss what you are not doing or cannot do.

Establish a Set of Personal Tenets

I have identified a list of tenets you can use, but in no way are they intended to be considered the only ones you can use. But we want you to get a head start, so I suggest (1) a personal philosophy that clearly states your commitment to the learner and his or her ability to generate and critically reflect on what knowledge is and how it is heard; (2) an understanding of how your philosophy is intricately linked to what you think and feel and how, ultimately, you act in a local and global community context; (3) a commitment to creating a learning environment in which the learner and you the teacher, are coauthors of information and knowledge generation; (4) an understanding of the subject matter and its place within social, economic, and political arenas; and (5) a commitment to exploring the polyrhythmic realities of the learner and you the teacher, along with determining how the realities of both of you are interwoven with the ways in which you behave, think, feel, and learn.

Establish a Set of Questions

The facilitator should establish a series of questions aimed at engaging individuals in a discourse around the topic of race and racism. For instance, you can begin by using the questions we outlined in Chapter One and made use of as we engaged in conversations about race and racism, or you can use others established by your group members. One thing I would add is a question about what act or set of actions the individual will perform as a result of having participated in this process. Three questions that will help guide the establishment of voice are these: "What is my role and function as an educator or facilitator?" "What is the role of the participants?" "How will our lived experiences, our racial identities or positionalities, impact the engagement in learning or planning of all participants, including the facilitator?" Additional questions that you might use are listed later in this chapter, under the "Black Feminism in Practice" section.

Giving Voice

Using small- and large-group discussions, encourage participants to share something about the self. I use the chart displayed in Figure 21.1 at the beginning of the dialogue to encourage people to get to know something about each other. There are other strategies, but I offer this one as a way to help you get started.

Participants are asked to add as many additional circles as needed to describe themselves to each other in the group. Once they complete

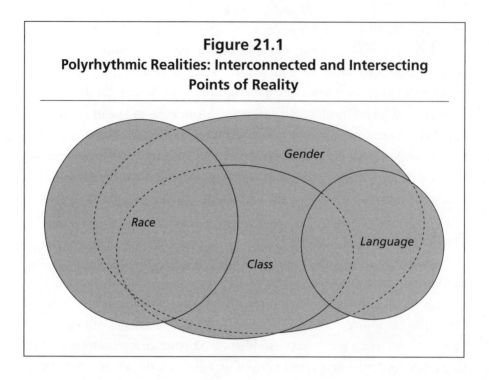

Figure 21.1
Polyrhythmic Realities: Interconnected and Intersecting Points of Reality

this activity, they work with a partner or two, in groups of two or three. They share with each other how these realities have affected their values and their thinking about themselves as well as others. I have used this activity and have discovered over the years that it allows people to talk about themselves and who they are as well as their perceptions about each other in a more nonthreatening way. As a result of this, as well as the activities offered throughout the class, students have noted that giving voice has enabled them to (1) not be silenced or feel marginalized; (2) gain a sense of power and locus of control; (3) feel as though they matter; (4) make a transition cognitively, developmentally, personally, and socially; (5) feel a sense of empowerment; (6) decrease or eliminate stereotypes about others; (7) respect the uniqueness of individuals and groups; (8) recognize universal, individual, and collective responsibility; and (9) seek new connections and commonalities with others (Sheared, 1996).

Other Things to Consider

In addition, the following observations highlight important aspects of establishing a space in which people can engage in the sometimes very difficult conversations about race and racism that can lead to improved relationships among men and women of all races, languages, religions, sexual orientations, classes, and other groups. Start a dialogue; because we are social beings, engaging in dialogue is an essential aspect of changing ideas and perceptions. Provide symbols, books, videos, and speakers; these tools can help people engage in intellectual conversations, which sometimes offer a safe place to begin. Offer role models reflective of the group members' race, gender, ethnicity, language, sexual orientation, religion, or age. Consider the arrangement of desks and chairs and the features of the room and building; the physical setting may present barriers to engaging in dialogue that are not immediately apparent. Finally, focus on the learning styles of group members to ensure that you use a variety of styles that reflect inclusion.

There is no magic wand, other than you. You, the facilitator, must examine your values, your tenets, and your reasons for engaging in a discourse about race and racism. Once you have those answers then you will be ready to give voice to others' experiences.

JUANITA: BLACK FEMINISM IN PRACTICE

Working to empower our learners can alter the ways we talk about race in our classrooms. In my classroom, when I teach about race I am attempting to make change, attempting to open up a dialogue and to create understanding. As a Black feminist educator, I am seeking to create an educational setting that is conducive to transformation.

There are two main theoretical approaches in the literature relating to transformative learning, the one purported by Mezirow and the one that has developed around Friere's *conscientization* (Merriam & Caffarella, 1999). Transformational learning as set forth by Mezirow was introduced in the field of adult education in the 1970s and is a theory that speaks to how adults use learning to make meaning of life events. The theory is based on Mezirow's major study (1978) on how a group of reentry women incorporated new learning gleaned from life-changing events. Ultimately, it is a theory about change—about how lives are forever altered by circumstances. The process, according to Mezirow, involves three phases: critical reflection on the assumptions held at the time of the life event, the use of a language or discourse to speak about or make sense of the event, and the development of a new schema that is incorporated into one's life.

It is set forth that a *disorienting dilemma* triggers the process that forces learners to begin self-examination of their set of assumptions or beliefs. Eventually, learners will realize the universality of their experience and will use their new perspective to look for new solutions. Overall, Mezirow's theory is individualistic and any extrapolation of his theory to the community or societal levels is problematic. Mezirow (1997) asserts:

> Thinking as an autonomous and responsible agent is essential for full citizenship in democracy and for moral decision making in situations of rapid change.... The adult educator must recognize both the learner's objectives and goal. The educator's responsibility is to help learners reach their objectives in such a way that they will function as more autonomous, socially responsible thinkers [p. 8].

This indictment discounts the positional and social relations of the students and the teacher and naively assumes that we live in a just, fair, and power-neutral society, placing an extremely heavy burden on the educator to create a perfect classroom environment for the allegedly willing and fully participating learner. The teacher in Mezirow's world acts with the highest degree of integrity and is caring, empathic, and sincere, while creating a safe, trusting, and learner-centered environment (Taylor, 1997).

In the idealized Freirean world, the teacher and student relationship is devoid of power imbalances and is reciprocal in nature. Dialogue is to Freire as discourse is to Mezirow. While Freire does consider how the context of the learning affects the learner, he still brings an idealized notion of the educator and learner to the conceptual table, believing that by freeing the minds of learners an educator can jumpstart the process of transformation. This conscientization discounts an important variable, the weight, trauma, and dailiness of oppression, placing the onuses of liberation squarely on the backs of the oppressed. Freire asserts the importance of dialogue to the process of change and empowerment, but does not realistically trouble the notion that language and therefore dialogue does not easily reside with the powerless, or in Friere's case the low literate.

Despite my need to wrap my curriculum around my students (Sealey-Ruiz, 2007), there are several standard beliefs and practices that I always build into my courses. First, I believe that the curriculum must always be about reading and writing. It is my personal belief that nothing makes a student stretch and grow more than reading challenging materials and being required to critically reflect upon, trouble, and react to the new information. So my classes involve tons of reading and writing.

Second, standard practices for me include needs assessment, agenda posting, and midsemester evaluations. Needs assessment is essential to making sure the course is responsive and fulfilling to students. I feel an obligation to find out what my students need, then build these requirements into the syllabus. Agenda posting simply supplements needs assessment by allowing students to negotiate the prioritization of materials and assignments that require more explanation, discussion, or debate. And despite all the best-laid plans, adjustments might be necessary. Therefore my courses routinely include midsemester evaluations to allow for any needed changes. Being responsive to the students' needs does not negate inclusion of the canon.

Also implicit in my teaching, which is rooted in social justice, is a critique of Western rationality, androcentric theories, and structured inequalities. I teach within a political framework that attends to and encourages the following: (1) a caring and safe environment, (2) consciousness raising, and (3) activism. My approach has evolved from my personal experiences. I have been in positions of enfranchisement and disenfranchisement and in positions of privilege and underprivilege. Each circumstance continues to shape what I bring to the classroom and to my students. There are few unexplored spaces in the classroom. Those who venture in will find acceptance, openness, and an atmosphere of constructive and energetic discourse. I will do my best to teach them, and they have never failed to teach me.

For several of the editors on this project, women and minorities are the "other." This *otherness*, as Beauvoir (1968) has stated, is defined against the norm of maleness and in today's context is additionally extrapolated and defined in contrast to the normalcy of Whiteness. Baker and Copp (1997) state the dilemma more succinctly: "faculty members who violate the white male, able-bodied stereotype must also experience students' contradictory expectations regarding gender, race, ethnicity, sexual orientation, and physical abilities" (p. 42). Baker and Copp (1997) go on to state that students not only actually see the "otherness" of professors who do not fit their stereotypes as inferior but also see the professors' various positionalities as "liabilities."

As an adult educator who attempts to practice a liberatory peda-gogy, where the idea of authority is made even more complex by the field's mandate to facilitate rather than to teach as authority figure, I acknowledge the importance of the concept of facilitation to our discipline (Apps, 1991; Brookfield, 1995; Knowles, 1992), and indeed I view the facilitator's role as a compatible and important compo-nent of feminist pedagogy. Yet I also understand and acknowledge the difficulty of using facilitation as the primary way of conducting and negotiating classrooms where we are not necessarily seen as having authority. When I facilitate and abandon the active authority role of the teacher, I provide students with the opportunity to control and order the environment.

When this occurs, students often recreate the larger social context where places are allotted along gender, class, and racial lines and where authority goes to those who resemble the "norm." This recreation of the rank order of the outside world can disadvantage professors of color and students of color. This predicament is aptly expressed by Smith (1999):

> I am alone but in charge. But am I really in charge? What shapes students' perceptions of their teachers? Why am I concerned about their perceptions? Can I be an authority and a minority in practice and theory? In theory, I am both; however, in practice I am often, foremost, a minority [p. 69].

What recommendations can be drawn from my experiences? I would like to share the following recommendations with educators who are concerned about creating a space where power structures are examined, societal *isms* are addressed, and the voices of our learners are validated and affirmed.

Making Statements That Instruct Behavior, Give Voice, and Encourage Risk

I feel it is important that students not be allowed to hurt, dominate, intimidate, or silence their classmates. Although I would never abdicate or deny that this is my responsibility, one tool that I have found very useful in achieving this is "Ground Rules for Class Discussion," a list of nine rules excerpted from an article by Lynn Weber Cannon (1990) at the Center for Research on Women, Memphis State University. (This list can be easily accessed from a number of course Web sites on line.) On more than one occasion I have defused and managed impossible discussions and rage by stopping the class and referring to one of the rules as a mediation tactic. In particular, rules 1, 3, and 7 have been very important:

1. Acknowledge that racism, classism, sexism, heterosexism and other institutionalized forms of oppression exist. (Other institutionalized forms of oppression include age, ethnicity, disability, religion, color, national origin, physical appearance.)

3. Agree not to blame ourselves or others for the misinformation we have learned in the past, but accept responsibility for not repeating misinformation after we have learned otherwise.

7. Share information about our groups with other members of the class and never demean, devalue, or in any way put down people for their experiences.

One constant concern that I struggle with in the classroom is the dilemma posed by students who speak up often and students who don't speak often. To make sure that all learners can contribute to the learning environment I try to build in varied means for fulfilling the participation requirement. This is important because 10 percent of my students are international learners who actively practice silence. So in each class where participation is assessed in determining the overall grade, students are told in a handout that I believe that active participation in the course is essential and that, because not all students are comfortable speaking aloud in class, participation can be verbal or nonverbal. Other acceptable forms of participation are suggesting outside readings, recommending out-of-class films or television programs, and attending and reporting in writing or on video on related campus activities. My syllabi, especially for classes that involve the difficult and controversial topics of race and racism, always contain a variation of this statement that addresses the issue of risk:

> This course is designed to be collaborative and interactive, with the promise that I will try to provide a safe environment for us to share our doubts and apprehensions about the ambiguities and pitfalls of working in the constructivist paradigm that undergirds academic research. That being said, I will attempt to be constructive in my critique and transparent regarding my knowledge, concerns, and experiences.

Using Questioning and Group Debriefing

It is significant to make the taken-for-granted power structures visible to the students by offering opportunities for collective debriefing on the verbal and nonverbal dynamics in class. For example, when male students take extensive class discussion time, I may invite the class to observe the interactive speaking patterns. Who listens? Whose comments are being attended? Or, as part of my introduction on the first day, I may make students aware of their own stereotypes by addressing pivotal questions such as these:

Have you ever been taught by a woman of color before?

How can a teacher's gender and racial background affect the course?

How do you perceive me as an instructor? How can your perceptions affect my credibility and power as a teacher in the classroom?

These questions usually help to sensitize students to their own stereotypes, and create a reflective opportunity to explore the impact of sexism and racism.

In addition to articulating questions directly related to power structures, I purposely alter the class dynamics by inviting White male and female guest speakers. I then encourage students to collectively reflect on the different behaviors they have demonstrated with these speakers and with me and then discuss their rationales behind the varying interactions. My belief is that this debriefing process allows students to reflect on, attend to, or make sense of their here-and-now behaviors as opposed to forcing them into accepting my interpretation of the classroom dynamics. Many teachable moments may emerge as a result of group debriefing.

Using Media Accompanied by Scholarly Writings to Further Conversations

The new generation of students in my classroom, who are in their twenties, not only love media but have a healthy respect for media, seeing in them the "truth seer" of our society. And so I embrace this preference and find ways to incorporate visual media as an aid, especially when the subject matter is race and racism. A good example of this strategy is my use of the Public Broadcasting Service (PBS) six-part documentary series

Africans in America, which has a companion study guide, to trace how historical events have shaped adult education for African Americans in the United States. The written scholarly complements I use are several articles from the *Adult Education Quarterly,* one of which, fortuitously, also quoted these well-known words of W.E.B. DuBois:

> The silently growing assumption of this age is that the probation of races is past, and that the backward races of to-day are of proven inefficiency and not worth having. Such an assumption is the arrogance of peoples irreverent toward Time and ignorant of the deeds of man.... So woefully unorganized is sociological knowledge that the meaning of progress, the meaning of "swift" and "slow" in human doing, the limits of human perfectibility, are veiled, unanswered sphinxes on the shores of science.... *Your country? How came it yours? Before the Pilgrims landed we [African Americans] were here* [DuBois, 1903/1995, p. 189].

The words, "Your country? How came it yours? Before the Pilgrims landed we were here," were used in the haunting musical refrain that introduced each part of the documentary series. Such teachable moments must be embraced by teachers in an effort to add scholarly and historical dimensions to classroom conversations about race and racism that are too often bound in personal anecdotes and experiences.

Claiming Our Authority

My liberatory pedagogy, as informed by Freire's critical pedagogy (1970), often suggests that instructors can democratize the teaching setting by sharing power with students. However, the power structures of the classroom often mirror those of the society. What purpose do the actions of sharing power serve when students are privileged by the social structures and, hence, have more power than women of color professors? If the instructors share power in order to resist against the existing power structures, should disenfranchised instructors work first to establish authority?

Facilitating the Process of Understanding New and Contradictory Knowledge

As discussed by McIntosh (1995), Whites are often taught not to see the oppression of others. Education is one of the institutions in which the oppressive social structures are reproduced by generating and disseminating Eurocentric knowledge. Therefore, when students eventually encounter knowledge and opinions contradictory to their traditionally accepted Eurocentric ideology, many manifest various types of emotions, ranging from guilt, anger, feeling betrayed, and resisting to denial. I believe that it is crucial to acknowledge students' difficulty when processing new and contradictory knowledge. In addition to sharing similar personal experiences to facilitate the learning, I also realize the necessity of providing materials and activities that address both the cognitive and affective components of the learning process. Being aware of how the society's interlocking systems operate and one's role in the system is a major transformational learning experience, which can cause pain, anger, and distress in students. Faculty members interested in equity and social justice education need to see this transformational experience as an emotionally embedded growth process for adults.

Selecting Culturally Diverse Materials

Curriculum development is a political decision in that it involves the inclusion and the exclusion of certain materials. This political decision is often informed by the individual instructor's positionality. A curriculum that acknowledges the cultural backgrounds of diverse learner populations will incorporate various cultural perspectives. A culturally diverse curriculum may serve to broaden the base of students' knowledge and understanding as it relates to who these students are within their integrated multiple identities and how they relate to others in society. It is also crucial to select materials that portray the experiences of the various populations or materials that center the curriculum around a group's lived experiences. As instructors we need to ask: How often do the readings for class actually reflect diverse experiences? Are my students' images or experiences represented in the selected readings? If a group's images are presented in the readings, do the readings serve to empower the group or to perpetuate stereotypes about the group? We need to be conscious of whose interests are served by the selected curriculum and materials.

STEPHEN: RECOGNIZING AND CHALLENGING WHITE SUPREMACY

So, are giving voice, changing perspectives, understanding other ways of knowing, and exploring new epistemologies enough to ensure that we have the type of dialogue required to begin the healing process caused by racist acts and racism? There are those Euro-Americans who have begun to have a dialogue about their role in either perpetuating or eliminating racist acts or racism in the United States and elsewhere. They have begun to discuss and use phrases like *White privilege, antiracist practices,* and *White supremacy* as a way to engage each other in a dialogue about race and racism. For some, the *ideology of White supremacy* has become the term used to explore racist acts and racism as perpetuated upon people of color. Although not new, White supremacy is and has been globally dominant over the past few centuries.

Even though the anticolonial movement of the last century kicked out the European occupiers of Third World countries, the march of imperial invasion and global capitalism continues apace. And the drill sergeant of this march is White. So challenging and dismantling the ideology of White supremacy—an ideology that has endured so successfully—is going to be difficult work. The White authors of the chapters in Part Two, on Whiteness, wanted to explore the things we Whites can do in the micropractices and micropolitics of our daily lives to fight this ideology and the practices and injuries it perpetuates. Calling out racism when we see it, in the manner explored by Elaine Manglitz and Ron Cervero, is one step. No one should underestimate the power of naming racism in the moment. The physical and psychological push-back when this happens illustrates just how powerful and threatening to racism this act is. Focusing on the racialized identities of Whites is another. In the decade-long history of conversations among the members of the European-American Collaborative Challenging Whiteness (ECCW), in Doug Paxton's outline of White epistemology, and in Lisa Baumgartner's analysis of White racial identity models, we can see examples of adult educators intentionally trying to become aware of their own racial formation and of the constituent psychopolitical elements of their own White racial identity. It is foundational in this kind of work that Whites recognize their own racial identity and the way the world is racialized to reflect this.

All the authors writing about Whiteness in Part Two emphasize the importance to antiracist work of striving to work with colleagues of color in ways that interrupt the narrative of White supremacy, and of addressing frankly the ways racism manifests itself. In my experience, one of the hardest things to do is confront, and make public, one's own racism. As I have shared, I don't particularly like to do this, and when I do it with my White students, I often tell myself that I am seeing racism where it doesn't exist and that I shouldn't be so hard on myself. However, it seems to me that a sustained owning up to one's racism is a crucial part of the work Whites need to do. One thing that makes this work easier is the systemic understanding of racism we advocate in this book. If racism is seen as an act of individual choice or individual sin, then acknowledging one's racism becomes mixed up with viewing oneself as an evil purveyor of hatred and bigotry. But if students become used to seeing racism as a systemic phenomenon, an ideology that is embedded and routinized in practices, habits, and structures that we are exposed to from an early age, then it become obvious that for Whites not to have learned racism is impossible. So constantly clarifying the systemic nature of racism is an important teaching act.

Dealing with Racial Microaggressions

One of the things that has been most helpful in my practice has been the concept of racial microaggressions. Racial microaggressions are the daily examples of racism that are expressed in the minutiae of small-scale interactions—tone of voice, gestures, meeting behaviors, news reports, media images, conversational speech, and so on. The more regularly we expose these, and the more we identify our own committing of such aggressions, the more students will understand their ubiquitous nature. This is something that one has to do routinely, and it has to become a part of one's habit. Although I know this, I do regular audits of my microaggressions for students to teach them how these aggressions are present at a subliminal level, and one of the tasks I set for students is for them to identify the racial microaggressions I commit and then to extend this analysis to their own behaviors. For example, I try to identity when I have overlooked a student of color in a class discussion, when I have used language in a racist way, when I have omitted to acknowledge other racially based intellectual traditions, or when I have actively discounted or misrepresented these same traditions. Articles such as the one by Sue et al. (2007) are useful teaching tools for showing the nonintentional nature of everyday racism.

Challenging White Epistemology

A general step the Part Two chapter authors discussed was challenging the dominance of White epistemology in the field of adult education. Scholarly and intellectual border crossing is overwhelmingly a one-way movement of traffic. Black scholars are expected as a matter of course to be familiar with critical theory, transformative learning, andragogy, and so on. No such requirement is placed as a matter of course for White scholars to know the central tenets of Africentrism, to know the difference between an Africentric and an Africanist scholar, to understand the diverse views in African American intellectual life over the validity of the Africentric paradigm, and so on. Black scholars are expected to know White scholarship fully before they can be allowed to do their thing and explore Africentrism, Black nationalism, and the dynamics of the Black liberation struggle. The converse is not true; White scholars' interests are the unproblematized norm, and publishing in these areas is seen as a natural direction for scholarship.

One thing we can do is to make clear in our writing and teaching that we are striving to understand other racially based intellectual traditions rather than just teaching how they contrast with Eurocentrism. Teaching about different racial traditions should not be something reserved only for scholars of color. Whites need to step up and take responsibility for educating themselves about these traditions and being willing to teach about them. We want to strive for a situation in which teaching seriously about a range of contrasting racial traditions is viewed as an example of responsible scholarship, irrespective of the racial identity of the educator. Of course when the teacher has racial membership of the tradition she is teaching about, she has an experiential as well as an intellectual credibility that teachers of other racial identities don't have. In my own case, for example, I feel I must strive to be properly informed about Africentrism so that if no other colleague is available to do it, I could lead students in an engagement with this perspective.

Refocusing on What Scholarship Is

Because of an ignorance of the rich diversity of scholarship produced by communities of color, White adult educators easily fall into two traps. First, they focus on African American scholarship, believing that this somehow represents all scholarship of color. When this notion is broadened to include Latino and Latina scholarship and scholarship of the Asian Diaspora, Whites fall into the habit of talking about "the African American, Latino and Latina, or Asian perspective" as if there were a unitary philosophy evident in each of these cases. This position shows a lamentable ignorance of the vigorous diversity of intellectual debate among communities of color. Skin pigmentation does not produce philosophical unanimity. For example, although we explore an Africentric perspective on adult education in this book, it should be stated that many African American intellectuals deny that there is any such thing as a unitary Africentric or African American philosophy. This is well illustrated in the interviews in Yancy's (1998) *African-American Philosophers,* where the editor, George Yancy, eschews any "ontological essentialist foundationalism that forms the sine qua non of African-American philosophical identity and thought" (p. 10) and observes that what emerges in his book is "a complex set of philosophical positionalities and thoughts exhibiting areas of commonality and diversity broadly informed by, though not simply reduced to, African-American culture" (p. 10).

There is a wide-ranging debate within African American philosophical circles surrounding the validity of the Africentric philosophical paradigm, a debate that illustrates a range of principled positions on the issue. Molefi Asante and Cornel West both write about racism and the African Ameripean (Colin III, 1988) experience, but one grounds his work in African cultural values, the other in European critical theory and American pragmatism. Both bell hooks and Angela Davis draw heavily, like West, on neo-Marxist critical theory informed by contemporary racial analysis. To speak of three colleagues in adult education with whom I have cotaught or coauthored, Scipio A. J. Colin III explores racism from an African-centered perspective; our dear colleague Elizabeth Peterson explored it from the standpoint of critical race theory; and Ian Baptiste views it from a perspective of informed critical eclecticism. So to talk of African American philosophy as if it were a distinctive, unified body of work is inaccurate and condescending. One would not talk of British philosophy as if everyone born in Great Britain with White skin philosophized in the same way. African American philosophy exhibits the same kind of subtlety, difference, and disagreement as does the philosophizing of any group of people. Whites who do not appreciate this, and I have been one of them, talk about the need for a Black perspective on things without realizing they are torpedoing their own good intentions. By assigning a false uniformity to the discourse produced by members of a community of color, that discourse is actually marginalized. Once all Black people are represented as thinking the same way, the unfortunate implication is that all we need to do to create racial balance in an adult education program is to add a module called "Black Philosophy."

Untangling and Breaking the Stranglehold

One way the Part Two authors tried to break the stranglehold of Eurocentric epistemology in their own practice was to work in multiracial teaching teams, modeling for students the analysis of racial dynamics and the struggle to confront racism. When a multiracial teaching team talks out in front of the students about the ways in which the racial identities and traditions of the team members enter into course and lesson planning, syllabus and curriculum construction, the choice of resources, the design of evaluative mechanisms, the assignment of teaching duties, and so on, it models for students the holding of conversations across different racial identities. White students need to see examples of racial dialogue in multiracial groups to show them that such conversations, although difficult and sometimes raw, are possible. Of course White adult educators can also strive to include resources authored or constructed by people with a broad range of racial memberships, and I believe they should do that. But there is no substitute for seeing a multiracial teaching team exhibit equal knowledge and fluency in a variety of racial perspectives and traditions.

Using a Critical Incident Questionnaire

In terms of specific classroom practices, one of the most helpful instruments I have found for bringing the discussion of race and racism into the classroom is the *critical incident questionnaire* (CIQ) that I use to gather anonymous data from students in all my classes. This is a one-page sheet containing five questions about engaging or distancing moments and helpful or confusing actions, and I ask students to fill it out once a week at the end of class (http://www.stephenbrookfield.com/Dr._Stephen_D._Brookfield/Critical_Incident_Questionnaire.html).

The responses on these forms are strictly anonymous, so I have no idea who has written what. I collect and read these forms and prepare a summary of the main themes students raise on them. The next time I meet with the group I provide a summary of their comments. I have often found that students who feel uncomfortable about a racial incident but too intimidated to speak up about it in class, or students who feel they don't know how to raise questions having to do with racism in discussion, will often record their reactions and questions on these anonymous feedback forms. This feedback is presented to the class as questions to be addressed.

Finally, from the perspective of Whites, one of the things we labor against is the expectation—so dominant in White epistemology—that every problem has a solution that can be discovered and applied to address the problem. Books like this illustrate the long march that antiracist work represents and caution against false hopes that with the election of an African American U.S. president centuries of successful racist ideological socialization and manipulation will magically be undone. Those Whites who try to fight racism, however unsuccessfully and sporadically they do this, need to say publicly that just because magical solutions don't appear doesn't mean you give up. They also need to make it clear that anyone doing this work should not expect recognition or approval from colleagues, whether they be White colleagues or colleagues of color. You do the work because it needs to be done, not because it will bring you plaudits for being what the ECCW calls the *good White person.*

FINAL REFLECTION: FROM THE KITCHEN TABLE TO THE CLASSROOM

It is the belief of the editors of this book that there is still much work to be done if people of varying races, geographic locations, languages, genders, religions, and sexual orientation in the Americas as well as globally are going to begin to learn how to honor and respect each other. We in no way intend this book to be a catchall for every idea or the end of the dialogue on race and racism. However, we believe that we all have to start somewhere, and we believe that the authors in this book have given all of us much to consider, reflect, and act upon. While we believe that dialogue is essential to increasing people's awareness and understanding, we recognize that it is each person's own ability to change how he or she engages, speaks, and acts that is the real test.

The lived experiences and the theories, practices, and recommendations that each of us writing for this book shared emerged from our personal and professional intersecting realities as we dealt with each racist act or acts of racism uncovered or discovered as we found ourselves practicing and living against the grain. Above all, while our classrooms are places where we make space for knowledge production, where we make space for all voices—including our own—and where we make space for deferred and unexpressed dreams, it is around the kitchen table that our values, beliefs, and ideals were formulated. We encourage an exploration of all the spaces in which all of you who are reading our words have lived and or operated as mothers, sisters, daughters, sons, fathers, professors, and administrators, and the list continues. This is our truest definition of liberatory pedagogy. We ask that as you think about the beliefs, feelings, and ideas and the dialogues and practices shared in this volume, you take the time to send us thoughts or notes about what you are doing in your practices to move your discourse and practices toward the incorporation of multiple voices and experiences into your classrooms and into your communities.

As you note from our book cover, we acknowledge that all that should be at the table are not, but we believe we have met our objective of establishing a place for everyone. *Please accept our invitation.*

REFERENCES

Apps, J. W. (1991). *Mastering the teaching of adults.* Malabar, FL: Krieger.

Asante, M. (1988). *The Afrocentric idea.* Philadelphia: Temple University Press.

Asante, M. (1990). *Kemet, Afrocentricity and knowledge.* Trenton, NJ: Africa World Press.

Baker, P., & Copp, M. (1997). Gender matters most: The interaction of gendered expectations, feminist course content, and pregnancy in student course evaluation. *Teaching Sociology, 25,* 29–43.

Beauvoir, S. de. (1968). *The second sex.* New York: Modern Library.

Brookfield, S. D. (1995). *Becoming a critically reflective teacher.* San Francisco: Jossey-Bass.

Cannon, L. W. (1990). Fostering positive race, class, and gender dynamics in the classroom. *Women's Studies Quarterly, 1–2,* 126–134.

Carruthers, J. H. (1999). *Intellectual warfare.* Chicago: Third World Press.

Colin, S.A.J., III. (1988). *Voices from beyond the veil: Marcus Garvey, the Universal Negro Improvement Association and the education of African Ameripean adults.* Unpublished dissertation, Northern Illinois University, DeKalb.

Colin, S.A.J., III. (1992). *Culturally grounded programs.* Unpublished manuscript.

Colin, S.A.J., III. (1994). Adult and continuing education graduate programs: Prescription for the future. In E. Hayes & S.A.J. Colin III (Eds.), *Confronting racism and sexism* (New Directions for Adult and Continuing Education, No. 61, pp. 53–62). San Francisco: Jossey-Bass.

Colin, S.A.J., III. (1999/2007). It's not what you call me, but what I answer to. In *Through the eyes of Ethiopia: Africentrism and culturally grounded research* (chap. 1). Unpublished manuscript.

Colin, S.A.J., III. (2002a). Marcus Garvey: Africentric adult education for selfethnic reliance. In E. Peterson (Ed.), *Freedom road: Adult education of African Americans* (pp. 41–65). Malabar, FL: Krieger.

Colin, S.A.J., III. (2002b). *The pillaging of a paradigm: Africentric and Africanist scholars and scholarship under siege.* Unpublished manuscript, National-Louis University, Chicago.

DuBois, W.E.B. (1995). *The souls of Black folk.* New York: New American Library. (Original work published 1903)

Freire, P. (1970). *Pedagogy of the oppressed.* New York: Continuum.

Giroux, H. A., & McLaren, P. (1986). Teacher education and the politics of engagement: The case for democratic schooling. *Harvard Educational Review, 56,* 213–238.

Gyekye, K. (1987). *An essay on African philosophical thought: The Akan conceptual scheme.* New York: Cambridge University Press.

Hayes, E., & Colin, S.A.J., III. (1994). Editors' notes. In E. Hayes & S.A.J. Colin III (Eds.), *Confronting racism and sexism* (New Directions for Adult and Continuing Education, No. 61, p. 3). San Francisco: Jossey-Bass.

Hord, F. L. (Mzee Lasana Okpara), & Lee, J. S. (Eds.). (1995). *I am because we are: An introduction to Black philosophy.* Amherst: University of Massachusetts Press.

Jones, W. R. (1977/1978, Winter/Spring). The legitimacy and necessity of Black philosophy: Some preliminary considerations. *The Philosophical Forum, 9,* 149–160.

Karenga, M. (1980). *Kawaida theory: An introductory outline.* Inglewood, CA: Kawaida.

Knowles, M. (1992). *The adult learner: A neglected species.* Houston, TX: Gulf.

McIntosh, P. (1995). White privilege and male privilege: A personal accounting of coming to see correspondences through work in women's studies. In M. A. Anderson & P. H. Collins (Eds.), *Race, class, gender* (pp. 76–87). Belmont, CA: Wadsworth.

Merriam, S. M., & Caffarella, R. (1999). *Learning in adulthood.* San Francisco: Jossey-Bass.

Mezirow, J. (1978). *Education for perspective transformation: Women's re-entry programs in community colleges.* New York: Teachers College Press.

Mezirow, J. (1997). Transformative learning: Theory to practice. In P. Cranton (Ed.), *Transformative learning in action: Insights from practice* (New Directions for Adult and Continuing Education, No. 74, pp. 5–12). San Francisco: Jossey-Bass.

Oruka, O. (1991). Sagacity in African philosophy. In T. Serequeberhan (Ed.), *African philosophy: The essential writings* (pp. 47–62). New York: Paragon.

Outlaw, L., Jr. (1996). *On race and philosophy.* New York: Routledge.

Sealey-Ruiz, Y. (2007). Wrapping the curriculum around their lives: Using a culturally relevant curriculum with African American adult women. *Adult Education Quarterly, 58*(1), 44–60.

Serequeberhan, T. (Ed.). (1991). *African philosophy: The essential writings.* New York: Paragon.

Sheared, V. (1994). Giving voice: An inclusive model of instruction—A womanist perspective. In E. Hayes & S.A.J. Colin III (Eds.), *Confronting racism and sexism* (New Directions for Adult and Continuing Education, No. 61, pp. 27–37). San Francisco: Jossey-Bass.

Sheared, V. (1996). Giving voice in an adult education context. *College of Education Review* (San Francisco State University), *8*, 97–103.

Sheared, V. (1999). Giving voice: Inclusion of African American students' polyrhythmic realities in adult basic education. In T. Guy (Ed.), *Providing culturally relevant adult education: A challenge for the twenty first century* (New Directions for Adult and Continuing Education, No. 82, pp. 33–48). San Francisco: Jossey-Bass.

Smith, R. (1999). Walking on eggshells: The experience of a Black woman professor. *ADE Bulletin, 122*, 68–72.

Sue, D. W., Capodilupo, C. M., Torino, G. C., Bucceri, J. M., Holder, A.M.B., Nadal, K. L., et al. (2007). Racial micro-aggressions in everyday life. *American Psychologist, 64*(2), 271–286.

Taylor, E. W. (1997). Building upon the theoretical debate: A critical review of the empirical studies of Mezirow's transformative learning theory. *Adult Education Quarterly, 48*(1), 34–59.

Walker, A. (1983). *In search of our mothers' garden: Womanist prose.* Orlando, FL: Houghton Mifflin Harcourt.

Weiler, K. (1988). *Women teaching for change: Gender, class and power.* New York: Bergin and Garvey.

Yancy, G. (Ed.). (1998). *African-American philosophers: 17 conversations.* New York: Routledge.

INDEX

critique of liberalism in, 178; effects of racism on, 113; Hispanics in, 62; immigrants and, 236–237; interest convergence and, 177–178; legislation evolving from, 114, 190; seeds of White supremacy and, 107

Clark, S., 113, 240

Clark, S. M., 57

Clark, S. P., 249

Classroom environment: dynamics in, 74; effects of racism on, 114; effects of stereotypes on, 250; feminist studies and, 72, 74, 79; for giving voice, 353, 355; of Maori students, 91; in multicultural studies, 79; positionality and, 195; preventing aggressions in, 164; for real conversation in real time, 279; as safe space, 48, 79, 91; society reflected in, 248; student participation and, 360; to support African-centered paradigm, 322; for transformational learning, 357–358

Clinton, H., 335

Closson, R., 168–169, 173–174, 260

Cobb, A., 37

Coconut, 36

Colin, S. J., III, 1, 5, 12–13, 17, 19, 142, 180, 191, 206, 223, 254, 296, 319, 324, 334, 343, 344–350, 368

Collaborative inquiry, 253

Collective community: in African-centered paradigm, 323–324; of Mexica people, 37–38

College admissions, 11

Collins, P., 173, 252, 274

Colonization, 32–34, 39; Afro-Caribbean identity and, 201–205, 207–212; bipolar model of, 89; commonalities of, 88–89; effects of, 202; of Maori people, 87–88, 89

Color blindness: from critical race theory perspective,

176, 178, 179; and critiques of liberalism, 178; definition of, 192, 247; description of, 76; effects of, 113; racial language and, 278; in White racial consciousness development, 108, 109, 312

Columbus, C., 31, 32–34

Commercialism, 178

Commission on Professors of Adult Education (CPAE), xxvii–xxviii

Commitment, 311, 312, 313

Communalism, 320

Communism, 232

Communities of practice, 253–254

Community activism: activist scholarship and, 63; authors' experiences with, 62, 63; citizenship schools and, 241–242; immigrants and, 237; versus professorship, 98

Community project, 233, 349

Community support, 225–226, 301

Community-based organization, 237

Compassion, 91, 129

Competency, 114

Complementarity, 319–321, 322

Concentration camp, 298, 299

Conceptual disobedience, 268

Confronting Racism and Sexism (Colin & Hayes), 350

Connections, discourse of, 110

Conscientization, 355, 357

Constitution, U.S., 177, 206

Constructivist pedagogy, 222–223

Contact stage, of White identity development, 107–108, 309

Control, of life, 31–32

Conversation. *See* Language; Racism, discourse about

Cook, D. A., 203, 205

Cooper, A. J., 173

Cooperrider, D. L., 236, 241

Copernicus, 125

Copp, M., 358

Corcoran, M., 57

Cornish, L. T., 269, 307

Corporate social responsibility, 120

Counselor, school, 59

Counterstory: authors' experience with, 14–15; definition of, 14; description of, 176

Crabtree, R. D., 73

Cranton, P., 249, 302

Credibility, 114, 217, 246

Crenshaw, K., 168, 174, 178, 190, 193, 274, 280

Crisis, 311, 312, 313

Critical Democrat, 112–113

Critical discourse analysis, 276–277

Critical humility: challenge of, 152; definition of, 147; questions to guide, 147–148, 150–152; rationale for, 155; reflection-in-action and, 148–155; scope of, 156

Critical incident questionnaire, 369–370

Critical legal scholars, 174–175

Critical professionalism, 212

Critical race theory (CRT): in adult education, 179–181, 212; versus Africentrism, 181; applications of, 190–191; central construct of, 174; components of, 168; versus critical white studies, 247; in curriculum, 212; definition of, 168; description of, 174, 175–178; father of, 175; foundation of, 247; immigrants and, 235–237; initial publications about, 175, 190–191; origins of, 174–175, 190; permanence of racism and, 169; primary tenets of, 168, 176; professional development in, 212; queer crit and, 189–195; SASHA model and, 223

Critical Race Theory: The Key Writings That Formed the Movement (Crenshaw et al.), 175

Critical reflection: adult educators' engagement in, 5; in

connecting theory to, 141–142; giving voice and, 280–281, 352; learning from, 128–129; queer crit and, 193–194; realms of, 284, 290

F

Face, 111

Faces at the Bottom of the Well: The Permanence of Racism (Bell), 52, 175, 176

Facilitation, of learning, 358

Faculty: authority of, 74, 75, 362; in citizenship schools, 240; competition among, 64, 65; complaints of racism by, 64–65; critical professionalism of, 212; critical reflection of, 5; embedded racist consciousness in, 15; filing of grievances by, 64–65; importance of racial discourse to, 113–115; internalized racism of, 218; needs of, 78; positionality self-assessment of, 189; in real conversation in real time strategy, 280; recruitment of, 137; reflections on homosexuality by, 187–188; responsibilities of, 40; role of, in critical English education, 48; undoing of miseducation by, 40–41

Faculty, African American: challenges of, 77; empowerment of, 79; feminist pedagogy and, 73–80; internalized racism of, 222; internalized racism strategies for, 220–227; number of, 51; people's assumptions about, 44–46, 51; racist language regarding, 273–274; requirements of, 366; scholarly work of, 161–163; self-reflection of, 80; stress of, 318; students' challenging of, 75; students' perceptions of, 114; tenure of, 114; White faculty's gratitude to, 160–161;

White faculty's promotion over, 317–318

Faculty, female: emotions of, 95–96; empowerment of, 79; healing of, 97–99; loss of enthusiasm by, 96–97; place of work for, 98; self-reflection of, 80; shared experiences of, 97–98; support for, 96; well-being of, 78, 79; White versus minority experiences as, 105–106

Faculty, Hispanic: authors' experiences as, 64–67; challenges of, 56, 57, 64–66; internalized racism of, 222; number of, 56–57; scholarly work of, 161–163; self-reflection of, 80; stories of, 56; tenure of, 114; truth of, 56; White faculty's gratitude to, 160–161

Faculty, of indigenous origin: ancestral teachings and, 91; authors' experiences as, 83–88, 90, 92

Faculty, White: authors' experiences as, 135–142; challenges of, 139; conceptualization of Whiteness by, 107–113; credibility of, 246; critical reflection by, 14; disengagement of, 97; freedom of choice for, 141; gratitude of, 160–161; importance of racial discussions for, 113–115; inclusion of, in book about racism, 102; need of, to be correct, 163; perpetuation of White privilege by, 146–147; recognition of achievements of, 113; as representatives for African initiatives, 317–318; responsibilities of, to challenge racism, 141–142, 251–255; students' perceptions of, 114; tenure of, 137; use of minority faculty's scholarly work by, 161–163; White privilege and, 245–247

Failure, 164

False disclosure, 153–154

False humility, 154

Family: discourse, in White people's conversations about race, 110; importance of, in academic achievement, 60, 61; as metaphor in adult education, 182–183; versus theory, 92; views of poverty by, 60

Fanon, F., 176

Farahmandpur, R., 212

Farmworker: authors' experiences as, 58–59, 63; civil rights actions for, 63; in Peruvian culture, 232

Feagin, J. R., 205, 206, 207

Fear, 232–233

Feminism. *See* Black feminism; Women's rights

Feminist pedagogy: African American faculty and, 72–80; definition of, 73; goals of, 73; guides for, 73–74; perspectives on, 73–74

Feminist scholarship: classroom instruction and, 72; definition of, 73; engaged pedagogy and, 79; ethnicity of students in, 72; importance of the home environment in, 80; otherness in, 66; perspectives on, 73–74; women of color and, 74–79

Fifth World, 39

Finding Forrester (film), 315

Fire, element of, 37

First Nation people, 88–89

Fixed reality, 33–34

Fix-it discourse, 110

Flowers, D., 268–269, 271, 278

Flowers, R., 89

Fone, B.R.S., 193

Fong, T., 298, 300

Ford, B., 269, 283

Foreclosure, 311–312

Frankenberg, R., 106, 107, 136, 138, 156–157

Freedom Road (Peterson), 180

Freedom Writers (film), 315

Freeman, A., 178

discrimination, 205–206; of Maori people, 87–88, 89; of multiple perspectives, 233; one-dimensional, 196; ongoing process of, 136–137; rightness and, 127; situational nature of, 233–234; transgressions of, 89; of White people, 107–108, 248

Identity achievement, 313–314

Identity diffusion, 311

Identity foreclosure, 311–312

Identity formation, racial, 309–315

Identity status, 311

Imel, S., 50

Immersion/emersion stage, of White identity development, 108, 310

Immigrant, 138, 202; in Asian American history, 298; challenges of, 238; citizenship process of, 238–241; civil rights of, 236–237; community action and, 237; critical race theory and, 235–237; government policies regarding, 238; labels for, 241; positionality of, 237; racial identity issues of, 232, 235–236, 239; retained sense of identity of, 239; social constructionism and, 235, 236. *See also specific immigrant groups*

Imperialism. *See* Colonization

Imus, D., 2, 107, 276

Inclusiveness: citizenship school and, 238; in higher education classrooms, 41–42; for Maori students, 91; precedent for, 41; in racial literacy development, 50–51

Indigeneity, 88

Indigenous people: connection of land to, 84, 88; denying of culture by, 85; importance of theory to, 84; who break tribal rules, 84. *See also specific ethnic groups*

Indigenous spirituality, 123

Inpowerment, 330

Institutional racism, 109

Instructional methods: to address racist language, 278–280, 287–289; in African-centered paradigm, 322; to develop racial literacy, 48–51; to examine paradigms, 287–289; for giving voice, 355; politics and, 363–364; in racial development process, 308, 314–315; for student participation, 360; for transformational learning, 252–253. *See also specific methods*

Insult, 275–276

Intellectualizer, 112

Intention, of racial acts, 225

Interest convergence, 177–178

Internalized racism. *See* Racism, internalized

Internment policy, 298, 299

Interracial relationship, 136, 140

Italian immigrant, 138

J

Jacobs, D., 240

Jamaican people, 204

James, C., 240

James, C.L.R., 209–210

Japanese Americans, 298, 299

Jarvis, P., 113

Jenkins, E., 240

Jensen, G., 113

Jim Crow laws, 114

Johns, T., 170, 217, 220, 225, 260

Johnson, B., 240

Johnson, L. B., 107

Johnson-Bailey, J., 1, 5, 9–12, 11, 18–19, 73, 74, 75–76, 78, 105, 136, 138, 140, 142, 180, 181, 187, 188, 189, 195, 196, 211, 246, 296, 301, 324, 343, 355–364

Jones, J. M., 202

Jones, W. R., 348

Jump Street Odyssey activity, 49

K

Ka'ai, T., 88

Kambon, K. K., 319, 321

Karenga, M., 348

Karumanchery, L. L., 86, 89, 286

Karumanchery-Luik, N., 86, 89

Kasl, E., 253

Kassworm, C., 50

King Jr., M. L., 178, 255

Kitchen table dialogue, 333

Knapsack activity, 49–50

Knowles, M., 113, 358

Kong, L., 170, 231, 233, 239, 242, 260

Ku Klux Klan, 106–107

Kuhn, T., 122

Kumashiro, K. K., 188, 194

L

Ladson-Billings, G., 168, 174, 175, 176, 177, 178, 181, 187, 190–191, 192

LaDuke, W., 84

Lakota people, 39, 84

Land: indigenous people's connection to, 84, 88; in Maori culture, 88, 90

Land of the Cranes (Salt Lake City), 39

Language: assumptions about, 295; in bilingual education, 62; deficiencies of, 277; giving voice and, 280–281, 352; importance of, 275; in racial socialization strategies, 288–289; of theory, 280; in transformational learning, 356

Language, racial, 2; African American faculty's encounters with, 273–274; Americanization and, 36; assaultive types of, 275–276; civil actions regarding, 62; in college courses, 60; communication of prejudice through, 273; covert use of, 277–278; critical discourse analysis of, 276–277; effects of, on relationships, 275; function of, 274; instructional strategies to address, 278–280, 287–289; in Maori classrooms, 86; of parents, for academic achievement, 61;

in new racism, 284–285; protection of, 109–110; race card and, 286–287; White faculty's challenging of, 139; White students' discourse about, 109–113

White racial consciousness: emotions connected to, 129; epistemology and, 123–125; ontology and, 122–123; stages of, 108–109; transformation of, 129–130; in Whites' discussions of race, 109–113

White racism. *See* Racism

White supremacy: authors' experiences with, 14–15; challenges of queer crit to, 192–193, 194; critical white studies and, 247; global dominence of, 364; Maori identity and, 90; pre-assessment of, 287–288; religion and, 106; seeds of, 106–107; strategies to challenge, 364–370

Whiteness, 106; authors' experience with, 126–130;

binary opposite of, 320; classroom strategies to investigate, 253; importance of discussing, 113–115; invisibility of, 136; as property, 177; Whites' conceptualization of, 107–113

Whitney, D., 236, 241

Wholeness, 78

Whole-person learning, 253

Wiessner, C., 278

Williams, O., 289

Williams, P., 168

Williams, R., 289

Williams, S., 289

Williams, V., 289

Winant, H., 236, 238, 242

Wing, A. K., 168

Win-win situation, 163

Wise, T., 320

Witherell, C., 55

Womanist framework, 350–355

Women, value of, 38

Women's rights, 113–114. *See also* Black feminism

Women's studies: authors' experiences in, 71–72;

critical race theory in, 190; feminist pedagogy and, 73–80; goals of, 72

Woodson, C. G., 38, 322

Work ethic, 60, 336

Workplace diversity, 120–121, 126–129

World War II, 298–299

Worldview. *See Paradigm*

Writing, 357

Wu, F., 299

X

Xantotl (Mexica) people, 37

Y

Yale University, 348

Yamato, G., 225

Yancy, G., 105, 367

"Yes, but. . ." discourse, 110–111

Yorks, L., 253

Yosso, T., 175

Young, R., 210

Yu, H. C., 36

Z

Zavella, P., 66